Foreign Affairs
North Korea and the Bomb

Foreign Affairs September 2017

TABLE OF CONTENTS

THE CURRENT CRISIS

NOW WHAT?

Introduction

Gideon Rose

A gathering at Kim Il Sung Square in Pyongyang celebrating the successful test launch of the intercontinental ballistic rocket Hwasong-14, in this photo released by North Korea's Korean Central News Agency, July 7, 2017.

Much of the current brouhaha over North Korean weapons development is overdone. The geopolitics of the Korean Peninsula has been frozen in place for more than half a century and shows no signs of thawing soon. The regime in Pyongyang is what it has always been, an evil family business operating for generations in a tightly protected market. And for decades, that regime has been able to deter others from attacking it— just as it has been deterred from attacking others. Nobody knows how much this basic calculus will be altered by incremental advancements in nuclear and missile technology, but the answer is almost surely less than most newcomers to the issue assume.

So why is everybody so riled up?

Because history feels different to those living through it. Reflecting on the nuclear age in his final speech to Parliament in 1955, Winston Churchill expressed hope that "safety will be the sturdy child of terror, and survival the twin brother of annihilation." A few years later, however, the strategist Albert Wohlstetter warned that the balance of terror was not sturdy but actually delicate. "Deterrence …," he wrote, "will be neither inevitable nor impossible but the product of sustained intelligent effort, attainable only by continuing hard choice."

Generations of strategists and policymakers have tried to follow Wohlstetter's advice and stabilize matters as much as possible, and so far they have largely succeeded. Churchill now seems prophetic. But past performance is no guarantee of future results, as the saying goes, and only a fool would dismiss the pessimists' concerns.

At Foreign Affairs, we've been tracking Korea since before the peninsula was divided, and we've collected these highlights from our coverage to put the current uproar over Pyongyang's weapons program into proper context. A failure of deterrence would be devastating, so even small changes in the odds are worth watching closely. And new situations may call for new tactics to strengthen deterrence or seize opportunities for diplomatic progress. But as so often in the past when dealing with this problem, wise policymakers today would try to dampen tensions rather than escalate them. To understand why, read the book.

GIDEON ROSE is Editor of *Foreign Affairs*.

© Foreign Affairs

North Korea's New Offensive

Joungwon A. Kim

A U.S. Navy Lockheed EC-121M Warning Star.

Last year both South and North Korea celebrated the twentieth anniversary of their establishment as separate political entities. Each had, at its inception, claimed the entire Korean nation as its legitimate domain, and each vowed to rid the other of the foreign power that was said to have created it. The year 1968 was also an anniversary of two other events. It was the 4300th anniversary of the legendary founding of the Korean nation, and the 1300th anniversary of the Silla Unification in A.D. 668, when the nation was brought under a single, centralized political rule. The irony of commemorating concurrently two decades of cold-war division and thirteen centuries of unified nationhood under a highly centralized political system was not lost on the Korean people.

The three dynasties which had ruled Korea during its thirteen-hundred years of unification had brought about one of the most completely homogeneous nations in the world. No minority ethnic groups are present within the borders of Korea, which for centuries have remained unchanged. Almost every other nation in the modern world is faced with problems of ethnic division; in Korea, one national ethnic group has been divided between two régimes. The long historical period of unification also brought Korean linguistic and cultural unity. The minor distinctions of speech from one region to another are not greater than the differences in English spoken in Texas and Maine. Unlike most of the "emerging nations," there are no language barriers in Korea. Furthermore, there are no religious divisions of any significance. A large majority of the population belong to no organized religion; systems of belief and ethics have been transmitted almost exclusively through the family. Finally, until 1945 Koreans had been under a common political and social system throughout the peninsula for thirteen centuries.

Forty years of alien rule by the Japanese aroused a zealous sense of nationalism in the Korean people. It was stimulated by Japan's efforts to wipe out the national language, to outlaw the teaching of Korean history and to impose discrimination against the Koreans in education and employment. Predictably, the Korean reaction was a fiery defense of the national heritage and national identity, especially in view of the fact that the Koreans had historically considered the Japanese to be their cultural inferiors, as Chinese culture had been transmitted to the Japanese islands by way of Korea. This aroused sense of Korean nationalism is a heritage with which the North Korean leaders (no less than those in the South) must reckon in order to remain in power.

Kim Il-sung, the rotund leader of the North Korean régime, was born under the name Kim Song-chu on the outskirts of Pyongyang. His family emigrated to Manchuria during his early childhood. According to Kim's official biographers, his father was a medical doctor, a practitioner of traditional Chinese medicine, who was captured and tortured to death by the Japanese for Korean independence activities. Whatever the unverified truth of this story, Kim became involved in communist activities in Manchuria after his father's death, and spent a few months in jail at the age of seventeen-perhaps the cause of his apparent failure to graduate from high school. At twenty, he joined the Chinese Communist Party, operating in Manchuria, and became involved in guerrilla activities there during the mid-1930s. Eventually, he became the commander of a small unit, using the name Kim Il- sung, which he borrowed from a legendary Korean hero.

On one occasion in 1937, when he was twenty-five, Kim and about one hundred followers actually penetrated into Korea to the border town of Pochunbo, caught the Japanese off guard and destroyed the village. This skirmish has been exalted as a famous "battle" in North Korea's rewriting of the history of the independence movement, as Kim seeks to capture the mantle of Korean nationalism. By 1941, the Japanese had defeated the harassing guerrillas (whom they called "bandits") in Manchuria, and Kim and a handful of followers retreated into the Soviet Union. Entering a training school there, they emerged in 1945 as officers in the Soviet Army (Kim is said to have been a major) and returned to North Korea, where the Russians installed their Manchurian candidate at the helm of the Soviet-sponsored régime, backed by Russian occupation forces.

Originally imposed upon North Korea by external forces, and ruling less than one-third of the Korean populace, the North Korean régime is now well aware of the necessity of identifying itself with Korean nationalism in order to survive. In an effort to secure a nationalist image, Kim Il-sung has become the center of a cult of personality of ludicrous extremes. The "life and works of Kim Il-sung," which involve a heroic legend of his independence activities during the Japanese rule, must be absorbed by the populace in Leader Study Centers provided for all citizens (including Koreans in Japan). A sample extract from the Pyongyang press refers to him as:

> … the great Leader of the 40 million Korean people [North Korea has only 13 million], peerless patriot, national hero, ever-victorious iron- willed genius-commander and one of the outstanding leaders of the international communist movement and working-class movement, who had been confidently leading our revolution solely along the one road of victory, pulling through in person all storms, and taking upon himself the destiny of the fatherland and the nation for 40 years and more since he started his revolutionary activities in the early years.

Each time Kim's name is mentioned, the whole formula must follow again. The consequence is that every article is filled with continuous repetitive verbiage, leaving little space for anything else. Gaps are filled with odes and poems such as "Kim Il-sung is the Red Sun." Yet unlike Lenin, Mao Tse-tung or Ho Chi Minh, Kim's achievements before his sudden thrust into leadership were negligible, his "thought" is devoid of a hint of originality and his claimed commitment to the national interests of Korea is questionable, except where they serve the advancement of his own political career.

No government, in either North or South, can secure permanent legitimacy in a divided nation. So long as the division persists, Kim's position can be continuously undermined by the existence of an alternative focus of loyalty in the South. The continued possibility that one régime may be able to "outbid" the other in the competition for national loyalty derives from the influence of a nationalism which denies the legitimacy of the national division. Therefore each régime must go out of its way to "prove" that it alone represents genuine nationalism and that the other is a foreign puppet. North Korea must depict the Southern government as a "stooge of American imperialism," just as the ROK government must paint the Kim Il- sung régime as a "puppet of international communism." Indeed, the Southern government is no less pressured than is the Northern one to lay out a timetable for the national unification.

Recent crises-the attempted assassination of South Korea's President Park Chung Hee by a North Korean commando unit in January 1968, the capture of the American intelligence ship Pueblo and its crew two days later, the shooting down of the American EC-121 reconnaissance plane in April of this year, and the increasing harassment of South Korea from the North through stepped-up infiltration and shooting incidents-these provide indirect confirmation that North Korea's overall policy aims have not altered. Kim has mapped a consistent path for reconciling the basic needs of his survival with the reality of national division. To the extent that these conflict, the régime is left with little alternative but to pursue an aggressive policy to eliminate the division.

One of the costs is the tremendous burden of defense expenditures which drain the economies and manpower of both North and South. With a population of only 13 million people-as opposed to South Korea's 30 million-the cost to North Korea of maintaining an army poised against the South is overwhelming. The extent of the military burden is dramatically illustrated by a comparison with Communist China: although the total population of Korea is about 5 percent of the population of Communist China, the standing armies of North and South combined total one million men-which is over one- third the size of Red China's standing army. These figures do not include the "people's militia" of the North, whose claimed strength is 1,300,000, or the "home guard" of the South, just being formed, whose total strength is to be 2,000,000. Korea almost certainly carries the heaviest per capita military burden in the world; its two armies, exclusive of the militia forces, constitute the fourth largest standing army in the world, topped only by those of the United States, the Soviet Union and Communist China. (South Korea alone has the fifth largest standing army, the fourth place being held by India.) The two Germanys, with almost twice Korea's population, have less than half the combined armed strength of the two Koreas. Indeed, North Korea must be the most thoroughly militarized society in existence; it maintains an army more than two-thirds the size of South Korea's from a population not much greater than one-third that of the South, and its military expenditures are estimated at more than two and one- half times the defense budget of the South (in part due to the fact that North Korea invests heavily in military production). It is no wonder that Pyongyang's behavior appears erratic and that pressure to remove the cause of these conditions-the existence of an alternative government in the South- should lead to plans of war.

II

Korea was separated into two zones of operation in 1945 for the purpose of accepting the Japanese surrender. Russian troops which had entered the war in East Asia only a week before the Japanese surrender, occupied the area north of parallel 38°; American troops moved into the South a month after the war had ended. When the two superpowers departed in 1948, after three years of military rule, Korea was a divided nation.

The Soviet Union, utilizing Kim Il-sung and his small entourage, and a large contingent of Soviet-Koreans (Soviet citizens of Korean ethnic origin), quickly created a régime in the North. Kim assumed the post of first secretary of the North Korean Communist Party in December 1945; by February 1946, he was also chairman of the central "People's Committee," later to become the Council of Ministers (Cabinet). Thus, even before the opening in May 1946 of the futile U.S.-Soviet negotiations designed to create a unified trusteeship government, Kim had already been placed in a position of dual power.

In the early days of the Kim régime, subordination to Moscow was complete. Soviet-Koreans, still members of the Communist Party of the Soviet Union, acted on the orders of their superiors from home. It was only with the outbreak of the Korean War, and the entrance into Korea of Chinese "volunteer" troops, that Kim was able to begin the consolidation of internal political control which ultimately enabled him to resist blatant Soviet domination. Consolidation was effected in three stages. In the early war years, Kim managed to mobilize anti-Soviet sentiment among new recruits into the party to diminish the influence of the Soviet-Korean hierarchy; this anti-Soviet sentiment had developed as a result of Soviet unwillingness either to commit troops to North Korea's defense or to provide adequate air cover for the invasion of the South. His maneuvring apparently had the backing of the Chinese-trained Koreans and probably the tacit support of the Chinese military.

The second stage of Kim's consolidation was his purge, at the close of the war, of the major South Korean Communists who had been brought into the party in the North prior to the invasion. A number were executed-among them South Korean Communist Party chief Pak Hon-yong, one of the founders of the original Korean Communist Party established in 1925. No internal rival to Kim Il-sung would be tolerated.

So long as Chinese Communist troops remained in North Korea, Chinese policies were emulated in many fields. Collectivization of agriculture began concurrently with that in China, and followed the same "three-stage" pattern. When China took its "Great Leap Forward," North Korea undertook its parallel Ch'ollima ("Flying Horse") campaign. The acceptance of Chinese support in carrying out these policies did not bring North Korea under Chinese domination, but rather created an independent power base for Kim. Collectivization resulted in effective political reorganization and the emergence of a new élite owing its existence neither to the U.S.S.R. nor China but to the Pyongyang régime under Kim Il-sung.

In 1956, at the start of the move toward de-Stalinization, the Soviet Union acted to restore its control over the North Korean party. Under the guise of "collective leadership," the Russians encouraged a restoration of Soviet-Koreans in the higher party hierarchy. It was Leonid I. Brezhnev, representing the U.S.S.R. at North Korea's Third Party Congress, who told the North Koreans that they would have to establish collective leadership in the party and modify their economic plans. Encouraged by this apparent Russian endorsement, Soviet-Koreans and the Korean Communists from China began to criticize Kim Il-song's "cult of personality." In retaliation, they were purged from the party, but were then taken back, reportedly at the urging of Russia's Anastas Mikoyan and China's then Defense Minister P'eng Teh-huai, who commanded the Chinese forces in Korea (and was later purged himself, presumably for being too close to Moscow). As soon as Chinese troops withdrew in 1958, however, a thorough purge-the third stage of Kim's political consolidation-removed all the Soviet-Korean and China-trained Korean members known to be associated with the "anti-Kim" move. Since then, Kim's control has remained essentially unchallenged, and today the top leaders are all drawn from those who were associated with Kim in Manchuria before 1945; since October 1966, the Party Secretariat has been entirely composed of these Manchurian-Koreans.

Although the Pyongyang régime is committed to communism, it has not been able to avoid severe conflict with both of its giant neighbors. Given its geographic location bordering on the two most powerful communist régimes and its military and economic dependence on both, it is inevitable that North Korea should have found itself in a difficult position when the Soviet Union and Communist China were suddenly at each others' throats. Walking the tightwire between the two disputants, both of whose support Pyongyang needed, proved increasingly difficult. An even more important problem in North Korea's relations with its communist allies, however, has arisen from the discrepancies between the exigencies of rule in North Korea and the foreign policy objectives of both the U.S.S.R. and China. The major difficulties have resulted from Kim Il-song's commitment to unification under his rule.

During the Korean War the unwillingness of the Soviet Union to press for Korean unification at the risk of major war with the United States was unmistakably demonstrated. Russia's call for an armistice meeting in 1951 enabled Kim to mobilize internal resentment against the Soviet-Koreans who had controlled the régime, and to assume the actual decision-making himself. The Russian attempt to create "collective leadership" in 1956 further antagonized North Korea's rulers, for it would have undermined Kim's own power and the unity of leadership needed to carry out an effective offensive policy.

After the armistice Kim attempted to create an independent economic base in North Korea, despite Soviet insistence on integration of the economies of the communist-bloc countries; he stated quite bluntly that without economic independence North Korea could not hope for political independence.

Apparently convinced that the U.S.S.R. would not again endorse an attempt at military reunification of the country, North Korea hoped to achieve a capability to fulfill its goals by unilateral action.

When the Soviet Union failed to reverse North Korea's policy through economic pressures, it cut off economic aid in 1963. North Korea charged the Soviet Union with economic imperialism, and in an angry diatribe called the Russians "great-power chauvinists" who think that everyone else is ignorant and therefore can be ordered around. The U.S.S.R. then discontinued its military assistance.

Throughout the North Korean-Soviet dispute, Peking, involved in its own split with Moscow, sided with Pyongyang; and conversely, by virtue of its antagonism toward the Soviet Union, North Korea appeared to be endorsing the Chinese position. In 1965, however, Kim Il-song's régime and that of Mao Tse-tung came to a parting of the ways. The break was apparently the result of the U.S. commitment of troops to South Viet Nam and the effect of the Viet Nam war on South Korea, Seoul agreed in 1965 to send forces to South Viet Nam, dispatching some of them as early as September of that year and doubling its commitment in 1966. In exchange for its troops, South Korea began to receive increased military assistance from the United States. American support of South Viet Nam generated growing confidence in the willingness of Americans to defend South Korea, and brought new strength to the South Korean economy. Foreign investment began to flow in, and foreign loans became available to the Seoul government on favorable terms. Korean production of some materials for the war (e.g. combat boots) helped boost the economy. The evidence of real economic achievements and the American recognition of South Korea as an important Asian ally gave rise to a new South Korean élan.

All of this had a crushing effect on North Korea and seemed particularly serious because South Korea's military was receiving some modern weaponry, while North Korea was no longer getting military aid from Russia. Especially in view of his expansive goals, Kim Il-song could not afford to allow the North's military capacity to fall far behind that of the South. America's stepped-up assistance to South Korea was dashing North Korea's hopes of appealing to South Koreans on the basis of its superior economic achievements; without Soviet assistance the North's economy was faltering at the same time that South Korea was making genuine progress. Yielding to the pressure of strategic circumstances Pyongyang began to reconcile its differences with Moscow.

Swallowing its pride, Pyongyang accepted the advances being made by the post-Khrushchev government in Moscow, although Leonid I. Brezhnev, the man who had instigated the move to undermine Kim Il-song in 1956, now headed the Soviet Party. In 1965, North Korea and the Soviet Union concluded an agreement for military assistance, which was followed in 1966 by renewed economic aid. In view of old resentments and conflicting objectives, however, this reconciliation can be only temporary. North Korea continued to insist on its independence from Moscow, and, indeed, did not attend the summit meeting of communist parties held in Moscow last June, despite the fact that its relations with Peking were now acrid.

The goal of unification seemed to Kim so overriding, and its achievement would give him a so much better base from which to resist the tremendous pressures of his erstwhile allies, that he was willing to risk rupturing his country's ties with both China and Russia in order to achieve his objective.

III

North Korea's rulers have taken to heart the communist commitment to "transform" the economy and the society. Even before the Russian occupation troops had been withdrawn from North Korea and the government formally inaugurated, nationalization of industry, land reform and political and administrative reorganization had been carried out. Almost immediately the régime began to adopt economic plans, though only on an annual basis. Tremendous difficulties were encountered: not only was the previous integration with the Japanese economy ended, but the national division resulted in shortages of agricultural commodities and consumer goods produced in the South. Furthermore, the Soviet Union apparently took advantage of its dominance to exploit the resources of the peninsula—according to Kim Il-song's later accusations. The lack of adequate technicians, skilled labor or trained managerial personnel was also a tremendous handicap. As if this were not enough, the Korean War devastated the industrial base left by Japan. North Korea's first postwar economic plan, of three years' duration, could do little more than restore production to 1949 levels, even with the help of large amounts of economic aid from the Soviet Union, China and Eastern Europe.

The second postwar economic plan, North Korea's only Five Year Plan, was designed, according to party spokesmen, to create a socialist economic base, both in industry and agriculture. In 1958, midway in the plan, the Ch'ollima campaign was launched. Like China's Great Leap Forward, it was designed to mobilize the people for rapid increases in production. Economic growth was in fact quite rapid, and most of the plans were fulfilled more than a year ahead of schedule, although the consequence was a breakdown in coördination of different economic sectors and exhaustion of machinery and manpower. By 1960, North Korea was bragging that it would soon catch up with Japan in per capita production of some industrial products, including steel.

The overwhelming concentration of investment in heavy industry in the first two postwar plans produced dynamic industrial expansion but also resulted in an extreme shortage of consumer goods and a slow rate of growth in the agricultural sector. By the end of the Five Year Plan, sufficient housing had not yet been constructed to replace that destroyed in the war, and agricultural production had declined in proportion to the population. The goods available were of poor quality, and the press continually complained about work teams which over-fulfilled their quotas with goods of such poor workmanship that they were unusable.

As much to increase political control as to expand agricultural production, the postwar plans also provided for rapid collectivization of farms. Although this policy was not undertaken on a significant scale until 1954, by 1956 80 percent of all farmers had ceased to be classified as "private," and by 1958 all farmers were organized in collectives. Large numbers of farm workers were shifted into industry and the bureaucracy. Whereas in 1946 74.1 percent of the population had been farmers and in 1953 66.4 percent, by 1958 less than half were employed in agriculture and the proportion continued to decline. By 1960, 38.3 percent of the work force was classified as industrial. Between 1953 and 1967, the urban population grew from 17.7 percent to 47.5 percent of the total. The increase in central political control thereby achieved was evident from the tremendous growth of the Workers' (Communist) Party. From 366,000 members in 1946, and 750,000 in 1948, the party grew to 1,164,945 in 1956. By 1967, its 1,700,000 members constituted 13.7 percent of the population, higher than in any other communist society-more than five times that of Communist China. Kim Il-song justified the unusually large number of members on the ground that they would be needed to carry out the reunification of Korea.

The major occupational and geographic shifts which took place during the 1950s significantly uprooted old patterns of life and replaced much of the previous dependence on the family and clan with dependence on the political régime. Universal elementary education has created a literate, if highly indoctrinated, populace. The complete elimination of the Chinese writing system in favor of the 24-letter, purely phonetic Korean alphabet (originally invented in the fifteenth century by a Korean king interested in the science of linguistics) has made reading and writing readily accessible to all. And universal compulsory vocational education at the junior-high level was recently introduced, in order to instill in every member of society the mentality of a "worker."

The Seven Year Plan was introduced with much fanfare at the Fourth Party Congress in September 1961. Spokesmen for the government endorsed the plan as one which would insure North Korea's economic independence, provide a comfortable standard of living for all and prepare the way for national reunification. Almost immediately the plan ran into difficulties. Only the steel and electricity sectors seemed able to meet their annual quotas (based on annual growth rates in 1960). By 1964, after the termination of Soviet economic assistance, the plans had obviously been laid aside, and goals were set lower than the (unfulfilled) annual plans for 1963-in some cases lower than the realized output of 1963.

The end of Soviet military assistance destroyed any hopes of recouping the shattered plans. Citing what he said was the increasing hostility of the United States, Kim Il-song announced that the economic plans would have to suffer because of the need for greater military expenditures. Statistics on production, which during the 1950s had filled the newspapers and journals of the North, began to disappear from the press and were replaced by articles on "American atrocities," "South Korean militarists" and North Korea's need for an improved defense posture.

Renewed Soviet economic assistance in 1966 was accompanied by an extension of the Seven Year Plan to 1970.

Statistics did not reappear, however, and as recently as last March, Kim Il-song stated that economic planning in North Korea was "unsatisfactory." Current economic difficulties have led to attempts to divert popular attention to external crises. Kim cannot help but reflect that national unification would give him a more viable economic base.

IV

Kim Il-song has made it clear that he intends to unify Korea, under his leadership, by the time of his hwan-gap, or sixtieth birthday. In Korea, the sixtieth birthday has traditionally marked the end of an individual's first life cycle and the beginning of his second. A person's life goals should have been fulfilled by the time he reaches his hwan-gap. Kim was born on April 15, 1912; since Koreans count the first year of life (before the first birthday) as age one, he has only until early 1971 to fulfill his "life goal." Failure to achieve his objective would mean a loss of face rarely courted by an oriental leader.

A Westerner may easily dismiss this non-rational system of policy-planning; to a Korean, it is not only credible but familiar. For example, did not President Syngman Rhee, despite his Princeton Ph.D. and forty-year residence in the United States, promote as his successor Lee Ki-pung, a fellow clansman of the succeeding clan generation, much as a traditional monarch without heir would have chosen his successor? (Lee committed suicide when Rhee was forced to resign.) South Koreans were not being irrelevant when they knowingly observed that the American EC-121 was shot down on Kim Il-song's birthday. Therefore, the significance of Kim's hwan- gap is a part of the war of nerves with the South.

The selection of 1971 as the deadline for political unification is not based solely, however, on Kim's adherence to traditional cultural concepts. The year 1971 is a significant one for many reasons. In South Korea, a Presidential election is to be held, involving either an acute succession crisis or a divisive political fight to amend the constitution so that President Park may seek a third term-or both. Furthermore, American economic aid to South Korea is scheduled to be discontinued, and U.S. military assistance has been declining for some time, despite occasional increases in response to a crisis. U.S. military aid to South Korea declined from 72.4 percent of the national defense expenditures of the Republic of Korea as recently as 1962, to 26.7 percent in 1968. The increases in the financial burden of maintaining the world's fifth largest army and creating a national militia are surely enough to absorb the economic gains which the country has made in the past few years, leaving little actual improvement in the living standards of the South Koreans. Indeed, in recent talks with South Korean inductees, I found the most common complaint to be perpetual hunger, indicating that the South has begun cutting vital corners in its defense outlays. Another factor is that the first payments on many of the loans taken out by the South Korean Government during the euphoria of rapid economic growth in the first years of the Viet Nam crisis will fall due in 1971.

North Korea's current economic plan will end in 1970 and its military aid agreement with the Soviet Union will also expire then. Under this agreement, North Korea has acquired considerable military equipment, including 500 jet fighter planes, about 60 of them MIG-21s. The end of the economic and military aid agreements will give Kim the choice of recommitting himself to subservience to the U.S.S.R., or moving against the South immediately, before his large-scale hardware becomes obsolete or worn down. (Unlike the South, North Korea can produce most of its small-scale weaponry and ammunition.) Certainly, if Kim seriously intends to make another attempt to reunify Korea by military means, he must see the advantage in acting before American forces have been withdrawn from South Viet Nam. Also, controversy over the U.S.-Japan security treaty and the return of Okinawa may arouse opposition in the United States and Japan to America's Asian involvement, and complicate the movement of American forces in East Asia. Finally, Kim might be inclined to take advantage of recent trends in American public opinion: if public reaction was responsible for the cessation in the bombing of North Viet Nam, it might well prevent an American bombing of North Korea in retaliation for acts against the South. If the United States should also prove unwilling to cross the DMZ into North Korea again, in view of the fact that Pyongyang concluded bilateral defense treaties with both the Soviet Union and Communist China in the summer of 1961, then the North Korean régime might feel it would not be risking much by launching an offensive.

North Korea has been preparing its people for a renewal of war. Appealing to the reservoir of Korean nationalism, Kim Il-song has introduced as a policy slogan the concept of chu-che, roughly translatable as "autonomy." Pointing out that Korea cannot rely on others and yet maintain its own independence, Kim calls for both resistance to Soviet and Chinese intervention and an aggressive push to drive American influence out of the South. "It is clear that we cannot make a revolution by relying on others," he says, "and that no one can make the Korean revolution for us.... Chu-che in ideology, independence in politics, self-reliance in economy, and self-defense in national defense-this is the stand our Party has consistently adhered to." Under the slogan, "A Gun in One Hand and a Hammer and Sickle in the Other," every man and woman has been exhorted to be ready for mobilization against an "American invasion," and a militia of "Workers- Peasants' Red Guards," with a total strength of 1,300,000, has been formed of men and women between the ages of 17 and 45, each armed with a rifle manufactured in the North. In Pyongyang and other major cities, underground concrete bunkers and air-raid shelters have been constructed.

At the same time, offensive training for infiltration activities has been expanded. According to the accounts of Kim Shin-jo, the captured member of the unit sent to assassinate President Park, the key infiltration group, the élite 124th Unit of the North Korean Peoples' Army (NKPA), formed entirely of 2,400 officers and placed directly under the Chief of Staff of the NKPA, is divided into eight sections, each with responsibilities for a province in South Korea. Reports of other defectors and captured infiltrators indicate that the unit is intended to gather information, recruit adherents in mountainous areas of scant population and form an underground party. One infiltration tactic has been to include in four-man units one individual with relatives in the South. The aim is to secure coöperation of Southerners by threatening harm to remaining members of the family in North Korea. (Despite this tactic, infiltrators who make themselves known to their relatives are ordinarily turned in to the police.)

In 1968, infiltrators detected in an attempt to cross the DMZ totaled 1,087; it is impossible to estimate the number undetected. Agents discovered entering by the coast numbered 160. The level of infiltration has been stepped up in 1969. North Korea has also sought to recruit South Korean students abroad to return home and organize Southern intellectuals to press for reunification. It has gained the coöperation of some students by providing them with financial assistance to complete their education abroad. Several students returning from Europe have been arrested in South Korea for involvement in underground activities.

Kim Il-song's intention to create disruption in the South is evident. His willingness to risk war with the United States in pursuit of his goals has been demonstrated in recent crises. In large measure, his belligerency derives from the difficulty of maintaining his rule in the unique conditions faced by North Korea. Whatever the outcome, the cost of a new offensive is certain to be high for the Korean people.

© Foreign Affairs

The Man Who Would Be Kim

Byung-joon Ahn

REUTERS

Kim Il Sung with his son Kim Jong Il.

KOREA'S DANGEROUS FUTURE

The Korean peninsula has entered a period of grave uncertainty. The death of North Korean President Kim Il Sung on July 8 came at a critical moment. The United States had just resumed talks to probe whether North Korea would abandon its nuclear weapons program in return for diplomatic recognition and economic assistance. With Kim's death, the answer to that question, which will define the fate of not only the North but the entire peninsula, fell into the untested hands of his son, Kim Jong Il. It is a question that this oddly reclusive man cannot hope to answer. Having assumed power when he did, the younger Kim is caught in a bind that only his father might have had the power, if not the wisdom, to break.

Kim Jong Il's dilemma is this: the North's increasing isolation and impoverishment make political and economic reform imperative; but Kim may find reform impossible. His legitimacy rests almost solely with the mantle of extreme nationalism inherited from his revered father. Kim will have little choice now but to continue down that road. But the need for economic opening is so overwhelming, the North's isolationist course and pursuit of nuclear weapons so untenable, and Kim's apparent abilities so limited that his regime will almost surely be short-lived.

The Korean peninsula remains unique. It is a place where the strategic interests of China, Japan, and Russia intersect, and where the United States still keeps 37,000 troops to deter another war. A nuclearized North or its messy breakup can only be averted by strengthening the regional deterrence and defense capabilities of America and its East Asian allies now. A steady and consistent policy of quiet and credible action will help discourage any provocation by the North's insecure but substantially weakened regime. In the meantime, should a reformist clique emerge – one that takes its cues from economic necessity rather than the dangerous imperatives of an outmoded ideology – then a new era of reconciliation and cooperation can commence.

For the time being, the status of the North's nuclear program is likely to remain unresolved. Washington must be careful not to let Pyongyang divide the United States from its allies. Together they must make clear that a nuclear-armed North is unacceptable. It would not only disrupt the state of deterrence on the peninsula but also threaten East Asia's entire balance of power. The only resolution to the crisis is not merely to contain the North's current program but to roll back any nuclear weapons capability it may have already developed.

WHY KIM WON'T LAST

Kim Jong Il's greatest asset is that he is the North's only alternative. Given the suddenness of his father's death, the ruling North Korean Labor Party, the People's Army, and the state bureaucracy have had little choice but to rally behind him as their supreme leader.

After all, Kim was handpicked by his father, the so-called Great Leader. Groomed since the 1970s to be the "party center," he has cultivated his own support network of "revolutionary small groups" and assumed supreme command of the military in the 1990s. But how long Kim remains in power will depend on his health, whether he can preserve unity among the ruling groups and feed his people, and most important, how he handles the nuclear issue.

Little is known of Kim, who has been strangely shrouded from public view for most of his career. His health seems to be poor; he is known to have diabetes, high blood pressure, and heart problems. His competence and character remain sources of intense speculation. Kim is rumored to have orchestrated the bizarre kidnapping in 1978 of a South Korean actress with whom he had developed a peculiar fascination. He is also suspected of having directed the 1983 bombing in Rangoon that assassinated much of the South Korean cabinet when President Chun Doo Hwan visited there, as well as the 1987 explosion aboard a South Korean airliner that killed 115 people. He may have initiated Pyongyang's move to withdraw from the Nuclear Nonproliferation

Treaty (NPT) in March 1993, and from the International Atomic Energy Agency (IAEA) in June 1994. With the exception of Chinese President Jiang Zemin, former Chinese President Yang Shangkun, and Cambodia's Prince Norodom Shihanouk, he has rarely met foreign dignitaries. Except for his erratic behavior, Kim is largely an unknown entity.

It is this unheralded man who must now skipper the North's sinking ship through perilously unfamiliar waters. The end of the Cold War has placed the North in the midst of simultaneous political and economic crises. Both the Soviet Union (then Russia) and China have normalized relations with the South, increasing the North's isolation and challenging the rationale of the state. Today, China provides the North's only dependable support, supplying roughly a million tons of oil and a half-million tons of food each year.

The disappearance of communist allies and Pyongyang's autarkic mismanagement have devastated the North's economy. Between 1989 and 1993, gross national product shrank 20 percent to about $20.5 billion, roughly one-sixteenth the size of the South's $328.7 billion economy. The North's foreign trade declined another 1.1 percent in 1993 to a mere $2.4 million, exacerbating the foreign exchange shortage of a treasury that already owes $10 billion in foreign debt. As food and energy shortages worsen, North Koreans have been urged to eat only two meals a day, and factories reportedly operate at 30 percent of capacity. In December 1993, the regime acknowledged for the first time that it had missed the production targets of its third seven-year plan.

Thus, in all aspects except the nuclear field, the competition between the North and the South is over. The South has outperformed the North both economically and politically. The South's economy ranks fifteenth in the world in terms of gnp and thirteenth in trade volume. Although its politics remain volatile, the South has wrought a functioning democracy, electing Kim Young Sam in 1993 as the first civilian president in 32 years. The South, moreover, remains a faithful security ally of the United States, as well as being its seventh-largest trading partner.

Given these circumstances, Kim's primary goal will be survival. Domestically, that means preserving the name of juche ideology, his father's founding philosophy of self-reliance and exclusive nationalism based on the principles of independence and grand national unity in a "Koryo Confederal Democratic Republic." Unification policy will continue to be based on the rhetoric of "one nation, one country, and two systems, two governments." Foreign policy, however, will be based on two Koreas, in the hopes of protecting the legitimacy of the Democratic People's Republic of Korea as a state.

The North's economic crisis and the nuclear issue will seriously challenge Kim's skills as a political operator. Scenarios for his downfall are many. Intense debates could fracture his elite circle into competing power centers. Internal challengers may seek to undermine Kim's uncertain stature, exposing to the public tales of corruption or other more unsavory aspects of Kim's private life. The specter of mass starvation could spark popular rebellions. A leader as untested as Kim could also inadvertently provoke the kind of domestic or international crisis that would ultimately be his own undoing. Kim's power will remain relatively safe only so long as his competence commands the support of top military and party leaders, such as Marshal O Jin U, Prime Minister Kang Song San, and Kim Il Sung's younger brother Kim Yong Ju, who returned to the Politburo in December 1993 after an unexplained absence of some 20 years. But it is precisely Kim's competence that has long been called into question.

But the real crux of Kim's quandary is that, despite the overwhelming need for economic reform, he has little choice but to continue his father's outmoded policies. For nearly two decades, Kim justified his claim to power as being the heir to his father's mantle in what would be North Korea's first communist dynastic succession, even as the North's political and economic crises turned that inheritance into a liability.

Now, the more Kim tries to bolster his credibility by following the political imperatives set by his father, the worse his economic difficulties and diplomatic isolation will become.

Importantly, Kim lacks his father's charisma. Absent the same cult of personality, Kim's reign may not last too long. Kim Il Sung's near- deification as the founder of the Democratic People's Republic allowed him to transcend any challenge to his legitimacy, even as he presided over the North's isolation and economic ruin. The inheritor of that "revolutionary" legacy cannot hope to be as lucky. Kim cannot raise his people's standard of living, as Deng Xiaoping has done in China, without jettisoning his father's philosophy of self-reliance and diminishing the mantle of his inheritance. He cannot liberalize the political system, as Boris Yeltsin has done in Russia, without alienating military and party leaders and seriously jeopardizing his grip on power. As long as he "adheres to and brightens our style of socialism," as Foreign Minister Kim Yong Nam encouraged him to do in his eulogy for Kim Il Sung, Kim's own future will remain murky indeed.

AFTER THE FALL

It is not easy to delineate precise scenarios for the North after Kim Jong Il's demise. But two likely possibilities exist: the ascension of a reform-minded military-bureaucratic regime, or a violent collapse of the state. Which will occur depends primarily on the quality of the North's leadership, the cohesion of its elite, the leadership's ability to cope with the economic crisis, and how it manages the nuclear issue. One thing is clear: the regime under the Kim family is unlikely to survive for too long, and North Korea is bound to undergo some kind of structural transformation, with or without reform.

A military-bureaucratic regime would distance itself from the Kim dynasty, following China's example of top-down reform and economic opening. As of now, real reformers, a North Korean Deng or Yeltsin, do not exist. But over time, as the economic crisis deepens and North Koreans, popularly and within the party leadership, begin to question the viability of the Kim dynasty, perestroika may eventually find Pyongyang. Reform would most likely be carried out by a collective leadership and reflect consensus within the party. To maintain order, this new cadre would try to preserve a one-party system but carry out liberalizing economic reforms along the path taken by neighboring China or Vietnam.

Such a regime might be more accommodating of reconciliation with the South and of U.S. demands for nuclear transparency. It would have less difficulty abandoning the Kims' rationale of confrontation and isolation that serve as the organizing principles of the world's last surviving Stalinist state. To carry out a successful economic opening, a reformist regime would need access to trade and economic assistance from the United States and its East Asian allies. Freed of ideological baggage, it might be more likely to forfeit the nuclear program as a bargaining chip. Hence, a reformist clique is the most desirable scenario for initiating a new era in North-South relations and for the North's political and economic integration with the rest of the world.

But such a benign evolution is not guaranteed. For a nation so long closed, the path of reform is fraught with uncertainty. The limited skills and resources available to economic planners would make it difficult to satisfy rising consumer demand, especially if broader access to media and information expose the extent of the North's impoverishment. A reformist regime could also fall prey to a cycle of rising popular political expectations. Even for avowed economic reformers, "seeking truth from facts," as Deng has urged in China, carries political dangers, as the frustrated 1989 revolt in Tiananmen Square amply proved. A reformist regime in the North could find itself similarly tested, or even toppled.

Thus a violent collapse, initiated by an internal power struggle or civil strife, could befall either Kim or a reformist regime. As happened in the revolutions that unsettled old orders in Romania, Albania, and Bulgaria, the regime's collapse could produce a period of anarchy. But in the case of the North, it is highly unlikely that either a civil society or political pluralism would quickly spring up. Instead, chaos would likely drive millions of refugees across the Tuman and Yalu rivers and the demilitarized zone separating the two Koreas. Thousands of others could take to the seas. Such a scenario is among the worst possible outcomes and one that South Korea, China, Japan, and the United States would certainly like to avoid.

It is against this potentially gruesome backdrop that the United States, its allies, and Pyongyang itself must work toward the North's "soft landing" through gradual economic reform. Only when economic necessity prevails over the political imperatives of the Kim dynasty can such an outcome materialize. But given the rigid nature of

Kim's regime, a "crash landing" is more likely. Such an event could lead either to another attempt to construct a reformist regime or to a sudden and unstable reunion with the South.

PLAYING A WEAK HAND

In his game of brinkmanship, Kim Il Sung attempted to use the nuclear card to recast the North's survival and security. He sought to present the world with a fait accompli and to keep the nuclear weapons that his regime has, in all likelihood, already developed. Only in his final days, as Washington contemplated tough U.N. economic sanctions and former President Jimmy Carter made his "private" journey to Pyongyang, did Kim agree to freeze his ongoing nuclear program in return for resuming high-level talks with the United States. To avert further isolation, he attempted to bargain away the limited prospect of future inspections in order to extort political recognition and economic concessions from the United States, Japan, and other Western countries.

The North's future now hinges on his son. But judging from the Geneva accord that Kim Jong Il signed with the United States in August 1994, he has not changed his father's policies, and whether he will faithfully implement his ambiguously defined pledge remains to be seen.

The deal went as follows: Kim agreed not to reprocess the North's some 8,000 spent fuel rods and to halt construction of two nearly completed reactors, to seal and allow IAEA monitoring of a "radiochemical laboratory," and to remain party to the NPT; in return, Washington promised to provide two 2,000-megawatt light-water reactors (which produce non-weapons-grade fuel), to arrange for an interim energy source as the North's graphite-moderated reactors are dismantled, to refrain from using nuclear weapons against the North, and to establish diplomatic "representation" in each other's capitals.

In other words, Washington gave Pyongyang all that it wanted. Nowhere in the Geneva agreement is there a provision for special, let alone mutual, inspection of suspected nuclear facilities or waste sites to verify the North's past record. This is the reason South Korea and Japan are so unhappy over the accord, with South Korea's President Kim Young Sam stating that even "one-half" of a nuclear weapon in the North is unacceptable. While Washington has since insisted that the North commit itself to special inspection before construction of any light-water reactor can begin, the North has refused. Yet absent such a pledge, Washington would be mistaken to acquiesce in Pyongyang's policy of nuclear ambiguity.

Moreover, Kim's ability to implement what he has already agreed to must be questioned. Although the threat of sanctions would appear compelling, Kim depends first on the support of his military, which is currently led by old-style guerrilla-war partisans who may continue to regard nuclear weapons as their primary guarantee of security. Pyongyang is thus likely to remain determined not to allow any inspection of its past nuclear record. At some point, Kim may seek to use his regime's nuclear card to replace the U.N.-North Korean armistice that halted the Korean War with a peace agreement reducing or gradually removing U.S. forces from the South.

Three near-term decisions by Kim will give some indication as to the North's agenda and Kim's ability to carry out the Geneva accord. First, Kim must decide whether to reprocess the North's spent fuel rods, which contain about 40 kilograms of plutonium (enough for five atomic bombs) and to reload the North's five-megawatt graphite-moderated reactor with fresh rods, which Pyongyang has threatened to do. These decisions must be made soon, as the spent rods continue to deteriorate in the cooling pond where they are stored. The United States wants the spent rods placed under IAEA control and moved to a third country. The North has proposed "dry storage," that is, encasing them in cement within North Korea. Under the NPT, Pyongyang can legally reprocess the rods with IAEA inspectors present, although doing so would violate the North-South denuclearization agreement signed in 1991. Thus, reprocessing may yet proceed.

Kim's second decision regards the future of the nuclear program. Not only is the North's five-megawatt reactor awaiting refueling, but a separate 50-megawatt reactor in Yongbyon could begin operating in early 1995, and a third 200-megawatt reactor in Taechon could be completed in 1996. Once in full operation, the two larger reactors could produce enough spent fuel to reprocess plutonium for at least 20 to 30 bombs per year. In addition to the three reactors, a plutonium reprocessing plant is also nearly complete, and in March 1994 IAEA inspectors reported evidence that a second reprocessing line was being built in the same plant.

North Korea is thus at the threshold of becoming a major nuclear power. It remains to be seen whether it will indeed abandon these facilities, which have cost it more than $2 billion, in return for the U.S. pledge to supply two light-water reactors that will cost about $4 billion and take seven to ten years to construct. Besides, dismantling the North's existing reactors will itself cost an enormous amount of money. The North has reportedly said that it would continue building the graphite reactors until a light-water reactor becomes fully operational.

Finally, Kim must decide whether to allow international inspection of any undeclared nuclear facilities and weapons that the North has developed. The CIA believes that the North may have already produced one or two nuclear bombs. Vladimir Kryuchkov, former head of the KGB, reported to the Soviet Politburo as early as February 1990 that the North had developed a nuclear device. Most recently, on July 27, 1994, Kang Myung Do, a defector identified as the son-in-law of North Korean Prime Minister Kang Song San, told a news conference in Seoul that the North possesses five nuclear weapons and is trying to develop five more while it stretches out negotiations with the United States.

How Kim decides these issues will be revealed in the process of implementing the Geneva agreement, which itself is likely to require a long and arduous negotiation. Judging from the North's strategy so far, however, the real danger exists that Pyongyang has already succeeded in keeping any weapons it previously made while buying the time to build more. Washington's decision to freeze the North's nuclear program now while delaying negotiation of contentious issues like Pyongyang's past record and its medium-range ballistic missile and biochemical weapons programs may actually have worsened this danger.

SEOUL'S NIGHTMARE

Seoul has grown increasingly wary of the manner in which Washington's negotiations with Pyongyang have progressed. It harbors the very real concern that Washington is so preoccupied with freezing further development of the North's nuclear program that it may forgo purposeful action on Pyongyang's past record, much as Washington did with Pakistan. From Seoul's viewpoint, Washington had prompted the South to abandon its own reprocessing and enrichment of fissile material for nuclear weapons in 1991, and so it is now incumbent on Washington to make Pyongyang do the same. It worries that Washington may be tempted to pursue a policy that pulls back from the brink at the expense of ensuring a denuclearized peninsula. Seoul also fears that its interests in the negotiations will suffer from Washington's overriding concern with global nuclear nonproliferation – that Washington may be tempted to declare victory in order to bolster a sagging NPT, which is up for renewal in 1995, and thus forsake local deterrence and assurances on a denuclearlized North.

Indeed, Seoul fears that Washington may even strike a separate peace with Pyongyang, delinking its relationship with the North from its alliance with the South. Washington's efforts to set up a liaison office in Pyongyang, even before Seoul has one, have not helped matters. South Korean Foreign Minister Han Sung Joo visited Washington in September to emphasize that the North's relationships with the United States and the South should proceed in tandem. Washington acknowledged the need for both dialogues to complement each other but has also made clear that it will negotiate independently with Pyongyang if necessary.

Yet it would be difficult for Washington to reach and implement a satisfactory agreement absent Seoul's approval and cooperation. For example, it is the South that has committed to financing 70 percent of the cost of the light-water reactors through an international consortium, the Korea Energy Development Organization, to be launched under Washington's auspices. It is important, then, that Washington help the two Koreas normalize their relations. Washington's best tack is to work toward the long-term goal of consensual unification even as it seeks a short-term resolution of the nuclear issue.

Throughout their talks, however, the North has sought to maneuver itself between the United States and the South and to negotiate the nuclear issue with

Washington alone. Moreover, it has treated its relations with the South as necessary only to the extent that they improve relations with the United States. As long as South Korea remains fearful of being left out of an issue in which it possesses such vital stakes, relations with both the North and the United States are bound to deteriorate. Both Washington and Seoul must make clear to Pyongyang that normal relations with the United States depend first on normal relations with the South.

Seoul has other concerns as well. A nuclear-armed North would certainly upset the state of deterrence on the Korean peninsula. Seoul doubts whether Washington would indeed extend its own nuclear arsenal in case of attack, and even whether Washington would continue to maintain its forward troop deployment in the teeth of a North Korean nuclear threat. While the North's motivation may well be defensive, a nuclear capability nonetheless increases the likelihood of diplomatic blackmail by Pyongyang. It also greatly diminishes the prospect of consensual reunification through a gradual process of confidence-building.

In short, Kim Jong Il with a nuclear arsenal is the South's strategic nightmare. As such, Seoul can be expected to stand firm against permanent ambiguity for the North's nuclear status. Moreover, should the United States appear to acquiesce in letting the North keep nuclear weapons, the credibility of the U.S. security commitment as well as U.S.South Korean relations could only suffer.

BY DESIGN OR DEFAULT

At such a time of uncertainty, the United States and South Korea must reaffirm their alliance commitments and the goals of nuclear transparency and gradual reunification. This message should be clearly communicated to Pyongyang. Preventing a nuclear North will require Washington to exercise timely and decisive leadership with clearly defined goals, a consistent policy, and credible action. Seoul should consult with Washington and coordinate its own policies toward that same end.

Above all, the United States and the South must remain united in their goal of ensuring a denuclearized peninsula. This means getting a full accounting of Pyongyang's past record through both IAEA and mutual North-South inspections. At the same time, Washington must stem further growth in Pyongyang's nuclear program by compelling Kim to live up to the commitments that he signed in Geneva. The Clinton administration should make clear that it will withhold diplomatic recognition and economic cooperation, including a light-water reactor, unless Kim makes good on the accord. Such a policy would receive the support of the U.S. Senate, which has unanimously passed a bill stating that no funds be made available to North Korea "until the President certifies and reports to Congress that North Korea does not possess nuclear weapons, has halted its nuclear weapons program, and has not exported weapons-grade plutonium."

Washington must also make clear that Pyongyang must first normalize relations with Seoul before it can negotiate any peace with the United States. Any other policy would substantially undermine Seoul's attempts to improve its own relations with Pyongyang. Nor should Washington allow Pyongyang to chip away at the U.S.-South Korean mutual defense treaty, which has kept the peace on the peninsula for more than 40 years. In these areas, Washington and Seoul must speak with one voice. Otherwise, Washington will be playing into Pyongyang's hands by inadvertently strengthening the pillars on which Kim's failing regime now rests.

For those reasons, Washington must take care not to transform a third round of talks with Pyongyang into a long political negotiation. The more the North can prolong direct negotiations with the United States, the more it will try to relegate relations with the South to an ancillary status. Such a course would not only damage Washington's relations with Seoul but also diminish the chances for a political reconciliation between the two Koreas, on which an ultimate solution to the peninsula's crisis depends.

But it remains doubtful that Kim will live up to the Geneva accord at all, especially given Pyongyang's track record of reneging at the last minute even as others meet its demands. The best way to ensure compliance is for Washington and its allies to remain strong in the face of a progressively weakening, if unpredictable, Kim regime. Kim will only give up the perceived gains of his nuclear program if faced with a certain countervailing disincentive.

As U.S. Secretary of Defense William Perry has suggested, "a very firm stand and very strong actions" are the best way to deter any possible military provocation by the North. This means enhancing joint deterrence capabilities with the South. Coordinated, quiet, and firm action on the part of the allies should keep pace with any escalation in Kim's bluster. The Geneva accord, continued negotiation, and the threat of sanctions will not produce desired results from Pyongyang unless they are backed up by a clear demonstration of determination and strength.

A nuclear-armed North would upset East Asia's entire military balance, causing South Korea, Japan, and even Taiwan to consider developing equivalent deterrents. It is in the interests of all the region's powers, then, that the North be denied nuclear weapons. Washington should thus stem any tendency for others to "free ride" as it bears the burden and risks of diplomacy. China, especially, has opposed sanctions in favor of diplomacy, but without facilitating dialogue with the North. As it enjoys the best relations with Pyongyang, Beijing should be pressed to persuade Kim to abandon his nuclear ambitions. This issue is important enough that the United States and Japan should make progress in their bilateral relations with Beijing contingent on a truly constructive Chinese role.

Russia has said that it will support U.N. sanctions, provided that an eight-party conference be held first, an idea that the United States has reluctantly supported.

Japan, meanwhile, has made clear that it can only support sanctions if they come through the United Nations. Yet Japan shares a strong interest in preventing a nuclear-armed North. If China succeeds in blocking U.N. sanctions, the United States should at least enlist Japan and South Korea in imposing their own sanctions, and only when the North shows serious signs of scuttling the nuclear option should they provide generous economic and political assistance. In the meantime, the United States, China, Russia, and Japan should also strive to provide a stable security environment in Northeast Asia through a two-plus-four dialogue that includes both Koreas, as an important supplement to the region's discrete bilateral relationships.

What is at stake on the Korean peninsula after the death of Kim Il Sung is the very credibility of American foreign policy, which Washington's confused signals thus far have significantly eroded. Only by restoring a steady hand can Washington regain the trust and respect that will ensure peace on the Korean peninsula and its success in future efforts at global nuclear nonproliferation.

But ultimately, the Korean question must be resolved by Koreans themselves, through normalized relations and eventual unification. The death of Kim Il Sung has raised the hope that those goals might someday soon be attained. South Korea will continue to view unification as a slow process of confidence-building and reconciliation, even as the North pursues its chimera of a confederal state. But it would serve Pyongyang well to recognize that Korean unification can come by design, or it may just as surely come by default.

Byung-joon Ahn is Professor of Political Science at Yonsei University, Seoul.

© Foreign Affairs

July/August 1997

Why North Korea Will Muddle Through

Marcus Noland

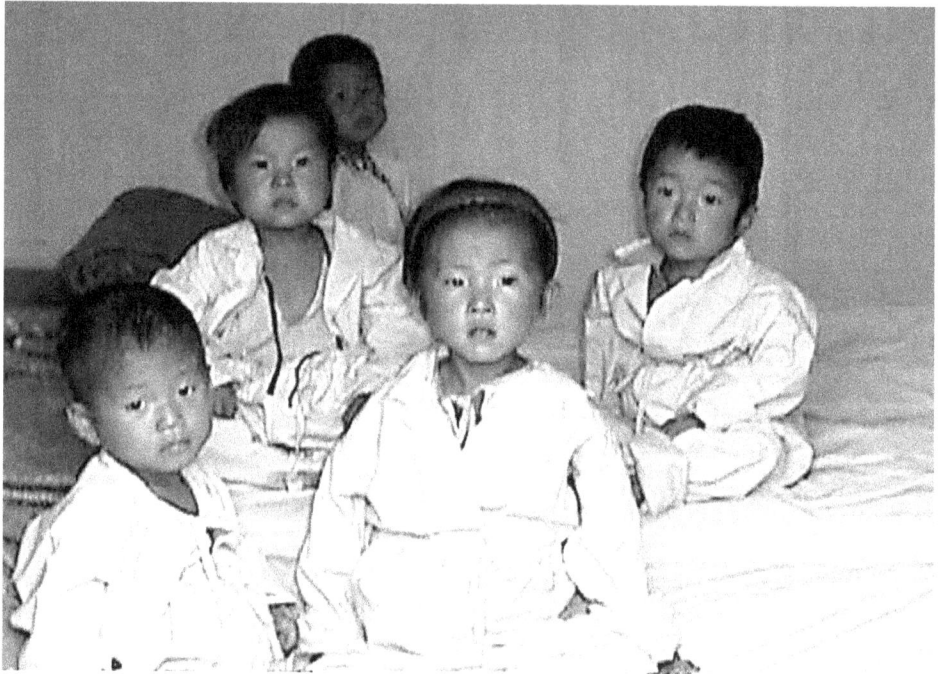

North Korean children sit on hospital beds suffering from malnutrition, Singapore, August 19, 1998.

APPARATCHIK CAPITALISM

After consulting with their superiors, the guards at Rajin harbor allowed us to exit. Apparently two Americans on a morning jog were not thought to pose a grave threat to national security. As we ran up the hill overlooking the harbor, I noticed a small military installation. On our way down I watched two soldiers stealthily working their way through the dilapidated structures, eventually reaching an isolated corner of the base, far from their comrades. Like two characters from a B movie, the soldiers looked left and right before kneeling. One removed his knapsack and placed it between them in the dirt. He opened it and withdrew two ...

Bananas. At that moment his colleague glanced upward and spied us on the ridge above. The soldiers leaped to their feet and turned their bodies to shield the bananas from our view. The presumably banana-laden knapsack was stashed at the base of a wall, and, checking that they otherwise had not been observed, the soldiers headed back toward the center of the base.

One can easily conjure up myriad interpretations of a surreptitious trade in bananas at an isolated North Korean military installation in the autumn of 1996. But any consideration of the state of the North Korean economy presents policymakers with two fundamental problems. First, there is an acute lack of information, a vast gulf between fragmentary anecdotal evidence on the one hand and highly uncertain estimates of economic aggregates on the other. Second, there is really no reliable theory linking economic distress or deprivation to political change. Even a reasonably persuasive analysis of the economy does not necessarily provide much guidance for political decision-making, much less for assessing the stability of the regime.

The North Korean economy is in bad shape, and a famine of unknown magnitude is under way in parts of the country, but it appears that minimum survival requirements can be maintained with little or no external support. Kim Jong Il's regime appears to have been largely successful in fusing juche (self-reliance) ideology to Korean nationalism, and unlike the countries of Central Europe, North Korea has no institutions capable of channeling mass discontent into effective political action.

Rather, in light of its domestic politics and geopolitical position, North Korea is likely to muddle through, along the lines of Romania in the 1980s, with support from China and possibly Japan and South Korea, which would like to avoid its collapse. Ironically, the reduction of North Korea to a dependency would represent the inversion of the ideology of its founder, Kim Il Sung, and a restoration of the status quo of much of the last millennium.

PROFITS FROM PACHINKO

The North Korean economy is organized like other centrally planned economies. Its distinguishing feature has been the extremes to which central planning has been taken under juche ideology. As a result, the economy is shrinking, but the margin of error for estimates of almost all economic aggregates of interest is on the order of hundreds of millions of dollars.

Foreign observers, including those from other socialist states, concluded that by the late 1970s the North Korean economy was experiencing serious problems when its ability to grow "extensively" through the mobilization of resources was reaching its limits. A series of macroeconomic shocks in the late 1980s—including the withdrawal of Soviet aid, economic disengagement with its former socialist allies in the Eastern bloc, and bad weather that worsened the crisis in agriculture—exacerbated those difficulties.

Assessing the degree of economic distress in North Korea with any precision is difficult. Virtually all economic and social data are regarded as state secrets. A number of individuals and organizations have attempted to estimate North Korean national income, but figures cited in public discussions are invariably the official South Korean estimates produced by the Bank of Korea. Those figures are apparently derived by taking classified data generated by South Korean intelligence agencies on physical output and then applying South Korean prices and value-added coefficients to indexes of physical production. Because the original estimates of physical output are classified, there is little opportunity to check their plausibility, nor is it obvious that South Korean prices and value-added weights are the most appropriate. Furthermore, the final growth rate figure is reportedly subject to interagency bargaining within the South Korean government.

With these caveats in mind, Bank of Korea data indicate that the North Korean economy shrank by roughly 30 percent from 1991 to 1996, certainly a significant amount, but not unprecedented for a transitional economy. However, the estimated fall in national income may well overstate the reduction in household welfare, since it is unlikely that such services as housing and education, which are undercounted in the socialist accounting system and are not amenable to physical measurement, have declined as much as manufactured output. These estimates of national income are therefore not necessarily indexes of hardship or political discontent.

Somewhat less uncertainty surrounds North Korea's external economic relationships. In principle one can obtain estimates of trade and capital flows by aggregating the data reported by North Korea's trade partners after adjusting for misreporting and transportation costs. Three conclusions stand out: North Korea runs large and chronic trade deficits, its trade is concentrated with a few partners, and, most telling, trade volumes are falling. If the deficits that North Korea runs with China—obtaining imports on concessional terms—and the surpluses that it runs with South Korea—generating export revenues—are considered in effect to be politically determined, China and South Korea together implicitly support most of North Korea's trade deficit with the rest of the world.

Still, North Korea appears to confront a financing gap on the order of hundreds of millions of dollars. Aside from exports, the largest source of hard currency earnings is probably remittances, principally from ethnic Koreans residing in Japan. Remittances have been variously estimated as the amount of currency that visitors from Japan could legally carry on their person, as profits from the pachinko industry, a form of gambling popular in Japan in which ethnic Koreans play an important role, and as the portion of the balance of payments that cannot be explained in other ways. Not surprisingly, given these varied approaches to tallying remittances, estimates of the annual total vary enormously, from the low millions to $2 billion, typically running in the hundreds of millions. The figure is probably less than $100 million, an assessment that Nicholas Eberstadt shares in his article in the May 1996 issue of Asian Survey.

In response to its current predicament, the regime has begun some modest and hesitant reforms, most notably the establishment of a special economic zone, modeled after China's southern and coastal provinces, in the far northeast of the country. But such tinkering, however politically contentious within North Korea, is unlikely to reverse the decline of the economy.

WITH A LITTLE HELP FROM CHINA

An alternative approach would be to ask what level of external assistance would be required to maintain the North Korean population at a subsistence level. With help from the Chinese or others, North Korea can avoid widespread famine. If catastrophic famine does occur, it will be due to political decisions made in Pyongyang, not shortages of food.

The government's attempts at food self-sufficiency were wrongheaded and unsustainable. The bureaucratic collectivist nature of North Korean agriculture is decidedly inefficient and has involved the inappropriate cultivation of land and application of chemical fertilizers. The denudation of hillsides has contributed to soil erosion and worsened the flooding that has recently plagued the country, wreaking environmental damage that will take decades to repair. In any event, North Korea should be exporting mineral products and manufactures and importing food, not trying to achieve self-sufficiency.

A variety of organizations and individuals have analyzed the North Korean food situation, and the consensus is that North Korea is experiencing an annual grain shortfall of roughly two million tons. That shortfall is partly due to bad weather and flooding, but its roots are structural, and the provision of food aid is only a short-run palliative in the absence of fundamental economic reforms.

As with agriculture, a lack of information clouds the energy picture. North Korea relies on imported oil for fuel and fertilizer. Foreign exchange shortages and the reduction in subsidized supplies from Russia and China have squeezed oil imports, although there have been recent reports of arms-for-oil deals with countries in the Middle East. The electrical system relies primarily on coal and hydropower and is hampered by difficulties extracting increasingly inaccessible and low-quality domestic coal reserves. The power grid—largely underground for security reasons—is said to suffer from extraordinarily large transmission losses. The 1994 U.S.North Korea Agreed Framework, which provides for fuel oil during the construction of light-water nuclear reactors and the rehabilitation of the electrical grid, will address some of these energy problems. Nevertheless, North Korea will need additional energy if it is to retain its estimated 1991 level of electrical consumption.

If these assessments of the agricultural and energy picture are correct and the Agreed Framework is implemented, the cost of purchasing shortfalls would not be very large, on the order of hundreds of millions of dollars. While anecdotal evidence suggests that both the central planning mechanism and the public food distribution system are fraying under the stresses of the ongoing crisis, these indications should not be overstated. The central government continues to act with a relatively high degree of coherence as well as the population's acquiescence. Starvation may be relatively localized and falling disproportionately on certain socioeconomic groups, particularly rural nonfarm workers, and could reflect conscious decision-making by the political elite.

Indeed, the sums of money required for the survival of the population appear to be within the margin of error of what is known about the North Korean economy. It may well be that North Korea can subsist with no or relatively modest external assistance. In the short run, China, Japan, or South Korea could keep North Korea afloat. Both Japan and China appear to have surplus government grain stocks that could make up the North Korean shortfall at minimal expense. Food is already flowing from China into North Korea. Some represents grant aid, some represents state trading on unknown terms, and the remainder is commercial exchange. North Korea has also had some success procuring food through barter.

However, it should be reiterated that this analysis is based on highly fragmentary information. A famine similar to that which took place in China during the Great Leap Forward may be unfolding in North Korea, and some U.S. intelligence officials already put deaths from starvation in the tens of thousands. Some of the worst (and least understood) famines in this century took place in socialist countries where governments were able to restrict the flows of information and people both internally and externally. North Koreans have been conditioned by nearly two generations of extreme regimentation. Given the country's terrain and the instruments of social control at its disposal, the current regime plausibly could prevent the mass population movements observed during famines in Africa and the Indian subcontinent. If a widespread famine were to occur in North Korea, the killers would be cholera and miscarriages, not kwashiorkor, and outside observers might not learn its full magnitude until a decade hence. If such a famine materializes, its roots will be in political decisions made in Pyongyang, not material resource constraints.

BETWEEN SHOCK THERAPY AND THE PACIFIC WAY

The North Korean leadership faces three broad options: it can adopt fundamental economic reforms in an attempt to reverse the economic decline, recognizing that reform may unleash forces that threaten the character of the political regime; it can stand pat and try to ride out the current crisis, risking collapse; or it can muddle through, making ad hoc adjustments as circumstances dictate. In the end, North Korea will most likely follow Romania in a form of apparatchik capitalism in which growth will follow the initial decline in output that results from the relaxation of central control.

REFORM

The reform option offers potentially enormous payoffs: North Korea could probably increase its output by more than half its pre- decline level under favorable conditions. However, the reform path would not be easy. A variety of considerations suggest that North Korea is unlikely to undertake wide-ranging reforms of its own volition.

Crudely put, the conventional wisdom has it that there are two ways to reform a centrally planned economy—the successful, Asian, gradual approach, and the unsuccessful, European, "big bang" approach. According to this view, North Korea is an Asian country, ergo it will adopt the successful, gradual approach and grow ten percent a year upon the commencement of reform. But gradual reform of a centrally planned economy requires resources to cushion adjustment in the heavy manufacturing sector. Auspicious initial conditions may have benefited successful agrarian countries like China and Vietnam, where the state-owned heavy industry sector was relatively small. Those countries were able to initiate reforms in the agricultural sector, where price liberalization spurred rapid efficiency gains, freeing up low-productivity surplus agricultural labor to be absorbed by the emerging non-state or semi-private light manufacturing and service sectors. In theory, these new, expanding sectors could be taxed to provide state revenues to cushion the transition in the heavy industry sector (though in fact few such transfers have occurred). But the initial conditions in China and Vietnam were unique, and such a path does not appear to be viable for more industrialized centrally planned economies. Piecemeal reforms have not been successful in those economies when they faced economic crises. The more interdependent nature of industrial enterprises means that a host of reforms—macroeconomic stabilization, rational pricing, liberalization of international trade and introduction of a convertible currency, and overhaul of the tax system, bankruptcy laws, and the social safety net—are a seamless web and must be carried out simultaneously to be economically successful and politically sustainable. Even in China and Vietnam, adjustment in the old state-owned heavy industry sector has proved difficult.

North Korea also faces the enormous ideological challenge posed by a prosperous, democratic South Korea. Once North Korea begins reforms, the state's raison d'àtre will be called into question. In Vietnam and China, Marxist ideologues were able to manufacture tortured rationalizations for market-oriented reforms. Maintaining such a facade is likely to be much more difficult for the North Koreans. The scale of change that will accompany significant liberalization is also likely to be tremendous. North Korea is probably the most distorted economy in the world. Liberalization would mean huge changes in the composition of output and employment. International trade would become far more important, and most of that trade would be conducted with South Korea and Japan, two countries with which North Korea maintains problematic political relations.

Finally, it is hard to imagine North Korea undertaking significant reform without a more secure external environment. Although the military—probably the most coherent institution in the society, with privileged access to economic assets—could be a prime beneficiary of change, it may well oppose reforms that it believes endanger the nation's security. Economic reform is therefore unlikely to occur before some rapprochement with South Korea.

COLLAPSE AND UNIFICATION

The regime's second option is to stand firm and do nothing. Although this path promises short-run political stability, if current trends continue, economic distress will eventually put a significant share of the population in peril, if it is not already. Moreover, North Korea differs in some significant ways from other socialist regimes that were able to survive self-inflicted famines earlier in this century. First, the Kim government is not a revolutionary regime, but the dynastic continuation of a leadership that has held power for nearly 50 years. Surely neither this government nor the governed have the same capacity for enduring hardship that would accompany a period of revolutionary fervor. Second, North Korea is a relatively industrialized, urban society, which curtails both its government's ability to squeeze resources out of the agricultural sector and the populace's coping mechanisms. Third, previous socialist famines have largely been precipitated by the introduction of counterproductive policies and could be solved straightforwardly by their removal. North Korea's current agricultural problems appear to be less a function of bad weather or the sudden introduction of misguided policies than the culmination of two generations of bad policy.

Even if the North Korean regime appeared to be teetering on the verge of collapse, the costs of unification would be so great that the South would try to prevent it. The most obvious point of comparison is German unification, which has involved more protracted and costly transfers than analysts anticipated at the time of unification. Even with that largess, East Germany has gone through a wrenching transformation: unification and the depression that ensued brought a collapse in the birth rate unprecedented in German history, including the interwar years and the period of military defeat, and a dramatic rise in the mortality rate. Although some of the declines in marriages and births presumably represent delay, not permanent reduction, the same cannot be said for the increase in mortality rates.

In some ways Korea presents a gloomier picture than Germany. North Korea's population is about half as large as South Korea's, while East Germany's was one-quarter the size of West Germany's. North Korea's per capita income is only around one-seventh that of the South; East German incomes were one-third to one-half those of West Germany. North Korea's economy is probably more distorted than East Germany's was, and South Korea is not as rich as West Germany. On the other hand, the combined Korean population is younger than the combined German population, and the North Korean population is younger than the East German population, which should facilitate adjustment with lower social expenditures.

Still, if South Korea were to absorb North Korea, the cost of unification, defined as the capital investment needed in North Korea to choke off the incentive for mass migration, would be on the order of $1 trillion—a figure so large as to be unfeasible, even if spread over a time period of 10 to 25 years. Even under optimistic scenarios, North Koreans will have powerful incentives to move to the South, and the potential for such migration is enormous: assuming that a person carrying some belongings could travel 20 miles a day, 40 percent of the population of North Korea lives within a five-day walk of the demilitarized zone. The level of migration will depend on whether political unification accompanies economic integration.

South Korea can discourage migration in two ways: by maintaining the demilitarized zone as a method of controlling population influx and by encouraging capital investment in the North to lessen the incentives to emigrate. While the former option is fraught with political difficulties—elected officials might hesitate before turning machine guns on a third of the electorate—the alternative has important implications for South Korean domestic policy. South Korean policy will strive to minimize the burden imposed on South Korean taxpayers by financing the economic reconstruction of the North. This task will require policies to encourage foreign capital, specifically foreign private capital, to flow into North and South Korea. Historically, South Korea has been inhospitable to both foreign direct and portfolio investment. However, in this case liberalization not only would bring its traditional benefits but would facilitate private capital inflows to unified Korea, or alternatively substitute in South Korea for capital invested in the North prior to political unification. South Korea needs to continue to improve its foreign direct investment regime and encourage the development of efficient domestic bond markets that are capable of mobilizing large sums of capital when the need arises. The capacity to mobilize global private capital quickly will be important if economic integration is accompanied by political integration and South Korean laws and institutions are extended throughout unified Korea.

Some international public capital should also be available. The World Bank, for example, maintains a special program for peace and sustainable development in the occupied territories in the Middle East. A similar program, scaled to the much larger North Korean population, would imply World Bank investments of $4.4 billion annually. Furthermore, North Korea and Japan have yet to settle post-colonial claims. Taking the 1965 settlement between South Korea and Japan as a base and adjusting for changes in the price level, population growth, and accrued interest, the Japanese payment would be about $12 billion. These amounts are small, however, relative to the $1 trillion that would be required.

MUDDLING THROUGH

Between the extremes of reform and collapse lies muddling through. Here the experience of Romania may be instructive. Romania and North Korea are similar in population, per capita income, social indicators, and sectoral distribution of labor, as well as central planning and its attendant maladies. Both combined rigid internal orthodoxy with symbolic independence in external affairs. Both experimented with socialism in one family; Nicolae Ceausescu's inspiration for the development of a cult of personality is said to have been a 1971 visit to Pyongyang.

Romania and North Korea both experienced economic problems in the 1970s as their central planning approaches began to fail. Although they were temporarily papered over by an inflow of recycled petrodollars, the underlying problems eventually manifested themselves in difficulties repaying accumulated external debts. One striking difference is that Ceausescu made the fateful decision to repay the debt, while Kim Il Sung defaulted on his Western creditors.

Romanian living standards began falling in the early 1980s as domestic consumption was compressed to free up resources for debt repayment, and conditions worsened in 1985, when the country was hit by severe weather during an energy crisis. Romanians were forced to live and work in freezing conditions, and draft animals were substituted for agricultural machinery. Nevertheless, mass unrest did not appear until 1987—six years after living standards began to decline—and it was not until 1989, with other socialist regimes collapsing and the economy going into free fall, that the Ceausescu regime toppled. That sequence of events suggests caution in drawing too deterministic a link between economic hardship and political failure, a caveat reinforced by the contemporary experiences of countries as diverse as Cuba, Iraq, and, until recently, Zaire. With the willingness of foreign powers to support North Korea's incumbent regime, that link may prove even more tenuous.

In Romania, Ceausescu's removal had more the air of a regime- preserving coup than a genuine revolution. Subsequent experience suggests that muddling through may indeed be a viable strategy. Both Romania and North Korea grew at a 2.5 percent rate in 1985. Romania subsequently suffered a sharper contraction in output than North Korea. However, once the reform process was initiated in 1990, the Romanian economy began to stabilize, and registered positive if unspectacular growth by 1993.

Similar economic and even political developments might occur in North Korea. The political and economic interests of the former Communist Party embodied in Ion Iliescu's recently ousted Social Democratic Party of Romania have strongly influenced that country's economic reform strategy. The state remains the dominant force in the economy. Political power is used to create and allocate excess profits that are channeled to politically influential groups and individuals, either openly or through corruption. Restructuring has proceeded at a slow pace. Kim Jong Il or his successor could well adopt similar policies to deal with economic hardship while satisfying the regime's political base. These favored constituencies would presumably be the Kim clique, the military, and possibly the upper echelons of the Korean Workers' Party. The regime could expect tutelage and material support from China, an advantage the temporizers in Romania did not have.

THE POWERS THAT BE

China, Japan, Russia, and arguably even South Korea may well prefer a muddling, domesticated North Korea to a capitalist and possibly nuclear-armed unified state on the Korean peninsula. China, Russia, and Japan may prefer continued economic engagement with South Korea and be willing to expend some resources to maintain North Korea as an allied buffer state. China has begun to pick up some of the slack left by Russia, North Korea's former patron, though the extent to which Chinese exports of food and other essentials are on concessional terms is unclear. Nor is it known what kind of economic or foreign policy conditions are attached to these exports. Beijing's dual goals of continued support for the North and enhanced economic engagement with the South is a delicate diplomatic conundrum, as was starkly apparent during the February defection of high-ranking North Korean official Hwang Jang Yop in the Chinese capital. Hwang's defection has made North Korea more suspicious of China's intentions and complicates the potentially constructive role China could play vis-‡-vis the North. Yet North Korea's diplomatic isolation is so profound that even a China walking a diplomatic tightrope between the two Koreas is still likely to be the North's most effective patron.

Unification along the lines of the German model would complicate strategic planning for China and Japan and further reduce Russian influence in the region. One can envision China giving North Korea aid and technical assistance, South Korea engaging China and possibly North Korea economically while protected by the American security umbrella, and concerns over a Sino-Japanese military imbalance submerged by the American counterweight.

The United States would bear little of unification's direct costs, and unification would hold the promise of eliminating the direct threat posed by North Korea to American troops stationed in northeast Asia and the prospect of ending North Korean proliferation of weapons of mass destruction. While there may be some benefit to the United States in playing the security role outlined above, long-run U.S. interests are surely better served by unification. In this regard the United States may be unique.

North Korea is not Romania, and such analogies should not be taken too far. A prosperous, democratic South Korea will make it much more difficult for Kim Jong Il to pursue apparatchik capitalism as a development strategy. Even in Romania,

Iliescu's party was driven from power last November. Nor do ad hoc measures ensure success—some of the muddlers among the states of the former Soviet Union have experienced declines in output of 50 to 80 percent. Nevertheless, the experience of Romania suggests that North Korea may muddle through for years before turning toward reform or chaos, especially if external powers find this solution to be in their interests.

Marcus Noland is a Senior Fellow at the Institute for International Economics.

© Foreign Affairs

How to Deal With North Korea

James T. Laney and Jason T. Shaplen

HEINZ-PETER BADER / REUTERS

Son Mun San, counsellor from North Korea to the International Atomic Energy Agency (IAEA) discusses the Yongbyon nuclear reactor, Austria, Vienna, January 11, 2003.

MIXED MESSAGES

Progress in reducing tensions on the Korean peninsula, never easy, has reached a dangerous impasse. The last six months have witnessed an extraordinary series of events in the region that have profound implications for security and stability throughout Northeast Asia, a region that is home to 100,000 U.S. troops and three of the world's 12 largest economies.

Perhaps the most dramatic of these events was North Korea's December decision to restart its frozen plutonium-based nuclear program at Yongbyon—including a reprocessing facility that separates plutonium for nuclear weapons from spent reactor fuel.

Just as disturbing was the North's stunning public admission two months earlier that it had begun building a new, highly-enriched-uranium (HEU) nuclear program. And then came yet another unsettling development: a growing, sharp division emerged between the United States and the new South Korean government over how to respond.

But recent events have not been entirely negative. In the two months prior to the October HEU revelation, North Korea had, with remarkable speed, undertaken an important series of positive initiatives that seemed the polar opposite of its posturing on the nuclear issue. These included initiating an unscheduled meeting between its foreign minister, Paek Nam Sun, and Secretary of State Colin Powell in July—the highest-level contact between the two nations since the Bush administration took office; inviting a U.S. delegation for talks in Pyongyang; proposing the highest-level talks with South Korea in a year; agreeing to re-establish road and rail links with the South and starting work on the project almost immediately; demining portions of the demilitarized zone (DMZ) and wide corridors on the east and west coasts surrounding the rail links; sending more than 600 athletes and representatives to join the Asian Games in Pusan, South Korea (marking the North's first-ever participation in an international sporting event in the South); enacting a series of economic and market reforms (including increasing wages, allowing the price of staples to float freely, and inaugurating a special economic zone similar to those in China); restarting the highest-level talks with Japan in two years; holding a subsequent summit with Japanese Prime Minister Junichiro Koizumi, during which Pyongyang admitted abducting Japanese citizens in the 1970s and 1980s; and finally, allowing the surviving abductees to visit Japan.

Viewed individually, let alone together, North Korea's initiatives represented the most promising signs of change on the peninsula in decades. Whether by desire or by necessity, the North finally appeared to be responding to the longstanding concerns of the United States, South Korea, and Japan. Equally important, Pyongyang seemed to have abandoned its policy of playing Washington, Seoul, and Tokyo off one another by addressing the concerns of one while ignoring those of the other two. For the first time, the North was actively (even aggressively) engaging all three capitals simultaneously.

Until October, that is, when North Korea acknowledged the existence of its clandestine HEU program—ending the diplomatic progress instantly. Once the news broke, Pyongyang quickly offered to halt the HEU program in exchange for a nonaggression pact with the United States. But Washington, unwilling to reward bad behavior, initially refused to open a dialogue unless the North first abandoned its HEU effort. In November, the United States went a step further: saying that Pyongyang had violated the 1994 Agreed Framework and several other nuclear nonproliferation pacts, Washington engineered the suspension of deliveries of the 500,000 tons of heavy fuel oil sent to the North each year under the 1994 accord. The Agreed Framework had frozen the North's plutonium program—a program that had included a five-megawatt experimental reactor, two larger reactors under construction, and the reprocessing facility—narrowly averting a catastrophic war on the Korean Peninsula.

In the weeks following the suspension of fuel shipments, the United States hardened its stance against dialogue with the North—despite the fact that most U.S. allies were encouraging a diplomatic solution to the situation. North Korea responded by announcing plans to reopen its Yongbyon facilities. It immediately removed the seals and monitoring cameras from its frozen nuclear labs and reactors and, a few days later, began to move its dangerous spent fuel rods out of storage. Pyongyang subsequently announced its intention to reopen the critical reprocessing plant in February 2003. On December 31, it expelled the inspectors of the International Atomic Energy Agency (IAEA). And on January 9, it announced its withdrawal from the nuclear Nonproliferation Treaty.

Although Washington, strongly urged by Seoul and Tokyo, ultimately agreed to talks, the situation appeared to be worsening almost daily. Depending on how it is resolved, the standoff could still prove a positive turning point in resolving one the world's most dangerous flash points. But it could also lead to an even worse crisis than in 1994. The proper approach, therefore, is to now re-engage with North Korea without rewarding it for bad behavior. Working together, the major external interested parties (China, Japan, Russia, and the United States) should jointly and officially guarantee the security of the entire Korean Peninsula. But the outside powers should also insist that Pyongyang abandon its nuclear weapons program before offering it any enticements. Only when security has been established (and verified by intrusive, regular inspections) should a prearranged comprehensive deal be implemented—one that involves extensive reforms in the North, an increase in aid and investment, and, eventually, a Korean federation.

THE NORTH GOES NUCLEAR

To understand how the most promising signs of progress in decades quickly deteriorated into nuclear brinkmanship, it is necessary to first understand the origins and motivation behind the North's HEU program and Pyongyang's subsequent decision to restart its plutonium program. Even before North Korea admitted that it was building a new HEU program, the United States had long suspected the country of violating its relevant international commitments. Three years ago, such concerns had led to U.S. inspections of suspicious underground facilities in Kumchang-ni. Although those inspections did not reveal any actual treaty violations—in part because Pyongyang had ample time to remove evidence before the inspectors arrived—suspicions lingered. These doubts proved justified in July 2002, when the United States conclusively confirmed the existence of the North's HEU program.

It now seems likely that Pyongyang actually started its HEU program in 1997 or 1998. Although Kim Jong Il's motives for doing so will probably never be clear (his regime has a record of confounding observers), there are two plausible explanations. The first focuses on fear: namely, North Korea's fear that, having frozen its plutonium-based nuclear program in 1994, it would receive nothing in return. Such a suspicion seems unreasonable on its face, since, under the 1994 Agreed Framework negotiated with Washington, Pyongyang was to be compensated in various ways for abandoning its nuclear ambitions. But from the perspective of a paranoid, isolated regime such as North Korea's, this concern was not without justification. Almost from its inception, the provisions of the 1994 accord fell substantially behind schedule—most notably in the construction of proliferation-resistant light-water reactors in the North and improved relations with the United States.1 North Korea may thus have started its HEU program as a hedge against the possibility that it had been duped, or, more likely, that new U.S., South Korean, or Japanese administrations would be less willing to proceed with the politically controversial program than were their predecessors.

A second, darker, and more likely explanation for Pyongyang's decision to start the HEU program holds that the North never really intended to give up its nuclear ambitions. Whether motivated by fear, honor, or aggression (the determination to stage a preemptive strike if threatened), Pyongyang views a nuclear program as its sovereign right—and a necessity.

Whichever of these theories is true, the North seems to have undertaken its HEU program slowly at first, ramping it up only in late 2000 or 2001. And it was able to hide the program until July 2002, when U.S. intelligence proved its existence. Although Bush administration officials insist otherwise, it is possible, as North Korean officials have suggested, that Pyongyang decided to step up its nuclear program in response to what it perceived as Washington's increasingly hostile attitude—a hostility demonstrated to North Koreans by President Bush's decision to include them in the "axis of evil" and to set the bar for talks impossibly high. This perceived hostility was further encouraged when the administration announced its new doctrine of preemptive defense. Notwithstanding the president's remarks to the contrary, Pyongyang views the new defense doctrine as a direct threat. After all, if Washington is willing to attack Iraq, another isolated nation with a suspected nuclear program, might it not also be willing, even likely, to do the same to North Korea?

This fear helps explain why the North decided to restart its plutonium program. Many within the senior ranks of the North Korean military believe that if the United States attacks, Pyongyang's position will be strengthened immeasurably by the possession of several nuclear weapons. North Korean planners thus reason that they should develop such weapons as quickly as possible, prior to the American attack that may come once Washington has concluded its war with Iraq.

HIGH-STAKES POKER

There are again two plausible explanations for why the North revealed its HEU program in October 2002. Since its earliest days in office, the Bush administration has made clear that it favors a more hard-line approach to North Korea than did the Clinton team. Even prior to the North's HEU admission, Bush's support for the

1994 Agreed Framework was lukewarm at best. His administration considered the accord a form of blackmail signed by his predecessor—even though, after a long review of North Korea policy in 2001, the Bush administration found it could not justify abandoning the pact without having something better with which to replace it. In short, Washington grudgingly considered itself bound by a diplomatic process it viewed as distasteful—if not an outright scam.

When U.S. Assistant Secretary of State James Kelly visited North Korea in early October, he took with him undeniable evidence of the North's HEU program. He also took with him very narrowly defined briefing papers, hard-line marching orders that reflected the influence of the Defense Department and the National Security Council.

Anticipating isolation and a worsening of already strained relations in the face of Washington's evidence, Pyongyang opted to play one of its few remaining trump cards: open admission of its nuclear program. This openness, Kim may have hoped, would keep the Bush administration from disengaging entirely. By acknowledging its HEU effort, Pyongyang essentially sent Washington the following message: "We understand that despite everything we've done over the past several months you want to isolate or disengage from us. Well, we admit we have a uranium-based nuclear program. You say you don't want to deal with us. Too bad—you can't ignore a potential nuclear power. Deal with us."

Another hypothesis to explain the timing is that Pyongyang simply miscalculated. North Korea watchers learned long ago to expect the unexpected, but even the most jaded observers were surprised in September 2002 when Kim admitted to Koizumi that the North had abducted 13 Japanese in the 1970s and 1980s to train its spies. Kim apologized for the abductions and, with remarkable speed, subsequently authorized a visit of five of the surviving abductees to Japan. In doing so, he removed a decades-old barrier to normalization of relations between the two nations (and to the payment of billions of dollars in hoped-for war reparations from Tokyo).

Kim's gamble on coming clean about the abductions appeared at the time to have paid off. Notwithstanding the predicted public backlash in Japan, further talks between Tokyo and Pyongyang took place in October (after the HEU admission).2 Having experienced better-than-expected results in admitting to the abductions, Kim may have hoped for the same by confessing to his HEU program. His thinking may have been that, in view of Washington's evidence, Pyongyang would eventually have had to come clean anyway. That being the case, it was better to do so sooner rather than later, thereby removing one of the primary obstacles to improved U.S.North Korea relations. Kim may further have surmised that the timing of such a revelation in October was advantageous, given recent progress in talks with Japan and South Korea. He probably hoped that Tokyo and Seoul would pressure Washington to mitigate its response.

In the weeks immediately following Kelly's visit, Washington made it clear that it did not see a military solution to the crisis on the Korean Peninsula. This left isolation, containment, and negotiation as the only viable alternatives. A policy of isolation would seek the North's collapse but would not address the HEU problem and would likely result in the North's restarting its plutonium-based nuclear program. Containment, or economic pressure designed to squeeze the North, would seek to punish Pyongyang while leaving the door open to future negotiation. It too would not address the HEU problem but, it was hoped, might maintain the freeze on the plutonium program. Negotiations, meanwhile, would seek to address the nuclear problem but could be viewed by some as a reward for bad behavior.

If a successful isolation or containment policy wins the day, the North will have miscalculated in coming clean. If, however, a policy of dialogue and subsequent negotiation ultimately emerges—or if isolation or containment fails (in part because Washington is unable to persuade China, South Korea, and Russia to endorse it over a sustained period)—Kim will have played his cards exceedingly well.

BEST OF A BAD SITUATION

Many pundits and policymakers in Washington, on both sides of the aisle, argue that the revelations about Pyongyang's clandestine HEU program prove that President Clinton's policy of engaging the North was a mistake. This argument maintains that giving in to blackmail leads only to more blackmail.

Although it is inherently valid, such analysis is too simple. In 1994, the United States was on the edge of war with North Korea. Washington had beefed up its forces in the theater, installed Patriot missile batteries in the South, and was reviewing detailed war plans. The White House had even begun to consider the evacuation of American citizens. The 1994 Agreed Framework, although deeply flawed, represented the best deal available at a far from ideal time. It remained so for several years. And although it has been disappointing on many levels, the agreement has not been useless.

Indeed, it averted a potentially catastrophic situation. Instead of a war (which the U.S. military commander in South Korea, General Gary Luck, estimated would have killed a million people, including 80,000 to 100,000 Americans), Northeast Asia has experienced eight years of stability. This has had vast implications beyond security. In 1994, South Korea's GDP was 323 trillion won; today, even after the 1997 financial meltdown, its GDP is approximately 544 trillion won.3 This transformation would have been unlikely in the face of imminent armed conflict. China has similarly experienced explosive growth, much of which might also have slowed had there been a major confrontation on its porous border with North Korea.

The Agreed Framework also provided the parties with critical breathing room, which has allowed new realities to emerge both within North Korea and among the

United States and its allies—developments that improve the chances for a better, more comprehensive deal today. To cite one example, in 1994, Kim Jong Il had only recently succeeded his father, North Korea's founder Kim Il Sung. Viewed as weak, mentally unstable, and without a power base of his own, Kim was expected to last a mere two weeks to several months. Today, however, he is acknowledged as the only power in North Korea and has established diplomatic relations with scores of nations, including many of Washington's closest allies in NATO and the European Union. This puts him in a vastly better position to strike a deal.

For its part, the United States in 1994 could not have counted on Russia or China to support its position toward North Korea. Today, however, Washington is likely to receive baseline support—albeit not carte blanche—from both. Indeed, although there has hardly been unanimity among the outside powers, there has already been evidence of such cooperation, in the form of a joint Chinese-Russian declaration issued in early December stating that the two powers "consider it important… to preserve the non-nuclear status of the Korean Peninsula and the regime of nonproliferation of weapons of mass destruction."

Another benefit of the breathing room created by the 1994 accord is the North's economic dependence on the South. South Korea today is North Korea's largest publicly acknowledged supplier of aid and its second-largest trading partner. Although not as successful as he would have liked, former South Korean President Kim Dae Jung's "Sunshine Policy" of engaging the North has, in conjunction with the North's economic collapse, given Pyongyang a strong economic interest in avoiding a crisis. (Although the numbers are much smaller, the situation is not wholly unlike that between Taiwan and China.) Should the North exacerbate current tensions, the economic fallout would be traumatic, and the loss of South Korean investment could destabilize the North.

THE WAY OUT

The timing of the steps now taken to resolve the current crisis will be crucial to their success. Indeed, timing is important to understand because the North's HEU program does not pose an immediate threat. Although it has the potential to eventually produce enough uranium for one nuclear weapon per year, it has not yet reached this stage and is not expected to do so for at least two to three more years, according to administration officials and the Central Intelligence Agency.

The North's decision to reopen its plutonium-based nuclear program at Yongbyon poses a more critical and immediate threat, however. Prior to its suspension in 1994, most experts believe this program had already produced enough plutonium for one or two nuclear weapons. The 8,000 spent fuel rods from the five-megawatt reactor contained enough plutonium for an additional four to five nuclear weapons.4 The IAEA monitored the freeze via seals, cameras, and on-site inspectors. It also canned the 8,000 existing spent fuel rods, placed them in a safe-storage cooling pond, and monitored them until its inspectors were expelled from North Korea on December 31.

The five-megawatt reactor, when operational, will produce enough plutonium for one or two additional nuclear weapons per year. But the 8,000 rods represent an even more immediate challenge. If the North follows through on its threat to reopen the reprocessing facility in February, it would take just six months to reprocess all of its spent fuel and extract enough plutonium to make four or five additional weapons. This would bring Pyongyang's nuclear arsenal to between five and seven weapons by the end of July. It could have enough plutonium for one to three weapons even sooner.

Thus there exists only a short window of opportunity before the North's recent action translates into additional nuclear-weapons material on the ground. The trick to unraveling the current impasse is to avoid rewarding the North for its violations of past treaties with a new, more comprehensive agreement. Blackmail cannot and should not be condoned. The starting point for future discussions should therefore be that the North must completely and immediately abandon its HEU and plutonium-based programs. This pledge must be accompanied by intrusive, immediate, and continuous inspections by the IAEA.

It is a tenet of all international negotiations, however—particularly those that involve the Korean Peninsula—that all crises create opportunity, and this one is no different. At its core—politics stripped aside—the current standoff will allow Washington to scrap the flawed Agreed Framework and replace it with a new mechanism that better addresses the concerns of the United States and its allies. In many ways, the North's HEU admission and its subsequent decision to reopen its plutonium program might therefore be viewed as a blessing in disguise. The Bush administration can finally rid itself of a deal it never liked and never truly endorsed and replace it with one that addresses all of Washington's central concerns, including the North's missile program and its conventional forces. Washington must, however, be willing to make such a deal attractive to the North as well.

Yet timing poses an immediate barrier to negotiating a new mechanism. Pyongyang has insisted it will give up its HEU and plutonium programs only after Washington signs a nonaggression pact with it. But the Bush administration, while publicly reassuring the North that it has no intention of invading, has justifiably insisted that Pyongyang give up these programs before there is any discussion of a new mechanism. The North seems unwilling to lose face by giving up this trump card without a security guarantee, and Washington is unwilling to take any action that appears to reward Pyongyang before it has fully dismantled its nuclear programs.

Those who think they can outwait Pyongyang by isolating it or pressuring it economically, as the Bush administration proposed in late December, are likely to be proved wrong. North Koreans are a fiercely proud people and have endured hardships over the last decade that would have led most other countries to implode. It would therefore be a mistake to underestimate their loyalty to the state or to Kim Jong Il. When insulted, provoked, or threatened, North Koreans will not hesitate to engage in their equivalent of a holy war. Their ideology is not only political, it is quasi-religious. Pyongyang also enjoys an inherent advantage in any waiting game: Beijing. Although China might initially support a policy of economic pressure, Beijing is afraid that it will face a massive influx of unwanted refugees across the Yalu River should the North collapse. To guard against this event, it will ultimately allow fuel and food (sanctioned or unsanctioned) to move across its border with the North. Similarly, South Korea, which also wants to avoid a massive influx of refugees, is unlikely to support a sustained, indefinite policy of squeezing the North. In mid-December, it elected by a larger margin than predicted a new president who ran specifically on a platform of expanding engagement with Pyongyang.

The way to cut the Gordian knot of who goes first is through a two-stage approach. The first stage would provide the North with the security it craves while also ensuring that Pyongyang is not rewarded for its bad behavior. To achieve this end, the four outside interested powers (the United States, Japan, China, and Russia—each of which has supported one side or the other in the past) would jointly and officially guarantee the security and stability of the entire Korean Peninsula. Washington may not be able or willing to convene a meeting of the four powers to this end. If not, back channels or unofficial initiatives should be used to encourage Moscow or Beijing to take the lead. Both Russia and China have sought to increase their influence on the Korean Peninsula in recent years. This plan would solidify their places at the table.

Once the security of the peninsula has been guaranteed by the outside powers, it will be time for stage two: a comprehensive accord, again broken into two parts. The North must completely give up its HEU and plutonium programs and allow immediate, intrusive, and continuous inspections by the IAEA; end its development, production, and testing of long-range missiles in exchange for some financial compensation; draw down its conventional troops along the DMZ (although there will be no reduction of U.S. troops at this time, and only a very limited reduction of U.S. troops in five years, should the situation permit); and, finally, continue to implement economic and market reforms.

In exchange for the above, Japan would normalize its relations with the North within 18 months of the agreement's coming into effect. This normalization would include the payment of war reparations in the form of aid, delivered on a timetable extending five to seven years. Both halves of the peninsula would also enter a Korean federation within two years of the agreement's coming into effect. And as soon as the IAEA had verified that the North has dismantled its nuclear weapons programs, Washington would sign a nonaggression pact with Pyongyang. This pact, which by prior agreement would automatically be nullified by subsequent signs that the North was not cooperating or was initiating a new nuclear program, would include the gradual lifting of economic sanctions over three years.

The United States, South Korea, Japan, and the European Union—the primary members of the Korean Peninsula Energy Development Organization (or KEDO, which was set up to administer the Agreed Framework)—would further maintain the organization and provide the two new light-water reactors stipulated in the original deal. KEDO would also resume delivery of heavy fuel oil until the first reactor was completed.

In addition to the above measures, China and Russia would agree to support the North economically via investment. All outside parties to the deal—the United States, South Korea, Japan, China, and Russia—would also contribute to the compensation the North would receive in return for ending its long-range missile program.

Finally, five years after the above accord is signed, a Northeast Asia Security Forum, consisting of the four major powers plus South and North Korea, would be created to ensure long-term peace and stability throughout the region.

The timing of the various parts of stage two will be critical to its success. To this end, the leaders of all the countries involved (or their high-ranking representatives) should meet in person to negotiate the deal. North and South Korea, Japan, China, Russia, and the United States must all sign on if the plan is to work.

Certain components of the comprehensive deal (such as the U.S.-North Korea nonaggression pact and the missile accord) should exist as separate agreements, referenced in but not attached as appendices to the main text. They should be fully agreed and initialed prior to signing the comprehensive deal. Immediately after signing the comprehensive agreement, the North would have to take the first step by fully dismantling both its HEU and its plutonium programs and allowing IAEA inspections to verify these steps. Only after the IAEA had certified the dismantling would the nonaggression and missile pacts be signed: in the case of the nonaggression pact, by Pyongyang and Washington alone, and in the case of the missile pact, by Beijing, Moscow, Pyongyang, Seoul, Tokyo, and Washington.

THE SUM OF TWO PARTS

Initially, Washington's response to North Korea's HEU and plutonium programs consisted mostly of condemning Pyongyang. Then, in early January, President Bush and Secretary of State Powell took steps to ease the tension. Following a trilateral meeting with South Korea and Japan (during which Seoul and Tokyo pressed for a diplomatic approach), Washington finally agreed to open a dialogue with Pyongyang. The Bush administration, however, limited the scope of the meetings to discussion of how North Korea could abide by its international commitments. It is now time to move beyond this narrow agenda to a policy of resolution—one that addresses all concerns on the Korean Peninsula.

Such a shift is particularly important given the very serious rupture that has opened between Washington and Seoul. At precisely the time that the situation in North Korea has reached a crisis stage, U.S.-South Korean relations have hit their lowest level ever. Korean anti-Americanism—far more than just a difference of opinion on how to deal with the North—was responsible for the election of Roh Moo Hyun as president in December. Roh beat a more hard-line rival specifically by distancing himself from Washington's position on the North and by promising to continue Kim Dae Jung's Sunshine Policy. More critically, he promised a new, more prominent role for South Korea in its relationship with the United States. America will therefore no longer be able to force its position on the more assertive and restless South Korean population.

The process above, fortunately, will address the major concerns of all the parties involved. It will assure North Korea of the underlying security it seeks, without requiring Washington to sign a nonaggression pact until after Pyongyang has dismantled its HEU and plutonium programs. If the North balks despite a security guarantee by all major outside powers and the prospect of a comprehensive accord, isolation or economic pressure by Washington and its allies will not only remain a viable alternative, it will be stronger and more fully justified than it would be otherwise, and will more easily win the unified, sustained support of major players in the region. The upside to exploring the path presented above is therefore massive, and the downside very limited. Doing nothing, meanwhile, could become the most dangerous option of all.

Footnotes

[1] The 1994 Agreed Framework called for best efforts to be made to deliver two light-water reactors to North Korea: one in 2003 and one in 2004. Even before the North admitted to having an HEU program—which has cast the future of the Agreed Framework into doubt—it had become unlikely that the first light-water reactor would be completed before 2008 or the second before 2009. To be fair, however, responsibility for the delay is borne by both sides, and primarily by the North, since it has frequently been intransigent on practical issues related to the agreement's implementation.

[2] The visit of the surviving abductees to Japan in October was originally scheduled to last two weeks. After the North acknowledged its HEU program, Japan refused to allow their return and pressed for their North Korean relatives to be allowed to join them. Interestingly, although the dispute remains unresolved, Tokyo and Pyongyang have opted to handle it quietly—even as Japan has made clear that future progress with the North is tied to this issue.

[3] In U.S. dollar terms these figures equal a 1994 GDP of $404 billion (using the 1994 exchange rate of 800 won to the dollar) and a 2001 GDP of $422 billion (using today's much lower exchange rate of 1,290 won to the dollar).

[4] Had the Agreed Framework not been signed in 1994, the North's plutonium-based program would by today have produced enough plutonium for up to 30 nuclear weapons. Critics of the accord should not ignore this fact.

James T. Laney is President Emeritus of Emory University and Co-Chairman of an independent task force on "Managing Change on the Korean Peninsula," sponsored by the Council on Foreign Relations. He served as U.S. Ambassador to South Korea from 1993 to 1997. Jason T. Shaplen was Policy Adviser at the Korean Peninsula Energy Development Organization (KEDO) from 1995 to 1999 and is a member of the task force.

© Foreign Affairs

The Fire Last Time

Scott Snyder

Army personnel and people gather at Kim Il Sung Square in Pyongyang.

This October marks the tenth anniversary of the Geneva Agreed Framework, which was signed by Washington and Pyongyang on October 21, 1994, ending the first nuclear standoff with North Korea. There will be no champagne toast, however, to celebrate the occasion. The Agreed Framework, sharply contested by Republican critics at its inception and never fully implemented, has been effectively dead since October 2002, when Assistant Secretary of State James Kelly visited Pyongyang. On that trip, the Bush administration's first high-level contact with the North Korean government, Kelly asked his North Korean counterparts about their covert attempts to develop a highly enriched uranium bomb program in violation of the Agreed Framework. The North Koreans responded angrily to Kelly's charge but, in the process, admitted that he was right, thereby igniting the second North Korean nuclear crisis.

Today, many of the events of ten years ago seem to be repeating themselves. Although this crisis has several striking differences from the last one, the Bush administration would do well to study carefully the drama of 1993-94 and reflect on President Bill Clinton's choices before making its own. Fortunately, Washington has a powerful new tool to aid it in this task: Going Critical: The First North Korean Nuclear Crisis, a comprehensive insider's guide to the first North Korean nuclear standoff and an essential tool for comparing today's events to the last round. As the book makes clear, the stakes and the confusion of the original crisis could not have been greater; during its climax in 1994, Clinton even compared it to the Cuban missile crisis. Going Critical also underscores the changing risks of nuclear proliferation in what Yale's Paul Bracken has called the "second nuclear age" and expands on earlier accounts to offer an authoritative discussion of the events of the first crisis as viewed from Washington. Written with the rare benefit of special access to U.S. government documents and incorporating the personal experiences of its three authors, all of whom played significant roles in the events of 1993-94, Going Critical recounts in detail the options that the Clinton administration considered at every stage of the story—and thus should prove invaluable to the Bush administration today.

LEAST BAD

Although Going Critical seems to have been written with an eye toward justifying the Agreed Framework as serving the U.S. national interest, its authors do not spin the story so as to defend the administration they served. Instead, Wit, Poneman, and Gallucci methodically recount every stage of their deliberations. Going Critical offers a detailed examination of the workings (and limitations) of the interagency process involved with trying to resolve a nuclear dispute and highlights challenges inherent in merging often radically different priorities into an integrated policy.

To their credit, the authors straightforwardly reveal the biases and problems in the Clinton administration's approach, even while they aggressively defend the logic that led to the final deal, which they describe as the least bad option. Keenly aware of the stakes, including the real possibility of military escalation, the Clinton team felt profound relief when it was finally able to gain essential concessions from its tough North Korean counterparts—even though these concessions were nowhere near enough to satisfy Seoul, Tokyo, and critics in Washington who opposed all concessions to Pyongyang. Indeed, the Agreed Framework was unpopular from the start and contested at every stage of its implementation. But as the authors point out, it also managed to keep North Korea from immediately going nuclear and it avoided a war—one that would have been costly for all sides.

There were two critical flaws with the American approach in 1993 and 1994, however, as the book—not to mention the intervening years—makes clear. First, although U.S. officials did convince the North Koreans to "can" and store their spent nuclear fuel, they were unable to persuade them to give up their nuclear components entirely, as they did with Kazakhstan and Ukraine. This failure gave the North Koreans easy access to spent nuclear fuel that could be reprocessed, which has proved to be their most significant source of leverage in the current standoff.

The Clinton administration also erred by allowing North Korea to delay its return to the nuclear Nonproliferation Treaty (NPT) by more than five years. This ambiguity in Pyongyang's status under the NPT made it much easier for North Korea to later declare, in January 2003, that it was no longer a party to that treaty and to exclude the International Atomic Energy Agency (which administers the NPT) from any role in the standoff. Wit, Poneman, and Gallucci assert that North Korea would not have accepted a return to full compliance with the NPT in 1994, but subsequent events have shown that these concessions were nonetheless a mistake; the Clinton administration should have pushed harder for subsequent revisions. Instead, within a year of the signing of the Agreed Framework, Washington had put the Korean Peninsula Energy Development Organization (KEDO), which administered the deal, on autopilot, and KEDO officials were left complaining that it was harder to get sign-offs from the United States than from Japan or South Korea. By 1998, under pressure from Congress, the Clinton administration reluctantly named former Defense Secretary William Perry as a special coordinator for policy toward North Korea in an attempt to salvage the process. But Perry's efforts only deferred the collapse of the framework until the end of the Clinton administration.

TOUGH TALK

Republican critics such as Senator John McCain (R-Ariz.) have charged that "the [Clinton] administration could have given less and received more" in 1994. The same thinking informs the Bush administration's current approach to North Korea, embodied in its call for "complete, verifiable, irreversible dismantlement" (known as CVID) as the only long-term solution to North Korea's nuclear weapons threat. According to Washington, anything short of CVID would leave open the possibility of a third North Korean nuclear crisis in the future. It is far from clear, however, whether the Bush administration has the tools, the attention span, or the temperament necessary to assemble the kind of regional consensus needed to achieve this goal.

To be fair, the Bush administration has learned from the last Korean crisis that a region-wide approach is necessary. The establishment of the six-party talks in August of 2003, which included China, Japan, Russia, and South Korea as well as North Korea and the United States, was thus a positive improvement on the bilateral approach used by the Clinton administration. Going Critical clearly illustrates the risks and burdens inherent in the Clinton approach, under which the United States sought to carry alone the full weight of negotiations with North Korea, indirectly representing the international community and allies such as Japan and South Korea—allies whose security interests were directly at stake. A decade ago, China was also still too closely tied to North Korea to play the kind of active mediating role it has this time.

Although the Bush administration has persuaded the other outside participants in the six-party talks to back CVID rhetorically, however, it has not been able to secure a working consensus on exactly what CVID would require North Korea to do, or how to get there. China, Russia, and South Korea favor signing a second agreed framework based on negotiations with North Korea. But the Bush administration seems uninterested in such an approach, convinced as it is that Pyongyang will dishonor its promises at every opportunity. If Washington truly opposes negotiation with North Korea, however, it needs to offer an alternative, such as coercive diplomacy. But so far, it has done little on that front either. The recently announced Proliferation Security Initiative and Illicit Activities Initiative may help limit North Korea's money counterfeiting, missile sales, and drug trafficking activities. But any successful coercive approach will require active Chinese and South Korean cooperation—something Washington has yet to secure.

The Bush administration apparently would rather that North Korea follow the example of Libya, which announced its intention in December 2003 to voluntarily give up its unconventional weapons and allow outside verification. (If Colonel Muammar al-Qaddafi can take such a bold step, some in Washington have reasoned, it should be even easier for a "general" such as Kim Jong Il.) The Libyan model is particularly attractive to Washington because it is the only way to guarantee sufficiently intrusive access to ensure real disarmament. It should also appeal to North Korea, since it is the only case of nuclear disarmament that has not also involved regime change. In addition, the Libyan path seems to offer serious economic benefits (in the form of a lifting of sanctions and increased trade), which Pyongyang covets. So far, however, the Bush administration has pushed for a sort of "Libyan model plus" with North Korea, the "plus" being requirements that North Korea also give up its other illicit activities, transform its economy, end its severe restrictions on and monitoring of food assistance, and become a "normal state." Such steps, however, would so loosen Kim Jong Il's political control that they would be tantamount to regime change. And North Korea is so isolated that no third country can play the honest-broker role that the United Kingdom played for Libya, serving as a proxy for the United States in preliminary disarmament negotiations.

Going Critical illustrates just how important it is that any approach toward North Korea involve Japan and South Korea; excluding these two countries was perhaps the biggest mistake made by the Clinton administration, and they remain weak links that North Korea has consistently tried to exploit. Much has changed, however, in ten years. A decade ago Pyongyang marginalized and insulted the South Korean leadership at every opportunity. Today, however, North Korea reserves its rhetorical blasts for President Bush while it woos South Korea, encouraging it, for example, to forge new economic ties by establishing an industrial zone in the border city of Kaesong. In return, South Korea has started cajoling the United States to take negotiations with North Korea seriously. If the six-party talks are to make progress, Washington and Seoul will have to repair their alliance, narrow their differences, and make a firm and unified stand to ensure that Pyongyang does not exploit their differences over whether to risk a military confrontation.

Although U.S. allies are important, the authors of Going Critical argue convincingly that Washington cannot contract out its foreign policy on an interest as vital as assuring nuclear nonproliferation. Given the alternatives—containment, military action, and regime change—the authors argue that negotiation remains the most effective way to secure U.S. interests in the region. The Bush administration's failure thus far to take such talks seriously enough has allowed the steady expansion of North Korea's nuclear program—a striking lapse, especially given new intelligence showing that North Korea poses a much greater threat to the United States than Iraq ever did. The only feasible approach to North Korea today is one that effectively integrates a range of threats and incentives and involves all the participants in the six-party talks. Achieving that objective will require full U.S. participation and sustained White House leadership. As Going Critical shows, Washington has been able to muster that kind of focus in the past, narrowly averting a crisis in 1994 through top-level attention supported by effective interagency coordination. Since then, however, North Korea has benefited from American neglect and inattention. If this lack of focus persists, the second Korean nuclear crisis could reach a disastrous climax. Simply waiting for regime change—in Pyongyang, or in Washington—is not a sufficient strategy.

Scott Snyder is Senior Associate at the Asia Foundation.

Regime Change and Its Limits

Richard N. Haass

Pyongyang, North Korea.

ARMED AND DANGEROUS

Although a third of the "axis of evil" is now occupied by U.S. forces, the other two thirds—North Korea and Iran—remain clear threats to U.S. interests. Consider North Korea: in February 2005, Pyongyang announced that it had nuclear weapons, and it is now thought to have several of them, or at least the material to build them. Over time, if the United States does nothing, North Korea's arsenal will surely grow, as will the amount of its fissile material. The results of this growth will be destabilizing and potentially disastrous: a sizable North Korean nuclear arsenal might well stimulate similar weapons programs in both Japan and South Korea, diminishing the region's stability. The repercussions could also spread far beyond Northeast Asia if Pyongyang decides to sell its new weapons or nuclear fuel for hard currency—as it has with drugs and missile technology in the past.

Iran, for its part, also has a nuclear weapons program, which may not be as advanced as North Korea's but is much further along than almost anyone realized only a few years ago. Building on efforts that began under the shah, Iran has assembled many of the elements needed for a uranium-enrichment program with military potential. Magnifying Washington's concern, Iran has a history of concealing its nuclear program, as well as supporting terrorism and developing medium-range missiles.

Thus far, the Bush administration has consistently shown that it would rather resolve all of these challenges through regime change in Tehran and Pyongyang. It is not hard to fathom why: regime change is less distasteful than diplomacy and less dangerous than living with new nuclear states. There is only one problem: it is highly unlikely to have the desired effect soon enough.

REVOLUTION AND EVOLUTION

Regime change allows a state to solve its problems with another state by removing the offensive regime there and replacing it with a less offensive one. In the case of North Korea or Iran, this would mean installing a regime that either would not pursue nuclear weapons or, if it did, would be so different in character that the prospect would be much less worrisome.

Using regime change as a policy panacea is nothing new. Nor are the challenges posed by repressive countries possessing threatening weaponry; these are certainly not exclusively post-Cold War or post-September 11 phenomena. Indeed, the Cold War itself can be understood as a prolonged confrontation with a state of precisely this sort; the Soviet Union threatened the United States by what it did beyond its borders and offended Americans by what it did within them. So had Nazi Germany and imperial Japan before it.

The Roosevelt administration ultimately chose to deal with Germany and Japan through a policy of regime change, seeking not simply to defeat them on the battlefield and reverse their conquests but to continue war until the regimes in Berlin and Tokyo were ousted and something much better was firmly ensconced. It took years of armed occupation and intrusive involvement in the internal politics of both countries—what is known today as nation building—to achieve that latter objective.

The U.S. approach to the Soviet Union, however, was markedly different. After World War II, when Moscow emerged as Washington's principal global rival and threat, "rollback" became something of a popular concept. Yet the potential for a nuclear war in which there would be no winners regardless of who struck first tempered U.S. policy. Seeking regime change, or rollback, was deemed too risky, even reckless, given what could result if a desperate Soviet leadership lashed out with all the force at its disposal.

Simply acquiescing to Soviet behavior at home and abroad, however, was not acceptable to Washington either. The result was a policy of "containment," which George Kennan (then a U.S. diplomat in Moscow) helped formulate in his "long telegram," which ultimately found its way into this magazine in 1947. Containment was never as modest a policy as its critics alleged. Although it prescribed resisting Moscow's attempts to spread communism and expand Soviet influence, it also had a second, less cited dimension.

"It is entirely possible," Kennan wrote, "for the United States to influence by its actions the internal developments, both within Russia and throughout the international Communist movement.... The United States has it in its power to increase enormously the strains under which Soviet policy must operate, to force upon the Kremlin a far greater degree of moderation and circumspection than [the Kremlin] has had to observe in recent years, and in this way to promote tendencies which must eventually find their outlet in either the break-up or the gradual mellowing of Soviet power."

In other words, containment's second, subordinate goal was regime change. It eventually achieved this end through incremental means. But this method was so gradual (it took more than 40 years to succeed) that it could better be understood as regime evolution, and it took a back seat to containing Soviet advances. Whereas regime change (as the Bush administration uses the term) tends to be direct and immediate and to involve the use of military force or covert action, as well as attempts to isolate both politically and economically the government in question, regime evolution tends to be indirect and gradual and to involve the use of foreign policy tools other than military force.

Advocates of regime change generally reject most, sometimes any, dealings with the regime in question, lest the process of interaction or engagement somehow buttress the offending government. Diplomacy is therefore marginalized, as it has been in U.S. Cuba policy for 40 years, and as it has been more recently in U.S. policy toward both North Korea and Iran.

Regime evolution, however, accepts the need for give-and-take. The United States carried out an active diplomacy with the Soviet Union throughout the Cold War. It mattered not whether the policy was characterized as "peaceful coexistence" or, somewhat more optimistically, as "detente"; either way, the United States was prepared to deal with the Soviet Union when doing so served U.S. interests. Containment took precedence over rollback, or regime change, and influencing Soviet foreign policy took precedence over influencing Soviet behavior at home. This did not mean the United States ignored questions of what was going on inside the Soviet Union—it did not, as evidenced by sustained U.S. support for radio broadcasts addressed to the Soviet people, for individual human rights cases, and for the right to emigrate. But Washington did not accord these issues the same weight as Soviet foreign policy.

To understand how this process worked, consider arms control, one realm of intense U.S-Soviet involvement. U.S. officials regularly negotiated with their Soviet counterparts and entered into agreements to limit weapons, particularly nuclear ones. Such a policy may have prolonged the Soviet regime, since it accorded Moscow a unique and prominent international standing and placed curbs on a costly arms race that might have hastened the regime's demise (given the country's weak economic base). Still, successive U.S. administrations prudently deemed avoiding war and regulating U.S.-Soviet arms competition higher goals.

A similar rationale motivated the United States' economic dealings with the Soviet Union. Concern that bilateral trade could buttress the Soviet government was overridden by the view that trade deals would also give the Soviets a stake in better relations with the United States and the West and thereby rein in any Soviet temptation to challenge violently the status quo.

In the end, the Soviet regime did change. Historians will continue to debate how much of this was due to internal flaws in the Soviet system and how much resulted from U.S. and Western policy. The easy answer is that both forces were effective. The important thing is that an end did come, and it came peacefully. The third great conflict of the twentieth century, like the first two, ended with the result desired by the United States. Unlike the outcomes of the first two conflicts, however, this one was achieved without total war.

EASIER SAID THAN DONE

The Soviet experience holds important lessons for current U.S. foreign policy. Removing odious leaders—"regime ouster"—is no easy thing. The Soviet Union survived for nearly three-quarters of a century. The United States found it difficult to locate and arrest Manuel Noriega in Panama in 1989 and impossible to oust Mohamed Farah Aideed in Somalia in 1993. Fidel Castro remains ensconced in Havana today.

Regime replacement, the second step in regime change, is even more difficult, however. In the end, toppling Saddam Hussein was easy compared with putting in place a new Iraqi government that could run a secure, viable country. Although the Iraq venture was made far more expensive and difficult than necessary by Washington's poor planning and questionable decisions, it is possible it would not have gone more smoothly even had Iraq's occupation been approached differently. And occupations elsewhere will not be much easier. The rise of nationalism, together with globalization (and the increased availability of powerful means of resistance), may have doomed prolonged occupations of foreign countries by sharply increasing their human, military, and economic costs.

Indeed, the uncertainties surrounding regime change make it an unreliable approach for dealing with specific problems such as a nuclear weapons program in an unfriendly state. Neither North Korea nor Iran appears to be on the brink of dramatic domestic change. A decade ago, many believed that North Korea was near collapse, yet the regime still stands, and it may persist for years more, notwithstanding North Korea's impoverishment, its cruel and eccentric leadership, and its utter lack of freedom. Iran, too, is unlikely to throw off its current clerical leaders, despite their unpopularity. Even if these assessments ultimately prove incorrect, regime change cannot be counted on to come quickly enough to remove the nuclear threats now posed by these countries.

Unless, that is, the United States is prepared to invade them. But the expense of this approach would be enormous. Pyongyang's conventional military power could inflict great loss of life and physical destruction on South Korea, and its nuclear weapons could obviously increase such costs dramatically. Many U.S. military personnel (including some of the more than 30,000 currently stationed in South Korea, along with reinforcements who would be sent) would lose their lives. The United States could and would win such a war, but only at great cost to itself, the region, and the rest of the world. The same goes for war with Iran. That country is roughly the size of Alaska and has 70 million people, roughly three times as many as Iraq—more than enough to make any occupation costly, miserable, and futile for the United States.

Using more indirect tools to bring about regime evolution, instead of change, might well work but would take years, if not decades. Achieving regime evolution requires the strategic use of television, radio, and the Internet. Admission to the World Trade Organization (WTO) could be offered in return for fundamental economic reforms, ones that are, by their nature, also political. Rhetorical support for change can also help, as can direct assistance to nongovernmental organizations and other elements of civil society. Economic and political incentives should be made available to the target country if it is willing to adopt policies that reduce threats and that create more freedom and space for independent economic and political activity; in the absence of such changes, targeted sanctions should be considered. Trade and personnel exchanges can open a closed society to new ideas. Over the past few decades, there have been dozens of cases of successful regime evolution in the former Soviet bloc, Latin America, and Asia, and there is no reason such patterns could not be repeated elsewhere if the United States makes the investment and takes the necessary time. Odious or dangerous regimes should never be neglected, but the safest and best way to encourage their moderation or implosion is to smother them with policies that force them to open up to and deal with the outside world.

MILITARY MEANS

One other alternative for dealing with Pyongyang's and Tehran's nuclear programs is the limited use of military force. Such attacks could take two forms. One is a preemptive strike, akin to what Israel did in 1967 when, learning of an imminent Egyptian attack, it hit the Egyptians first. For such an attack to work, however, the intelligence assessment of the threat must be near 100 percent accurate, confirming that the danger is in fact imminent and that there are no other available means to stop it. Under such rare circumstances, it is widely viewed that a state enjoys the right to strike before it is certain to be struck. This is preemption in the classical sense—something quite different from President George W. Bush's use of the term, which in fact is better understood as prevention.

The problem for U.S. policymakers today is that neither situation—neither that with North Korea nor that with Iran—is likely to satisfy the conditions that warrant a preemptive strike in the traditional sense. Instead, available intelligence will probably be questionable, the threats uncertain and in no way clearly imminent, and the military option but one of several policies available. Under such circumstances, any U.S. attack would be preventive, not preemptive—the use of force against a gathering but not imminent threat.

There are some precedents for preventive strikes, such as Israel's attack on Iraq's Osirak nuclear complex in 1981 or the U.S.-led invasion of Iraq some two decades later. But preventive attacks always pose serious problems. For one thing, it is all but impossible to get international support for them. For another, they are quite difficult to carry out successfully; indeed, given the secrecy surrounding nuclear programs, the level of intelligence needed to effectively cripple them through a military attack can be impossible to attain.

It is this last consideration—of feasibility—that is likely to determine the use of preventive strikes in the future. It is not just a question of what constitutes North Korea's nuclear weapons program or where it is. Washington could in principle strike other targets valued by Pyongyang to coerce it into meeting U.S. and international demands regarding its nuclear programs. It is not clear, however, whether Washington could get political support for such attacks or that they would have the desired effect. In fact, South Korea, Japan, China, and Russia are likely to oppose any action that could lead to a war on the Korean Peninsula that would kill hundreds of thousands and destroy the economy of South Korea and of the region more generally.

Using preventive strikes to destroy Iran's developing weapons program would also be much easier said than done, given the imperfect nature of the intelligence on Iran's program and the operational challenges of attacking its dispersed and buried nuclear facilities. U.S. strikes might succeed in destroying part of Iran's weapons program and set it back by months or even years. But even if this were to occur, Iran would surely reconstitute its program in a manner that would make future strikes even more difficult. Moreover, Iran has the ability to retaliate by unleashing terrorism (using Hamas and Hezbollah) against Israel and the United States or by promoting instability in Iraq, Afghanistan, and Saudi Arabia. A U.S. strike on Iran would also further anger the Arab and Muslim worlds, where many already resent the double standard of U.S. and international acceptance of Israel's and India's nuclear weapons programs. Much of the Iranian population, currently alienated from the regime, would likely rally around it in the case of a foreign attack, making external efforts to bring about regime change that much more unlikely to succeed. Attacking Iran would also lead to sharp and possibly prolonged increases in the price of oil, which could trigger a global economic crisis. Nor would the United States avoid these costs if Israel carried out the strike (a scenario suggested by Vice President Dick Cheney in January 2005), since Israel would be widely viewed as doing the United States' bidding.

TALK FIRST

Another alternative policy for meeting the nuclear challenge posed by Iran and North Korea would be to emphasize diplomacy. North Korea and Iran could be promised a number of benefits, including economic assistance, security assurances, and greater political standing, if they satisfied U.S. and international concerns regarding their nuclear programs. They could also be presented with clear penalties in case they fail to cooperate adequately. Such penalties could include diplomatic and economic sanctions and, in the most dire circumstances, military attack.

It is far from clear, however, whether any such agreement could actually be negotiated. North Korea may well decide that possessing nuclear weapons is the best way to deter a U.S.-led military intervention and to earn hard currency—and thus refuse to give up such weapons. Iran, too, may decide that nuclear weapons are too useful as a deterrent and a means to acquire regional influence. Even if these states agreed to give up their weapons, moreover, there is no guarantee that they would honor their agreements. North Korea has already breached a 1992 accord with South Korea to keep the peninsula free of nuclear weapons and violated the spirit (if not necessarily the letter) of the 1994 U.S.-North Korean Agreed Framework. Iran, for its part, has failed to fulfill its obligations to notify the International Atomic Energy Agency (IAEA) of its uranium-enrichment activities, as it is required to under a safeguards agreement Tehran signed pursuant to the Nonproliferation Treaty.

Given their records, North Korea and Iran could be expected to exploit the time any negotiation would buy them to enhance their nuclear capabilities. Even absent such bad faith, essentially rewarding a country such as North Korea with alternative energy sources and various political and economic benefits for its having once invested in nuclear weapons could have the perverse effect of encouraging proliferation elsewhere. It might give other countries an incentive to follow suit in the belief that they, too, will eventually be rewarded for their bad behavior.

Despite these problems, however, diplomacy remains an attractive option, both because it could succeed and because only by first making a good-faith effort will the United States have a chance of getting the necessary regional and international backing for then pursuing a more confrontational tack.

In fact, the United States (working with China, Japan, Russia, and South Korea) has already initiated a series of discussions with North Korea in order to convince it to abandon its nuclear weapons program. Pyongyang, however, rejected the incentives Washington offered it last year, and the failure to include any clear penalties in the deal put little pressure on North Korea to compromise. Neither the carrot nor the stick was adequate. In addition, the Bush administration lost valuable time by resisting the prospect of bilateral talks with North Korea. This was a mistake; it matters little whether China, Japan, South Korea, and Russia are physically in the room so long as the United States coordinates its policies with them.

The best path available now is to continue to work with these states on a diplomatic package that would give North Korea security assurances, energy assistance, and specified political and economic benefits in exchange for forgoing its nuclear programs (fuel and weapons alike) and agreeing to robust international inspections. Sequence matters in all this; it is unrealistic to expect North Korea to satisfy all nuclear-related requirements before it receives any benefits. Washington and its partners should also agree on what economic and political sanctions would be imposed on Pyongyang if it failed to accept such an agreement by a specified date or if it crossed a red line, such as by testing a nuclear device.

China's role is central to any such diplomatic undertaking. Although Beijing's influence on North Korea is limited, it is greater than any other country's. China is the source of much of North Korea's energy and is its principal trading partner. But Beijing, while willing to apply some pressure, seems reluctant to insist, possibly out of fear that if Kim Jong Il's regime begins to collapse, war will break out and refugees will flood China. As a result, China has seemed more interested in placing a lid on the North Korea problem than in actually resolving it.

Washington must try to persuade Beijing to use all of its influence to convince Pyongyang to abandon its nuclear weapons program. To this end, China's leaders should understand that the North Korea problem is a test case of China's willingness to become a true strategic partner of the United States. It would also help if the U.S. government were to reassure China's leaders about its long-term thinking on Northeast Asia, namely, that the United States is firmly opposed to the emergence of any new nuclear weapons state in the region, be it Japan, a unified Korea, or Taiwan.

Addressing Iran's nuclear program will require an international proposal offering Tehran the nuclear fuel it says it requires for power generation, but not direct access to or control of the fuel itself. Such an offer could be made to Iran alone. But to improve its attractiveness, the deal should be put forward as a new global policy, in which no entity other than the five acknowledged nuclear weapons states and the IAEA would be permitted to control nuclear fuel. To secure Iran's agreement, the country, which is currently subject to numerous U.S. economic sanctions, could be offered various economic inducements and security assurances akin to those being considered for North Korea. In exchange for these benefits, Iran (again like North Korea) would be expected to convince the world, by allowing intrusive inspections, that it is not developing nuclear weapons or producing the fissile material they require. U.S. policy currently seems to be headed in this direction, but Washington needs to offer more than simply ending its blockage of Iran's admission to the WTO or its purchase of spare parts for aircraft. For their part, Europe and Russia, as well as China, must commit to meaningful sanctions in the event Iran violates the agreement. This is a moment for creative specificity, not ambiguity.

Even if such tactics are used, it remains possible (some would say likely) that diplomacy with Iran will fail, either because of insufficient international support or because many in Iran want to proceed with uranium enrichment or develop nuclear weapons regardless of the cost. As with North Korea, however, the diplomatic option is nonetheless worth pursuing, given the costs of every other approach and given that the only chance for building international support for (or even acceptance of) a more aggressive strategy is to first make a good-faith effort to resolve matters diplomatically.

LIVING WITH PROLIFERATION

There is always the option of accepting a de facto nuclear status for North Korea and Iran. This is the default option if regime change yields no dramatic result, the military option is rejected, and diplomacy fails. And it would be similar to what has already become the U.S. and international approach to Israel, India, and Pakistan. There would have to be, however, one big difference: given the bellicose history and nature of both North Korea and Iran, the United States would need to introduce an extra element of deterrence to discourage either government from using a nuclear weapon or transferring critical technologies, fuel, or weapons to other states or to terrorist groups. To this end, the United States should declare publicly that any government that uses weapons of mass destruction, threatens to use them, or knowingly transfers WMD or key materials to third parties opens itself up to the strongest reprisals, including attack and removal from power. This message should be accompanied by a concerted diplomatic effort to get the other major powers to sign on to such a policy. Such moves would add teeth to Security Council resolutions and international conventions that already forbid states from facilitating nuclear terrorism in any way.

Even with such international statements, this approach would be inherently risky: accepting a North Korean nuclear arsenal might mean accepting the perpetuation of a desperate, failing government that could well try secretly to transfer nuclear material to terrorists in exchange for much-needed money. Accepting the existence of a nuclear-armed Iran implies a similar bargain. And in both cases, deterrence might not work.

What is more, even if deterrence did work, accepting and learning to live with a nuclear-armed North Korea or Iran would not be cost free. As suggested above, if North Korea is allowed to retain nuclear weapons, this could prompt Japan, South Korea, or other states to seek to acquire them as well. Keeping the peace in a nuclear Northeast Asia would be no easy feat given the historical animosities, the latent rivalries, and the lack of institutional mechanisms for promoting regional confidence and stability.

The same goes for the Middle East. A nuclear Iran could well cause Egypt, Saudi Arabia, Syria, and even Iraq to consider developing a similar capability, although it might take them longer to catch up due to their lack of an advanced industrial base. And keeping the peace between a half dozen nuclear-armed states that are suspicious of, if not downright hostile toward, one another would be extremely difficult. The emergence of new nuclear weapons states would also dramatically increase the risk that these weapons or their components would fall into the hands of terrorists, whether by accident or design.

ALL TOGETHER NOW

Regime change, limited military action, diplomacy, and deterrence can all be considered as alternative policies. They are better understood, however, as components of a single comprehensive approach toward states such as North Korea and Iran. Deterrence is a way to make the best of a bad situation. Military action or, more precisely, the threat of it can buttress diplomatic prospects. But diplomacy should be the heart of U.S. policy toward both countries—because it could succeed, because it must be shown to have failed before there is any chance of garnering support for other policies, and because all the other options are so unattractive.

As for regime change, it is best viewed as a complement to diplomacy and deterrence. It is essential to appreciate not only the limits of regime change but also its nature. A refusal to engage tyrannies allows them to wrap themselves in nationalism and to maintain control; offering regimes enhanced security and economic and political interaction if they meet specified requirements can deny them their rationale for tight control and their ability to maintain it. A foreign policy that chooses to integrate, not isolate, despotic regimes can be the Trojan horse that moderates their behavior in the short run and their nature in the long run. It is time Washington put this thinking to the test, toward what remains of the axis of evil. Delay is no longer an option, and drift is not a strategy.

Richard N. Haass is President of the Council on Foreign Relations. He was Director of the State Department's Policy Planning Staff from 2001 to 2003. This article is drawn from his recently published book, The Opportunity: America's Moment to Alter History's Course.

The Long Road to Pyongyang

Michael J. Mazarr

Army personnel and people gather at Kim Il Sung Square in Pyongyang, North Korea.

At first glance, the outcome of the North Korean nuclear standoff might appear to be a positive one for the United States. Under the February 2007 nuclear deal negotiated by the Bush administration, North Korea will freeze its main nuclear reactor, at Yongbyon, and allow the return of International Atomic Energy Agency (IAEA) inspectors. The agreement also reawakens the slender hope that Pyongyang is on the road to nuclear disarmament.

More broadly, Bush officials have pointed to the outcome of the North Korean saga as evidence that the administration has defied—or, as some would have it, never deserved—its caricature as a bellicose, preemption-obsessed neoconservative clique. After the initial confrontation over North Korea's nuclear program, the diplomacy quickly assumed a multilateral dimension and never lost it. Japan has been a valued partner of the administration, its voice influential on North Korea policy; China was fully engaged. Outright military solutions were never seriously considered, and the process was built around negotiations designed to test North Korea's willingness to surrender its nuclear ambitions.

But a look back at the history of the Bush administration's approach to North Korea highlights a somewhat different aspect of the White House's foreign policy. The portrait that emerges is not one of a confrontational, militaristic administration; what instead becomes apparent is an image of a White House with extremely poor conceptual strategies and decision-making processes.

From the beginning, President George W. Bush, as the nation's chief strategist, has failed to articulate a coherent policy for dealing with North Korea. The administration as a whole entered office without a clear foreign policy doctrine. The president himself appears to have been attached to a number of basic principles: the importance of strength and credibility, the universal appeal of democracy, a Reaganite belief that dictatorships are morally reprehensible and cannot be trusted. But beyond those core attitudes, in the North Korean case the basic elements of strategy—ends, means, and the balance between them—were not lucidly expressed or rigorously debated at the most senior levels of the U.S. government. The result was a strategic muddle, a swirling debate not guided by any clearly calculated long-term vision. And after six years, the process has wound up almost exactly where it started—except now North Korea appears to have tripled the amount of nuclear weapons material in its possession and has become a declared nuclear power.

REGIME CHANGE VERSUS REDEMPTION

During the transition between administrations in late 2000 and early 2001, a team of Clinton administration national security officials traveled to the home of the secretary of state designate, Colin Powell, to brief him and the national security adviser designate, Condoleezza Rice, on North Korea policy. Powell expressed a desire to pick up on the progress that had been made during the Clinton administration—progress achieved through extensive bilateral negotiations culminating in a 1994 accord, the Agreed Framework, that froze the North's Yongbyon nuclear facility and its five-megawatt nuclear reactor. The Kim Dae Jung government in South Korea seemed equally hopeful that it could bring the new administration around to a Clinton-style policy on North Korea, an intention that reportedly emerged during a February 2001 telephone call between the two national leaders.

But from the outset, Bush's one overriding view was that Kim Jong Il, the North Korean leader, was a loathsome tyrant who did not deserve to be in power. The president, according to several officials who dealt directly or indirectly with him, felt very strongly about this. Beyond this instinctive reaction, however, Bush had no strategic concept for dealing with North Korea and little background in the situation on the peninsula or the details of the nuclear issue. He agreed that abandoning the centerpiece agreement of the Clinton years—the Agreed Framework—would be too provocative and risk U.S. alliances in Asia. And as a believer in redemption, he was in some ways sympathetic to arguments for giving even Kim's North Korea an opportunity to change its ways, an instinct that went against the advice of his hard-line advisers.

A stark difference of opinion was soon on display between Bush and South Korean President Kim. Kim was scheduled for a state visit on March 7, 2001, without a final U.S. Korea policy having been developed. When, on March 6, Powell spoke to the press about the visit, he predicted, as Kim had hoped, that the Bush administration would "engage with North Korea to pick up where President Clinton and his administration left off." This seems to have produced some prompt discussions at the most senior levels of government, and the next day Powell was forced to leave the presidential summit and comment to waiting reporters about the new administration "undertaking a full review" of policy and developing policies "unique to the administration." And when Bush and Kim emerged sometime later, the U.S. leader made pointed comments distancing his administration from the idea that Kim's "sunshine policy" toward the North—engaging Pyongyang in order to moderate and gain leverage over its behavior—could achieve its goals.

Ironically, a policy review process was already under way, and it had determined that the Bush administration would uphold the Agreed Framework unless North Korea violated it first. In effect, then, Powell was largely correct in describing the initial policy decisions as ones to continue Clinton-era policies. The problem was saying so publicly.

The problem also may have been an early competition to become the lead spokesperson for the president's foreign policy. As secretary of state and a far more experienced senior official than Rice, Powell naturally assumed it would be him. But as the national security official closest personally to President Bush and as the coordinator of his overall policies, Rice, some officials believe, wanted to reserve the last word on U.S. foreign policy for her own office.

This episode reinforced two emerging themes of Bush administration policymaking. One was that the president had very strong instincts about issues—and that those instincts would override the policy process, even making the whole notion of a process quite beside the point once the president was sure of what his "gut" was telling him. A second theme was that Powell was misinformed about just how poorly he and the president understood each other's worldviews and personalities—and the degree to which he, as secretary of state, would run the administration's foreign policy. Officials such as Powell, who came into office expecting a more normal interagency policy experience, had no idea yet how combative, personalized, and undisciplined the national security process of the new administration was going to become.

A formal review of North Korea policy concluded in June 2001. The basic outline of the Bush administration's national security policy process, NSPD-1, specified that regional issues would be handled by regional assistant secretaries in the State Department and functional issues would be overseen by functional senior directors on the National Security Council. Because North Korea was seen as a combination issue,

Rice created a joint review process, with James Kelly from the State Department's East Asian Bureau and Robert Joseph from the NSC's nonproliferation directorate sharing responsibility. Some in the State Department saw this as a power grab by the hard-liners (who held a number of key seats in the nonproliferation offices) to ensure they would have a strong voice on North Korea. For their part, the hardliners and the nonproliferation specialists saw a combined effort as only logical given the proliferation stakes involved. Ultimately, the nonproliferation specialists did use the combined working-group model to do everything in their power to influence, even control, the process.

Some of what followed was a fairly straightforward interagency process—background papers, deputies meetings, and an evolving dialogue leading to policy. The majority of the officials involved, however, describe an ideological debate and a fragmented interagency process that simply could not be resolved. This fight pitted the East Asian Bureau of the State Department (and some within the NSC), arguing for negotiations with the North, against a critical mass of hardline voices, arguing against the validity of the Agreed Framework or any dialogue with the North. The formal interagency dialogue stalled, and the writing of the policy had to be centralized, with NSC officials reporting to Kelly and Joseph. They generated a proposed document that was run through the interagency process, cleared, and finalized in early June 2001.

CAMP FOLLOWERS

There were different camps in the debate over North Korea policy from the beginning. The hard-line, or hawkish, group reflected some areas of strong consensus. This camp eventually came to include such officials as Undersecretary of State John Bolton, the NSC's Joseph, aides to Vice President Dick Cheney and the vice president himself, and selected senior Defense Department officials, including Secretary of Defense Donald Rumsfeld. They viewed the North Korean government as a brutal, Stalinist tyranny and believed that any economic or political engagement with Pyongyang would merely serve to prolong the life of an evil and dangerous regime. This hard-line group held to the view that because North Korea would not give up its nuclear weapons, there was almost no prospect of a negotiated settlement's achieving its goals. The only sensible option, they believed, was to put Pyongyang in a vise—to create a situation in which the North Korean leadership felt it had no choice but to surrender its nuclear weapons and agree to a painfully intrusive verification regime. Accordingly, the hard-liners felt that the Agreed Framework negotiated by the Clinton administration was a terrible mistake and ought to be undermined; some remarked openly that anything they could do to bring it down would be a step in the right direction.

What was needed, in the hard-liners' minds, was not engagement but sanctions—anything to strangle the North Korean economy and push it to the point of collapse would serve the long-term interest of peace better than steps that extended the life of Kim's murderous regime. The hard-liners, echoing the arguments of the American

Enterprise Institute economist Nicholas Eberstadt, argued that by roughly 1999, North Korea had come very close to collapse and was only saved by new influxes of outside aid and investment. Some officials recall the hard-liners saying in meetings that if China could only be brought along, North Korea could be cut off from most trade and aid and would collapse in short order. Several State Department officials mentioned a memorandum Rumsfeld had reportedly sent to President Bush arguing for just such a strategy: enlist the Chinese, he allegedly proposed, in an effort to topple Kim.

An alternative school of thought within the administration would be reflected by such people as Powell, Deputy Secretary of State Richard Armitage, the NSC's Michael Green, Kelly, and (in the second term) the NSC's Victor Cha. These more moderate officials favored a strategy of tough dialogue rather than isolation and regime change. They recognized the importance of regional relationships and alliances to solving the North Korean issue—and the constraints that those relationships and alliances placed on U.S. policy. Some among this pragmatic, pro-negotiation group seem to have been content to pick up the Clinton process where it lay. Others shared the hard-line critique of the Clinton policy but believed, as the hard-liners did not, that negotiations could still be useful.

Rice fell somewhere between these camps—but closer to the pragmatists than to the hard-liners. In a 2000 Foreign Affairs article outlining Bush's prospective foreign policy, she was restrained in her criticism of the Agreed Framework. "Any U.S. policy toward the north should depend heavily on coordination with Seoul and Tokyo," she wrote. "In that context, the 1994 framework agreement that attempted to bribe North Korea into forsaking nuclear weapons cannot easily be set aside." The United States, she concluded, ought to approach North Korea "resolutely and decisively." But that did not suggest urgent efforts at regime change: "These regimes [North Korea and Iraq] are living on borrowed time, so there need be no sense of panic about them."

The landscape of the strategic debate on North Korea policy within the administration, therefore, was a complex one. When the February 2007 agreement was announced, many conservative commentators declared it a sellout, a complete reversal of administration policy toward the North since 2001. In many ways, this was true. But in another sense, the 2007 accord merely represented the victory of a strain of thought that had been very much alive—even if submerged—within the administration all along. In a second-term Bush administration anxious for a foreign policy victory, this secondary approach would be taken up, dusted off, and put into play by Rice, newly empowered as the secretary of state.

A HOSTILE POLICY?

That phase of Bush's North Korea policy, however, was still six years off when, in June 2001, the administration's first policy review came to a conclusion. The policy that was eventually approved by the principals' committee emphasized two main themes—denuclearization and strong alliances—and listed four areas of interest that the United States would pursue with the North: nuclear weapons, the conventional military balance, missile technology, and human rights. "I have directed my national security team," Bush's June 13 announcement said, "to undertake serious discussions with North Korea on a broad agenda…. If North Korea responds affirmatively and takes appropriate action, we will expand our efforts to help the North Korean people, ease sanctions, and take other political steps."

The basic paradox of the administration's North Korea policy was thus right out in the open: Bush had directed his national security team to pursue negotiations with a North Korean regime that he believed to be evil and dishonest. In fact, no real policy decision had been reached. The public statement seemed to welcome talks, but most senior U.S. officials bitterly opposed them, and in fact no coherent U.S. strategy toward North Korea was being assembled at all. North Korea's response to the administration was predictable: the United States had a "hostile policy," it said to U.S. officials through low-level channels, and Pyongyang had no interest in dialogue. And then, in January 2002, the president's State of the Union address pushed the North even further away from the bargaining table with its infamous reference to an "axis of evil" that included North Korea.

Still, notwithstanding the "axis of evil" barb, in early 2002 there was a new round of discussions on North Korea policy in Washington. A great deal had happened since the first policy review—most notably, September 11 and the onset of the war on terrorism. U.S. government officials worked up a "road map" for negotiations with Pyongyang—an intensely detailed document of 20 or 30 pages spelling out step by step the specifics of what both sides should do in each of the four issue areas laid out by the first policy review.

In February 2002, President Bush traveled to South Korea. He spent more time with Kim Dae Jung and met with U.S. military officials to discuss the challenges of the regional war plan. His administration was also now embroiled in the war on terrorism, the invasion of Afghanistan, and early planning for the invasion of Iraq; perhaps as a result, his comments in Seoul reflected a notable shift in tone. Speaking side by side with Kim, Bush said of their conversations, "I made it very clear to the president that I support his sunshine policy. And I told him that we, too, would be happy to have a dialogue with the North Koreans." (And yet, a year later, once the six-party talks were under way, key U.S. officials would work late nights and weekends to ensure that such a direct dialogue never occurred.)

Back in Washington, presented with the road-map document, Bush balked—not at the idea of talking to the North but simply at the interconnected complexity of the proposed approach. If the United States intended to offer the North a basic choice—change its ways or face even more isolation—why not make the alternatives as simple as possible? Bush sent his aides back and directed them to develop a "bold approach"—a large-scale offer on a few basic issues.

Of course, huge unanswered questions remained. What possible reason did Washington have to expect that Pyongyang would accept the deal? What would it do if the North declined—or took the offer as an invitation to enter into an extended negotiation? At the State Department, the reaction was quizzical. What was meant by "bold approach"? What was the goal? The response, as some in the State Department heard it, was that the principals would "know it when they saw it." Once again, the gut reactions of the president and his most senior aides would be allowed to substitute for wide-ranging staff work and strategic thought in the development of policy.

Meanwhile, a parallel notion that had been germinating within the administration from its relatively early days was gathering momentum: the idea of putting pressure on North Korea by undercutting its various illicit trading activities, such as drug smuggling, counterfeiting, and exporting arms. Interest in this plan seems to have developed in earnest in late 2001 and early 2002, pushed by a number of officials across the government but most especially by David Asher, working in the office of Kelly in the East Asian Bureau at the State Department. Asher assembled an interagency task force to study North Korea's illicit activities and develop tactics to interdict them. Some who favored negotiations approved of this "pressure points" effort, hoping that it would furnish additional leverage in talks. Reactions to the plan varied: some pro-negotiation officials, for example, hoped that by endorsing and even leading this effort, they would recapture some hard-line credibility.

These two lines of policy—negotiations and pressure—would progress within the Bush administration for the next three years. They would collide openly in September 2005, when efforts to put pressure on the North helped scuttle an emerging accord on its nuclear ambitions.

THE HAWKS' ASCENDANCY

Through the spring of 2002, staffers at the NSC built a concept paper for the "bold approach," and the United States began sounding out the North Koreans about a meeting to broach the new deal. The bold approach was an effort to assemble a grand bargain that would test North Korea's willingness to do two things: denuclearize and make a strategic choice to begin moving in the direction of domestic reform and joining the world community. Kelly was set to travel to North Korea in the early summer of 2002 to deliver the offer.

That meeting, however, would never occur. Two events intervened—the first would delay the meeting, and the second would kill it. On June 29, 2002, patrol gunboats from the two Koreas engaged in a short firefight in the West Sea, and a South Korean patrol boat was sunk with some loss of life. And then every hostile instinct of the hard-line coalition in the U.S. government seemed to be confirmed. During the Clinton administration, evidence had emerged that North Korea was intent on acquiring centrifuges to enrich uranium for nuclear weapons—as distinct from the plutonium it was acquiring from the reprocessing of spent fuel at its Yongbyon nuclear reactor. Then, in June 2002, U.S. intelligence agencies assessed that there existed "clear evidence" that the North had "acquired material and equipment" for a centrifuge facility.

Outside the government, there has been some debate about just how significant the North Korean uranium program in fact was. Later public reports suggested that the 2002 intelligence was built on evidence that Pakistan, through the Pakistani nuclear scientist A. Q. Khan's network, had sold North Korea about 20 centrifuges. The accuracy of these public reports, however, cannot be confirmed, and one is left to wonder why such a small number of machines would generate a sizable U.S. response. The alarm may have stemmed from suspicions that the North intended to clone them and make hundreds or thousands more. Even if this was the fear, however, no evidence has publicly emerged to suggest that North Korea—while it may have been busily engaged in the purchase of the components of a centrifuge capability—was anything but years away from an actual capability to produce significant quantities of highly enriched uranium.

But regardless, the intelligence assessment reawakened still unresolved debates at the core of U.S. policy and strategy toward the North. The hard-liners viewed the moment as a perfect opportunity to kill the Agreed Framework by eliminating the heavy fuel oil deliveries still being made by the framework's implementing organization, the Korean Peninsula Energy Development Organization. The moderates advocated a more measured response, but the seeming obviousness of the cheating and the emotionalism of the principled position won out after a peremptory debate. In a famous October 2002 session with a delegation led by Kelly—which the North Koreans thought was aimed at discussing the "bold approach" agenda—Washington unveiled its evidence of the uranium program. The North Korean delegation appears to have confirmed that Kelly's accusations were accurate.

To punish the North, the administration secured a multilateral agreement to suspend fuel oil shipments, and North Korea reacted quickly—more quickly, several officials say, than the administration expected—with a series of provocative steps. In December, it reactivated the nuclear reactor at Yongbyon, removed IAEA seals and cameras from its facilities, and expelled the IAEA inspectors. In January 2003, it withdrew from the Nuclear Nonproliferation Treaty.

The Bush administration struggled to adopt a tough stance with the North, including threatening UN Security Council sanctions. Pyongyang, meanwhile, was carrying out a threat to remove the 8,000 spent fuel rods that had been sitting in cooling ponds near the Yongbyon reactor, which the Agreed Framework had shut down. North Korea claims that these fuel rods were reprocessed by July 2003; the reactor, meanwhile, was refueled, and two years later its spent fuel was again removed. What is known in the unclassified world is this: at the time of the Agreed Framework, in 1994, the North was assessed to have one to two bombs' worth of plutonium; from the cooling ponds, it acquired spent fuel that could generate between two and six additional nuclear bombs' worth of plutonium; and from the subsequent operation of its reactor, it generated as much as two more bombs' worth of the material.

INTERAGENCY SPOILERS

Between October 2002 and January 2003, it became apparent in Washington that new ideas were needed, and momentum began to build for a multilateral approach. After a long-drawn-out discussion within the administration involving a wide range of options and a series of meetings with key regional powers, the United States and other governments settled on an initial U.S.-Chinese-North Korean trilateral session in Beijing in April 2003, followed by the beginning of a six-party format that would include Japan, Russia, and South Korea.

In Washington, Powell reportedly found some opposition to the idea of multilateral talks. Rice supported the line of thinking, but Secretary of Defense Rumsfeld and others entered the debate at this point to argue against the process and in favor of a much more confrontational policy toward the North, even extending to efforts to collapse the regime. Their arguments were rejected. With that broad decision having been made, the interagency process would crank up again—with the old tensions reappearing immediately. One official described the resulting process this way: Powell would work something out with the president, Rice would agree—and then the policy would have to be fought through the interagency process, where staffers sympathetic to the hardline view and doing the bidding of Rumsfeld, Cheney, and others would do their best to prevent any deal from actually being struck with North Korea.

The defining example of this in the lead-up to the trilateral talks was the debate over the scope of Kelly's negotiating instructions. One day in April, an initial State Department draft of the instructions, which granted Kelly wide latitude, was circulated roughly at noon, according to one account. But Cheney's office and Joseph, of the NSC, quickly intervened, concerned that North Korea would exploit any bilateral dialogue with the United States to buy itself strategic breathing space. By 4 PM, the State Department draft had morphed into a set of more restrictive instructions issued from the NSC: Kelly would have no ability to speak directly to the North Koreans on any bilateral basis—which, according to many accounts, the Chinese had explicitly promised Pyongyang would occur. As a result, the North Korean delegation stopped participating in the talks long before they were scheduled to conclude.

After the trilateral meeting, the six-party talks opened in August 2003. U.S. negotiators were squeezed on both sides—on one by the North Koreans and on the other by the hardline coalition within the administration. Yet State Department officials found that as the six-party process moved forward, Bush seemed to gain confidence in it. The other parties were actively participating, in many cases putting pressure on North Korea, and the multilateralism of the effort was having an effect.

In June 2004, the momentum toward direct dialogue led to the preparation of the most elaborate formal offer to North Korea yet assembled by the administration. Some U.S. Asian allies, especially Japan, reportedly believed that the time had come to put North Korea on the spot with a strong proposal. Accounts described the offer as proposing, in part, that China, Japan, and South Korea furnish energy aid to the North in exchange for the North's freezing its nuclear sites, fully disclosing its nuclear activities, and opening itself up to IAEA inspections—all within three months.

The North Korean response was pleasant but noncommittal. In fact, the timing of the proposal should have made this hardly surprising: by laying its best offer on the table less than five months before a presidential election, the Bush administration was all but inviting the North Koreans to stall for time and wait to see if the Democratic candidate, John Kerry, won and offered them better terms. In an interesting sideline at the meeting, North Korean negotiators told the U.S. delegation that forces within their country were pressing for a nuclear test. If matters were not resolved, they warned, hard-line elements might have their way. At the time, it seems, Washington dismissed this threat as a negotiating ploy.

A RETURN TO ENGAGEMENT

In Bush's second term, the style and substance of the approach to North Korea changed markedly. This was the product of a number of gradual shifts: changes in the political context, changes in personnel, and an acceptance of the reality on the ground. Many of those involved in the policy insist on its fundamental consistency—its multilateralism, its emphasis on diplomacy, its desire to test North Korean intentions. That claim is accurate, as far as it goes, and one has to admire the commitment of those second-term officials, such as the negotiator Christopher Hill and Cha, who diligently pursued negotiations and at a minimum brought U.S. policy back to the starting point from which it had veered so dangerously. Still, judged by such standards as the degree of engagement of North Korea, the force and frequency of U.S. negotiating offers, and the willingness to tolerate Pyongyang's misbehavior, there can be no doubt of a significant shift in tone in the second term—and an eventual collision with many of the core principles the administration had stated from the beginning.

Within the administration, Rice replaced Powell as secretary of state, and by the end of 2006, Rumsfeld had left the Defense Department, replaced by Robert Gates. Cheney's office remained influential, but less so, in part because it was in turmoil due to the high-profile trial of his former chief of staff, Lewis "Scooter" Libby. Meanwhile, Bolton's nomination as UN ambassador had to be abandoned. The domino effect of senior staff changes resulted in the weakening of the once-dominant hard-line coalition on North Korea.

Rice quickly made it clear that as secretary of state she saw her role differently from as national security adviser: now, when she wanted to take charge of an issue, she would do so. North Korea became just such an issue, and she has been described as a sort of "super North Korea desk officer" because of her focus and involvement from 2005 on. Rice went looking for an energetic, effective diplomat to replace the well-respected Kelly as lead negotiator, and she found Hill. His experience as a Balkan negotiator was appealing, as was his reputation as a tireless and determined diplomat.

With the Rice-Hill team in place, there was a powerful force advocating a new round of negotiations. Movement toward a negotiated settlement may have been helped along by political considerations: many reports suggest that there was a growing feeling in the administration that a foreign policy success story in North Korea would be of major value, especially as the situation in Iraq worsened between 2004 and 2006.

These powerful drivers, however, still ran firmly against the strong and oft-expressed conviction of many key foreign policy officials, including the president himself, that North Korea was simply not a regime that could, or should, be dealt with. An agreement would contradict powerful rhetoric that had been in play since the administration's first days in power—and would have to overcome the continuing, although far less intense, bureaucratic games of a hard-line faction that remained unpersuaded of the need for a deal.

Still, at least from a negotiating standpoint, the energetic Rice-Hill efforts began paying dividends quickly, during the summer and fall of 2005. An announcement came on September 19: the United States had offered a nonaggression pledge and, in principle, to normalize relations with the North, and it had reopened the possibility of delivering a nuclear reactor of "light water" design to the North at some point. North Korea, in turn, had made an allegedly novel promise to fully denuclearize and open itself to inspections. The agreement represented more of an "agreement to agree": a minefield lay ahead of the September 2005 announcement in the best of circumstances—and the best of circumstances were not to emerge.

The first shot across the bow of the new deal came from Pyongyang. Within days, the North was backtracking, claiming it had been promised a light-water reactor immediately and would only begin implementing the deal when construction began. The second shot came from Washington. The Treasury Department had made an announcement of its own: based on evidence that North Korean counterfeit U.S. currency was being laundered at a Macao-based bank, it had issued a draft notice designating an obscure financial institution called Banco Delta Asia as a "money laundering concern." This caused a run on the bank, which led Chinese officials to freeze its assets, including some $24 million of North Korean funds. Pyongyang called the financial action an attack on its sovereignty and stalked away from the negotiating table. The second track of U.S. policy—the pressure-points strategy—had veered sideways and crashed into the nonproliferation strategy. More than a year would pass before the talks would begin again.

With negotiations having collapsed, North Korea apparently made the calculation that the time had come to cross some very prominent red lines. In July 2006, it conducted a test of a long-range missile, and on October 9, it crossed the biggest threshold of all, testing an underground nuclear device. Global condemnation was swift, and the United States immediately urged a package of UN sanctions. Yet the U.S. rhetoric was muted. Bush reaffirmed his commitment to diplomacy; in one press conference, he used some version of the word "diplomacy" 17 times. This seems to have reflected the dominant reaction to the underground test within the administration: concern, mainly, that an overreaction would play into the hands of a North Korea determined to provoke the United States and, at the same time, a refusal to recognize the North's nuclear status and an attempt to get the North back into denuclearization talks as soon as possible.

The UN Security Council did pass two resolutions, including Resolution 1718, which levied controls on any North Korean trade having to do with weapons of mass destruction or luxury goods and allowed for the possible inspection of goods going to and from the North. But this hardly seemed a punishment fit for the crime, and reporters were soon sending back accounts of bustling trade at North Korea's border with China.

The six-party talks had gotten under way again in December 2006, with a fruitless round that ended in failure. Cha, of the NSC, by chance ran into the North Korean delegation at the Beijing airport; the North Koreans, anxious to break something loose from the stalled talks, suggested a bilateral round of U.S.-North Korean negotiations somewhere besides Beijing. Cha could make no commitments and promised only to raise the idea back in Washington, which he did—reportedly in the form of a memo arguing in favor of such bilateral negotiations. According to published reports, his argument relied on the principle of testing North Korea's intentions. Cha told a reporter that Bush "wanted to see if the North Koreans were serious about implementing the September 2005 joint statement." Cha's memo prompted a series of intense discussions within the administration. On the one hand, bilateral talks would constitute a complete reversal: as recently as October 12, Bush had again castigated the Clinton policy of direct bilateral negotiations and insisted resolutely that his administration would never pursue them. On the other hand, in informal venues within the six-party talks, the administration had already been holding what amounted to bilateral talks for some time.

Cha's case for testing North Korea's intentions reportedly carried the argument, and Bush approved the most formal set of bilateral dialogues yet—and in a richly symbolic location, Berlin, where the Clinton administration had conducted some of its own negotiations with North Korea. Hill met North Korean officials there in mid-January 2007 and produced the outlines of a possible deal. Rice reportedly spoke by telephone with Bush and her successor as national security adviser, Stephen Hadley, about the potential agreement; both of them endorsed it. The Berlin meetings generated only the framework of a deal; nothing was finalized until February 2007, and the six-party process then got back under way. Having conducted a bilateral dialogue, however, proved important: other parties could now tell the North Koreans that patience with Pyongyang's stalling was at an end, in part because the North had gotten the bilateral dialogue it had long demanded.

Back in Washington, meanwhile, the hard-liners, accustomed to being the ones privy to key inside information and able to influence the most important decisions at the last minute, found themselves on the outside looking in. They complained that the resulting deal had not been subjected to a comprehensive interagency vetting. "There was no process here," one disgruntled opponent complained to The New York Times. "Nothing." Advocates of a negotiated solution were the ones feeding the last-minute papers to the key decision-makers. The world had, in many ways, turned upside down inside the Bush administration's policymaking process.

STRATEGIC MUDDLE

With the victory of the Rice-Hill approach, Bush's foreign policy on North Korea came to reflect the triumph of pragmatism over principle. But the Bush administration's Korea policy has long reflected something much more than that: an essential lack of strategy and (at least in the first term) a decision-making process that was alternately fragmented, bitterly ideological, and impelled by top-down, instinct-driven mandates.

Participants in the process, especially in the second term, will point to what they see as a strategy that is now in effect: the six-party talks. We have employed multilateral diplomacy to offer North Korea a strategic choice, they claim. That is a strategy, and it has worked.

But negotiations are a tactic and a process, not a strategy. They have not resolved the immense contradictions in the administration's attitude toward North Korea—for if what the president says about its moral character is true, it is not a regime with which the United States can reliably negotiate. Pursuing talks leaves open huge questions about such issues as what the ultimate ends of U.S. policy are—what degree of certainty, for example, about North Korean disarmament will be enough? Most fundamental, beyond the nuclear issue, the administration has never articulated a coherent strategy toward North Korea as a whole, and as long as that question remains unanswered, U.S. strategy toward the nuclear issue will remain hostage to unresolved issues as basic as whether or not Washington is willing to live with the North Korean regime.

This strategic muddle was in part a consequence of key policymakers' thinking in principled rather than strategic terms—a major feature of the Bush administration. Many officials made policy based on moralistic grounds rather than strategic ones, arguing that the United States "must do X or Y" (because, for example, North Korea is an "evil" regime) instead of thinking in terms of a strategy to achieve specific, carefully designed ends.

It was also a consequence of the personalities that drove the strategy process. It is often said about foreign policy that there is only one real policymaker—the president. The North Korean case reinforces this well-known lesson: whenever President Bush got involved, his preferences, instincts, and reactions overwhelmed the process; the system, in the end, responds decisively to one individual. This can create opportunities but also enormous risks.

To fill his cabinet- and subcabinet-level posts, moreover, Bush gathered together a combination of realists, neoconservatives, classical conservatives, radicals, pragmatists, and others—all of which added up to an incoherent advisory personality, and bureaucratic warfare often broke out. The result was an often fractured, disjointed process—policy incoherence caused by a collision of contradictory approaches from ideologically opposed officials whose combat was often unregulated. In order to get something done in this environment, the typical pattern in the administration was to centralize the decision-making process and cut people out of the loop. In the by now very well-publicized Iraqi case, it was the State Department that was cut out; in the North Korean case in the second term, hardliners at the NSC and elsewhere were the ones brushed aside.

A related lesson—hardly unique to this case—is that at least in the first term, the office of the national security adviser did not adequately do its job. There was no effective strategy-making or critical analysis, no merging of views into a coherent whole, no resolving of debates. One way of conceiving the resulting problem was as a mismatch of process (and national security adviser) and president. In the first term, Rice seemingly decided to be a personal policy adviser to the president rather than the manager of a coherent policymaking process. That model can work, but only with a president who is a master strategist. When a president is a moralist with scant interest in the nuances of international strategy, he needs a process that will make up for the natural shortcomings of such a style—an inattention to second-step thinking, an allergy to detail, a tendency not to see the point of having dissenters, a habit of allowing certainty to override considerations of risk. It is a national security adviser's responsibility to fill a president's strategic gaps, not to exacerbate them.

Finally, and perhaps somewhat ironically for such a tough-talking administration, the North Korean case demonstrates that the administration—when confronted with repeated North Korean sallying across numerous red lines—abandoned its principles in favor of pragmatism when those principles proved inconvenient. Tough talk was not backed up; commitments were not fulfilled. The administration said that it would not tolerate a North Korean nuclear program—and then tolerated a substantial growth of that program. It called the regime evil—and then volunteered aid. It disparaged bilateral talks only to eventually engage in them. It refused to negotiate over the financial issues surrounding the Banco Delta Asia—and then returned the money. Those hard-liners, such as Bolton and Joseph, who expressed public exasperation at such reversals were right about one thing: the ultimate nuclear deal was a very public repudiation of many principles that the administration had enunciated on North Korea between 2001 and 2006.

In the end, an administration that had abandoned engagement for moralism ended up deserting its moralistic principles after all. Embracing full-scale engagement would have been anathema, of course, and so the administration turned instead to a meager denuclearization offer unlikely to break North Korea fully free of its entrenched position as a declared nuclear power. Meanwhile, Pyongyang appears to have acquired anywhere from three to eight more nuclear weapons than it had when Bush came into office—and it has exploded one of them right in the face of the world community. And still absent from the stage is any sense of true long-range strategic thinking or any real hope that the long-running saga of the North Korean nuclear issue can be resolved in any fundamental way. Without additional U.S. actions, the coming months and years will likely hold a series of half-step-forward, quarter-step-back negotiations, in which Pyongyang will use the February 2007 agreement as the basis for endless wrangling, partial payoffs—and the continued possession of its hard-won nuclear arsenal. From the perspective of today, life under the Clinton administration's much-maligned Agreed Framework looks very good indeed.

Michael J. Mazarr is Professor of National Security Strategy at the U.S. National War College. The views expressed here are his own.

Staying Alive

Why North Korea Will Not Change

Andrei Lankov

Kim Jong-il inspects a unit of the Korean People's Army, North Korea, April 7, 2008.

Fifteen years after taking over from his father, Kim Jong Il remains in full control of North Korea; he is still, at 66, the supreme ruler and "ever-victorious General." In the early 1990s, few outside observers expected him or his regime to survive this long. But he has persevered, thanks to his ruthless leadership, a gift for political manipulation, and his use of brinkmanship diplomacy—and also because no other member of the top leadership has been willing or able to challenge him. Kim is both the head of the Korean Workers' Party and, along with a three-person standing committee, the head of the state. Nepotism and a cult of personality ensure Kim's dominance over the party; the lack of administrative or judicial checks, independent social organizations, or a free press ensures the party's dominance over the whole country. North Korea's elites feel cornered and understand that unity is a major condition for their survival. Thus, they continue to support their leader with little regard for the plight of most North Koreans.

Pyongyang is often described as the world's last Stalinist regime, but for all practical purposes, North Korea's state-run economy of steel mills and coal mines is dead. Despite loud paeans to self-reliance coming from the regime, even during the Cold War the North Korean economy survived only thanks to Soviet subsidies, and it collapsed as soon as Moscow discontinued its aid in 1990. The crisis that followed cut industrial output by 50 percent within a few years. The Public Distribution System was suspended—a major blow to the population, which for decades had relied on government-subsidized grain rations as its main source of food. A disastrous famine from 1996 to 1999 killed between 600,000 and one million people.

The crisis has had many consequences. Until the early 1990s, the North Korean government strictly controlled private markets. However, things have changed. With the partial exception of the military industry, the only functioning parts of the North Korean economy are the unofficial private markets. Now, according to a North Korean trader, "There are two kinds of people in North Korea: those who have learned to trade and those who have starved to death." Indeed, in a country where the average monthly salary ($2-$3) buys only four kilos of rice, private economic activity is the only way to survive for a vast majority of the people. Even the bureaucrats, having realized that the government has no resources to reward their zeal, are looking for other opportunities. Corruption has exploded, making possible many things that were unthinkable 20 or 30 years ago, such as bribing the police for a travel permit or running a private inn.

The authorities have responded by reiterating their old antimarket rhetoric and staging frequent (but unsuccessful) campaigns against what they call "subversive, antisocialist activities." In 2005, Kim's government attempted to revive the comprehensive rationing system, but these efforts have been only partially successful, largely due to a shortage of funds and a general disruption of bureaucratic controls. It has since launched intense antimarket campaigns and increased security on the border with China to limit smuggling and unauthorized crossings by migrant workers. The regime in Pyongyang is doing its best to resist reform and maintain the domestic status quo for as long as possible—and with good reason, at least from its perspective. No amount of foreign pressure, from Beijing or Seoul, is likely to persuade the leaders in Pyongyang to jeopardize their standing by ushering in reforms anytime soon.

GOOD NEIGHBOR POLICIES

China and South Korea have taken the lead in exhorting Pyongyang to open up its economy. Pointing to the successes of Vietnam, which suffered a famine in the mid-1980s but by the mid-1990s had transformed itself into a major rice exporter, and China, the once-impoverished economic miracle, they argue that economic liberalization is in the North Korean regime's interest.

Beijing's and Seoul's motivations are pragmatic. The Chinese government would prefer to keep the Korean Peninsula divided and maintain the North as a strategic buffer zone, and it fears that North Korea might implode, which would produce refugee flows into China. On the other hand, it is tiring of pouring aid into the inefficient North Korean economy: Beijing gives a few hundred thousand tons of grain to North Korea every year and sells it a large amount of oil at heavily discounted prices. As a result, the Chinese government is promoting its own style of reform in Pyongyang: economic liberalization with limited, incremental political change. During an official visit to North Korea in October 2005, Chinese President Hu Jintao touted the Chinese model: "As proved in practice, the path of socialism with Chinese characteristics is a correct way of leading China to prosperity, democracy, civilization, and harmony." Chinese diplomats are said to be even more assertive behind closed doors.

Seoul also has its reasons for preaching reform. It worries that if the North were to be reunited with the South, the costs of the North's reconstruction would wipe out the South's hard-won prosperity. In late 2007, a report prepared for the budget committee of the South Korean National Assembly estimated that the expense of unification would be $0.8-$1.3 trillion—a staggering amount and yet just enough to bring the North Koreans' average income to only half that enjoyed by South Koreans. South and North: Dead If United, a recent bestseller published by Seoul National University, argues that a German-style absorption of North Korea might deliver a mortal blow to South Korea.

On the other hand, Seoul no longer believes, as it did for decades, that the North poses a serious military threat. Even immediately after North Korea's nuclear test in early 2007, only 63.9 percent of South Koreans polled by the Social Trends Institute, a Seoul-based organization, said that they believed North Korea's nuclear weapons were a potential threat. Yet 90.4 percent of the respondents believed that if Japan developed a nuclear program, it would constitute a danger.

And so Seoul, like Beijing, would prefer to see a Chinese-style "developmental dictatorship" emerge in Pyongyang. It hopes that such a regime would maintain North Korea's stability while encouraging economic growth in order to gradually close the huge development gap between the two Koreas. The main goal of Seoul's so-called sunshine policy, which it has pursued since 1998, is to persuade Pyongyang that such a transformation is both feasible and desirable. In November 2007, South Korean President Roh Moo-hyun formulated this position once again: "We do not want to achieve unification through absorption of the North; neither do we consider it feasible…. The Government's support for and private investment in North Korea will continue simultaneously over a long period of time until the North Korean economy reaches a substantial level."

To create the environment necessary for such benign development, the South is engaged in a number of cooperation projects backed by large government subsidies, such as the Kaesong Industrial Park, a large industrial complex just north of the demilitarized zone where some 15,000 poorly paid North Koreans work for enterprises jointly run by the North Korean regime and South Korean businesses. In recent years, it has also essentially assumed responsibility for feeding the North Koreans. From 2002 to 2005, it provided 400,000-500,000 tons of grain annually, an amount equal to some ten percent of North Korea's average harvest. The North's agriculture is heavily dependent on mineral fertilizers that the country can no longer produce; about two-thirds of the fertilizer it uses comes from the South. Seoul may thus be essentially contributing as much as 40-50 percent of the calories consumed by the average North Korean.

MOINS ÇA CHANGE

Despite the leverage both countries have with North Korea, neither China nor South Korea has succeeded in persuading Pyongyang to change. In 2002, it briefly appeared as if Kim's government had belatedly decided to give the growing unofficial economy its conditional approval. In July of that year, the government issued the Improved Economic Management Measures, which decriminalized many market activities. Optimists worldwide hailed the measures as a sure sign that Pyongyang's long-awaited Chinese-style transformation had finally begun.

But the July measures were merely an admission of changes that had already occurred and that the authorities knew they could not control. And in the past few years, North Korean officials have walked back from even that concession and tried to turn back the clock to the 1980s by restoring extensive state controls. In October 2005, Pyongyang announced that the Public Distribution System would be fully reinstated and outlawed the sale of grain on the market (the ban has not been thoroughly enforced thanks to police corruption). Soon after, men were prohibited from trading at markets, a ban that has recently been extended to women below the age of 50. The message is clear: the able-bodied should go back to where they belong—in the factories of the old-style Stalinist economy.

This policy was never really intended to spur an economic revival, however, for most factories could not be restarted—and sure enough, after a brief spurt of very moderate growth, the economy shrank again in 2006. But returning people to the assembly lines made sense politically: government surveillance has long centered around work units. People were sent back not so much to the production lines as to interminable indoctrination sessions under the watchful eyes of police informers and away from the dangerous temptations of the marketplace. The North Korean authorities also greatly increased border surveillance and staged campaigns against the spread of smuggled foreign videos.

Pyongyang's stubborn refusal to embrace an apparently beneficial strategy of reform may seem to be driven by paranoia. But this is not the case. Considering the peculiarities of Pyongyang's situation, its current policies are perfectly rational. The North Korean elites know that the greatest threats they face are internal, not external, and that resisting reform is the most effective way to control the population.

Consider an important—and frequently overlooked—difference between North Korea today and China or Vietnam in the 1990s: North Korea borders a rich and free country that speaks the same language and shares the same culture; South Korea is, in other words, a real-life vision of what North Korea could and perhaps should be. The people of China and Vietnam, although well aware of the affluence of, say, the United States and Japan, do not feel that their experiences are directly comparable. Likewise, tiny Taiwan and Hong Kong have followed their own trajectories in the shadow of huge mainland China. But for the North Koreans, the comparison with South Korea hurts. The Bank of Korea recently estimated, for example, that per capita gross national income in the South is 17 times that in the North. By comparison, per capita gross national income in West Germany before unification was roughly double that in East Germany.

Were North Korea to reform, the disparities with South Korea would only become starker to its population. For decades, Pyongyang has based its legitimacy on its alleged ability to provide its people with a better material life. Even though for most North Koreans living well means eating rice every day, government propaganda has insisted that they enjoy one of the world's highest living standards and has presented South Korea as a land of destitution—a "living hell." It has managed to sustain the legitimacy of these claims with a self-imposed information blockade apparently unparalleled anywhere in the communist world, past or present.

Market reforms and increased foreign investment would unavoidably undermine this isolation. Many North Koreans, who have been exposed to South Korean videos and high-quality consumption goods smuggled in from China, already suspect that the official line about South Korea is misleading. But even they underestimate the extent of the government's lies. Faced with more graphic descriptions of the South's prosperity, the population would come to seriously question the North Korean regime's legitimacy. And this new awareness, combined with the intoxicating effect of unification talk, could imbue them with the belief—possibly naive—that their problems would be easily resolved under Seoul's tutelage or by the wholesale adoption of the South Korean model. When outsiders extol the benefits of reform for North Korea, they seem to assume that a transformed Pyongyang could continue to suppress dissent by improving the living standards of the majority of the population—much as Beijing appears to have done. But the Chinese government has not had to manage the kind of burst in popular expectations that Pyongyang would face.

REASONS IN MADNESS

Liberalization would have other challenging side effects as well. Adjusting to the market's demands would drive the North Koreans to pay less attention to party rituals and focus more on making money. The government would have to tolerate information exchange, travel between different areas of the country, and the growth of horizontal connections beyond its direct control. One cannot run a successful business in a country where it is illegal to leave one's place of residence without a travel permit issued by the police.

Another concern of the North Korean elite is that reform would precipitate a change of the guard. In most former communist countries, the collapse of the system did not undo the lives of party officials. On the contrary, many apparatchiks instantly remodeled themselves as capitalists and prospered. Thanks to a near monopoly on administrative experience, good educations, and de facto control over state property, they were the group best prepared to take over public assets and become the backbone of the new capitalist elite. Such a scenario is unlikely to unfold in North Korea. If the system collapses there, Kim's bureaucrats will have to compete with the resident managers of LG and Samsung and assorted carpetbaggers from Seoul. And without state backing, they would be certain to lose.

Many North Korean bureaucrats also fear a backlash against their brutal rule. There are at least 150,000 political prisoners in North Korean labor camps today, that is, one political prisoner for every 150 citizens—a ratio comparable to that in the Soviet Union under the worst of Stalin's rule. They also fear retribution from the South Koreans or their sympathizers. According to current North Korean regulations, even the grandchildren of those who collaborated with Seoul during the war are banned from living in major cities or attending college. So why, North Korean bureaucrats wonder, would the South Koreans treat them and their families any differently if they lost power?

Pyongyang makes no secret of its hope that it can keep things more or less as they are now. The Korean Central News Agency tells its readers how to think about reform: the South Koreans "want to use their pitiful 'humanitarian aid' to lure us into 'openness' and 'reform' in order to destabilize our system from within." In March 2007, an editorial in the official daily Rodong Sinmun warned against the consequences of contact with the outside world: "Imperialists mobilize their spying agencies and use schemes of 'cooperation' and 'exchange' through various channels in order to implant the bourgeois ideology and culture within the socialist and anti-imperialist countries." The elites in Pyongyang believe, seemingly with good reason, that they must all hang together or else they will surely be hanged separately.

SLOW BUT STEADY

Can Kim's regime hold on much longer? Some argue that the current situation is untenable because North Korea's economic system is inherently inefficient and the country is incapable of meeting its most basic needs, including feeding its people. But none of this is new, and the leadership in Pyongyang has nonetheless managed to retain its grip for decades. The North Korean economy was already unsustainable in the 1970s and 1980s and has been kept afloat largely thanks to aid grants, first from the Soviet Union and then from China and South Korea. The elites have good reason to believe that with skillful diplomacy such achievements can be repeated and some aid maintained. So far, they have deftly played on fears of a possible U.S.Chinese rivalry, as well as on Seoul's anxieties about the consequences of North Korea's implosion and the costs of unification, to secure a moderate but steady flow of assistance from their neighbors. If the aid money does dry up, mass starvation would be a risk again, but even the great famine of 1996-99, which killed as many as one million people, created no immediate domestic political challenge. Trained under the old system, deprived of opportunities to organize, and ignorant about the outside world, North Korea's starving farmers did not rebel. They just died.

Pyongyang can also continue to ward off international pressure for a while longer. Its nuclear blackmail paid off nicely in the 1990s—and it might again. This is one reason why Pyongyang is unlikely to completely surrender its nuclear weapons, even though some compromises, including the dismantling of some facilities, might eventually be reached; Pyongyang's nuclear arsenal is its only real leverage with the international community. A security guarantee from the United States would not help much: leaders in Pyongyang are painfully aware that they are much more likely to be overthrown by their own discontented citizens than by a foreign power.

This is not to say, however, that North Korea is doomed never to change. Although the famine of the late 1990s has not prompted much political reform so far, it has had an irreversible impact on the expectations of ordinary North Koreans. The old Stalinist economy cannot be fully rebooted; even the authorities seem to care more about asserting state control over the people than about restarting the Stalinist production regime. Information from the outside world is filtering in more than the regime ever thought would be possible. Small efforts at grass-roots capitalism over the past decade have also created a new mood. The North Koreans once accepted being completely dependent on the government. Now they realize that they might be able to survive without its handouts. They make items for sale at home, trade in goods smuggled to and from China, and resell any food aid they can get their hands on. This grass-roots capitalism has created a new (slightly) rich class and changed the aspirations of the young. A smuggler told me recently, "In the old days, people wanted to go to the army in order to join the party there, and so they would become cadres. But what is the use of this now? They can live better than cadres if they are successful at markets."

In all likelihood, China and South Korea will continue to provide virtually unconditional aid to North Korea, since Seoul and, to a lesser extent, Beijing believe that the consequences of North Korea's collapse would be disastrous. Granting humanitarian assistance to the North Koreans is one of the few issues on which South Koreans broadly agree. According to an annual poll by Seoul National University, in 1995 merely 25.2 percent of South Koreans thought North Korea should get economic aid; by 2007, the figure had reached 56.6 percent. During last year's presidential race in South Korea, both the conservative candidate, Lee Myung-bak, and the liberal-nationalist candidate, Chung Dong-young, emphasized their support for such aid programs, arguing that they are a way of maintaining peace in North Korea. For all of Seoul's rhetoric advocating economic liberalization in the North, the major, if understated, short-term goal of its assistance is to ensure that Pyongyang remains stable. Seoul hardly even monitors how its aid is distributed, allowing the North Korean government to divert large sums to its cronies and the security forces.

Things will play out very differently in the long run, however, for aid and cooperation—as well as spontaneous exchanges with the outside world—will eventually undermine Pyongyang. They will facilitate the spread of rumors about life in South Korea and thus erode the major pillar of Kim's legitimacy. The North Koreans will gradually learn that their brethren across the border enjoy material conditions and social freedoms that would be unthinkable in North Korea, and sooner or later the masses will be tempted to join in that prosperity—and quite likely by getting rid of the government whose policies have been disastrous. This change, however, will occur in very slow motion, for North Korea's leaders are in no hurry to introduce any reforms.

ANDREI LANKOV is an Associate Professor at Kookmin University, in Seoul.

The Once and Future Kim

Succession and Stasis in North Korea

By Jennifer Lind

KCNA VIA REUTERS

North Korean leader Kim Jong Un with scientists and technicians of the DPRK Academy of Defense.

At the historic Workers' Party meeting that took place in Pyongyang last September, North Korean leader Kim Jong Il anointed his third son, Kim Jong Un, as his successor. The decision recalled the words of King Lear, who, announcing his retirement, said he wanted "to shake all cares and business from our age / Conferring them on younger strengths, while we / Unburden'd crawl toward death." Today, the world watches, hoping that compared to Lear, Kim's judgment will be more sensible, his relatives less venal, and his eventual succession less bloody. Succession is always a regime's most difficult challenge, and Kim Jong Un will have many obstacles to overcome when he tries to take power. But powerful forces will encourage stability and the continued, sorry reign of the Kim family.

At first blush, the road ahead for the "Brilliant Comrade," as Kim Jong Un is called, does not look smooth. Said to be around 27 years old, he is young and inexperienced. He has two older brothers and an untold number of relatives who may be eyeing the crown. Outsiders do not know how news of his ascension was greeted by the elites who prop up the Kim regime—whether they share the views of eldest brother Kim Jong Nam, who told an interviewer, "Personally, I am opposed to the hereditary transfer to a third generation of the family." Perhaps most important, one wonders how the military feels about such a youthful figure suddenly being promoted to four-star general and handed the reins of power.

Aside from his internal challenges, Kim Jong Un will inherit a wreck of a country. Energy shortages continue to ravage North Korea's already frail economy. The 1995–97 famine killed more than one million North Koreans and created an undernourished generation wracked by cognitive disabilities. A 2008 U.S. National Intelligence Council study on global health reported that half of North Korean children are stunted or underweight, while fully two-thirds of young adults are malnourished or anemic.

To make matters worse, North Korea is encircled by powerful adversaries. To the east is Japan, a military and economic powerhouse that annexed and colonized Korea in the early twentieth century. Below lies South Korea, which has 20 times the GDP of North Korea, twice its population, and a military alliance with the global hegemon. South Korea's military is far more technologically advanced than North Korea's and is staffed with well-trained and well-fed soldiers.

Across North Korea's northern border is China, an erstwhile ally that regards Pyongyang with a warmth that ranges from jaw-clenched resignation to total exasperation.

However daunting all of this may seem, and however dim Kim Jong Un's prospects appear, several factors, both internal and external, will work in his favor. He will rely on the system designed by his grandfather, the founder of North Korea, Kim Il Sung—a system that, as Daniel Byman and I have written, was designed for resilience.

Kim Il Sung devised this system to deter revolution from below and military coups from within. An elaborate ideology confers legitimacy upon the Kim family: according to the country's founding myth, Kim Il Sung led a gallant band of guerilla fighters in the bitter winds of Manchuria to defeat the Japanese, liberate the Korean people, and establish the North Korean state. As historians such as Charles Armstrong and Bruce Cumings have argued, this genesis tale secures Kim Il Sung as the father, son, and holy spirit of the "religion" that is North Korea. Like his father, Kim Jong Un enjoys the legitimacy of Kim Il Sung's blood in his veins—and even bears a striking resemblance to his broad-cheeked grandfather. Kim Jong Un has allies who share his formidable pedigree. His aunt, Kim Kyong Hui (recently elevated to four-star general), is Kim Il Sung's daughter; her husband, Jang Song Taek, is, as the vice chairman of the National

Defense Commission, Kim Jong Il's number two. Kim Jong Un and these allies enjoy a great deal of legitimacy from this "great leader" (suryong) system.

Xenophobia is another ideological tool that helps prevent revolution. The regime's propaganda inspires fear of dire threats from predatory Japanese and perfidious Americans, who are aided by traitorous South Koreans. These supposed dangers justify the powerful political role of the military, which already enjoys a glow of legitimacy provided by the Manchurian tale. By keeping North Korea on a perpetual war footing, the regime justifies spending a massive share of its budget on the military (25 percent of GDP, compared to South Korea's four percent)—a great deal of which goes to internal security.

The risk of popular rebellion is also reduced by Kim Il Sung's social engineering. In the communist system that Kim Il Sung created, North Korea has neither a middle class nor a clergy—groups that are frequently instrumental in fomenting revolution. Students and intellectuals—other would-be revolutionaries—have been intellectually defanged by the regime's strict control of information. Heavily monitored, they are deterred from dissent by the threat of terrible punishment.

Indeed, perhaps the most important factor deterring revolution in North Korea is the government's threat or use of force. Informants from multiple security agencies watch for any stirrings of dissent. People who commit relatively minor transgressions—failing to dust their Kim family portraits, for example—undergo "reeducation": extra self-criticism sessions or more time forced to memorize the writings of the Great Leader. People who are accused of more serious disloyalty are exiled to harsh lives in the remote countryside, sent to brutal prison camps, or executed. North Korea's would-be freedom fighters know that, according to the government's "three generations" policy, they risk the arrest, incarceration, torture, and death not only of themselves but also of their parents and children. For all of these reasons, during the famine "North Korea's starving farmers did not rebel," Andrei Lankov noted. "They just died."

Although the military is a dictator's most important ally, it may also be his ultimate undoing. But the odds of a military coup in North Korea have been significantly reduced by Kim Il Sung's measures to "coup-proof" his government. From the inception of the regime in the 1950s, Kim selected political and military leaders on the basis of political loyalty rather than professional competence, installing his relatives and guerilla cronies in the most powerful positions. To maximize the intelligence he received about any brewing disloyalty, he designed multiple internal security agencies that competed with and watched one another, and all reported to him. In the event that these measures failed and a coup occurred, Kim Il Sung created a parallel military force to protect himself from the Korean People's Army.

Another factor reducing the likelihood of military coups is North Korea's class system, which is divided into three tiers. The "core" class consists of favored elites who have impeccable pro-regime credentials (such as relatives who were wounded while fighting for the North in the Korean War). A "wavering" class has more questionable bloodlines. Consigned to the "hostile" class are people whose relatives fought for the South in the war or supported the Japanese occupation of the peninsula.

Elites in the core class are co-opted with comfortable jobs, housing, and gifts (such as cognac, flat-screen televisions, and Mercedes-Benzes). They are also allowed to live in Pyongyang, which, during the famine, meant the difference between life and death. Since the regime gave more food to residents of the capital than it did to the wavering or hostile classes exiled to the hinterland, it thus targeted the famine on its opponents while sheltering its allies. Because of this class system and regime co-optation, any disgruntled member of the North Korean military elite knows that a failed coup attempt would result in his own execution and would forever relegate his family to the hostile class. As hostiles, family members would forfeit their good jobs and good schools, their plentiful food and luxury cars, in exchange for penury and—in the likely event of more food shortages—starvation.

"A prince," Niccolo Machiavelli wrote, "should have two fears: one, internal concerning his subjects; the other, external, concerning foreign powers." As a weak country surrounded by powerful neighbors, North Korea's external position looks dire. But as insecure as the country appears, Kim Jong Un will not face serious external pressure. In 1993, after Pyongyang announced its intention to withdraw from the Nuclear Nonproliferation Treaty, the United States contemplated cruise missile attacks on North Korean nuclear facilities but demurred for fear of war on the peninsula. Since then, two North Korean nuclear tests have provided an added deterrent.

But today, North Korea's greatest deterrent lies not in its power but in its weakness. The grim specter of the potential chaos associated with the collapse of the Kim regime in the event of war has led neighboring countries to treat it with kid gloves. Outside countries fear that the government's collapse could unleash a civil war; send refugees streaming into China, South Korea, and across the sea to Japan; and let "loose nukes" from North Korea's arsenal find their way onto the global black market. An already dangerous situation could grow far deadlier if—in order to stem refugee flows, track down weapons of mass destruction, or help starving North Koreans—China, South Korea, or the United States decided to unilaterally intervene and found their forces jostling together on the small peninsula.

As a result of these fears, when confronted with the latest North Korean outrage, countries have chosen to keep their swords sheathed. South Korea and others have sought to engage North Korea and have provided it with large amounts of aid, restricting retaliation to strongly worded condemnations and economic sanctions. Last March, such dovishness even dominated in response to a North Korean act of war: the sinking of the Cheonan and murder of 46 South Korean sailors.

can produce high-strength aluminum or steel alloys on its own, or that ring magnets, bearings, and vacuum valves were manufactured indigenously.

The most likely scenario is that the equipment was built and brought into operation over many years at a different location and then moved into the new facility. The items needed to manufacture the centrifuges were likely obtained through North Korea's complex and far-reaching procurement network—in which Pakistan likely played a significant role. Former Pakistani President Pervez Musharraf admitted in his memoirs that the Pakistani scientist A. Q. Khan delivered what amounted to an enrichment starter kit of 24 centrifuges around the year 2000. There were also reports that before A. Q. Khan's house arrest in 2004, North Korean scientists had cooperated closely with the Khan Research Laboratories, which provided hands-on training at their centrifuge facilities. In addition, in late 2001, the CIA reported to Congress that North Korea had attempted to acquire centrifuge-related materials in large quantities from Russia and Germany to support a uranium-enrichment program. It is also quite likely that the North Koreans fabricated at least some of the many components themselves.

And Washington cannot rule out North Korean cooperation with Iran, since the two have collaborated closely on missile technologies before. North Korea's centrifuge facilities appear to be more sophisticated than what Iran has shown to international inspectors, but it is well known that Tehran is developing next-generation centrifuges. Moreover, North Korea has much greater experience in uranium processing and reactor technologies than Iran, raising concerns that such expertise could flow from Pyongyang to Tehran.

These findings demonstrate the difficulty of accurately evaluating clandestine uranium-centrifuge programs. The small footprints and signatures of such facilities make assessment problematic. The best indicators of North Korea's progress were its procurement activities and technical cooperation with other countries—in this case, Pakistan. These markers led the CIA to conclude in 2002 that by mid-decade North Korea could produce two highly enriched uranium (HEU) atomic bombs annually. The George W. Bush administration used this evidence to confront Pyongyang in October 2002 in a manner that led to the termination of the 1994 Agreed Framework, which had foreseen eventual diplomatic normalization in exchange for denuclearization. Terminating the agreement provided North Korea with an excuse to withdraw from the Nuclear Nonproliferation Treaty, reprocess bomb-grade plutonium from the spent uranium fuel rods, and build its first bomb.

In retrospect, it was not faulty intelligence that led to the disastrous outcome of the October 2002 confrontation but rather the Bush administration's misguided political determination to end the Agreed Framework without preparing for the consequences. At Yongbyon, the North Koreans told us that they will eventually build larger power reactors, and although they anticipate difficulties because the technologies for the reactor and fuel are new to them, they are confident of success. Our Foreign Ministry host reminded us that they had previously threatened to build a LWR and do their own enrichment but that "no one believed us, including you, Dr. Hecker." He made it clear that, in their minds, they had no choice; U.S. actions had pushed them in this direction.

The existence of a North Korean light-water reactor poses its own set of policy challenges. Pyongyang has seriously pursued LWRs since 1985, when it struck a deal with Moscow to supply two such reactors. The Agreed Framework was an attempt to replace its gas-graphite reactors, which are useful for making bombs but bad for generating electricity. By contrast, LWRs, which are less suitable for bombs, are very good for electricity. Shortly after the North's April 5, 2009, rocket launch and the predictable UN condemnation that followed, an official government press release stated, "We will see a light water reactor, which is vigorously 100 percent running on our own raw materials and technology." Now, as promised, they have started construction on a small, experimental LWR designed to deliver roughly 25 to 30 megawatts of electric power.

I believe North Korea's expressed interest in nuclear electricity is genuine. Although it is technically possible that the LWR will be used to produce bomb-grade plutonium, such a scenario is unlikely. Plutonium from an LWR is much less suitable for bombs than the plutonium already produced in the existing gas-graphite reactor. In fact, if Pyongyang wanted more plutonium bomb fuel, it would simply restart that reactor, not build an LWR. Still, the construction of the reactor raises a number of policy issues: an LWR requires enriched uranium, and once enrichment capabilities are established for reactor fuel, they can be readily reconfigured to produce HEU bomb fuel—precisely Washington's concern about Iran's nuclear program.

In revealing these facilities, Pyongyang is sending a signal that policymakers must take seriously. In this case, the revelation appears to be part of a calculated plan developed around the time of the U.S. presidential transition to proceed with its nuclear program in a way that would influence the diplomatic situation in its favor. After the international community condemned North Korea's April 2009 rocket launch, Pyongyang officially terminated its participation in the six-party talks and conducted a second nuclear test to demonstrate to its own satisfaction and to the world that it had a functioning nuclear device.

At the same time, the North Koreans designed a small LWR and began building the enrichment facility by tearing down Yongbyon's fuel-rod-fabrication facility and building a centrifuge hall. They timed our visit to show off their completed project. With these moves, Pyongyang managed to justify its need for an enrichment program while moving toward its long-standing ambition of using LWRs for nuclear power.

The truth is that North Korea has run both plutonium and uranium programs in a dual-use mode—that is, for bombs and electricity—from the beginning. It favored the plutonium program for both weapons and electric power in the early 1990s, but it was willing to trade in the plutonium bomb program for electricity from LWRs to be supplied by the United States as part of the Agreed Framework. It appears to have rejuvenated its uranium program for bombs later in the 1990s, when A. Q. Kahn came calling and the Agreed Framework was moving along very slowly. By 2002, much as the intelligence reports indicated, the North was making major procurements of centrifuge materials and components. The October 2002 diplomatic confrontation allowed the North to accelerate the plutonium bomb program in 2003, and subsequent nuclear tests allowed it to demonstrate its success.

The modern centrifuge facility the North Koreans showed us this time indicates that Pyongyang never gave up on the uranium path to the bomb. The North must have been able to procure enough materials and components, fabricate and assemble them into working centrifuges, get them functioning in an undisclosed facility and then install them in short order at Yongbyon. The centrifuge facility we saw is most likely designed to make reactor, not bomb, fuel, because it would not make sense to construct it in a previously inspected site and show it to foreign visitors. However, it is highly likely that a parallel covert facility capable of HEU production exists elsewhere in the country.

The question now is how this affects Northeast Asia's security calculus. North Korea already has plutonium—by our estimates, enough for four to eight basic nuclear weapons. Possession of similar amounts of HEU does not fundamentally change the threat. HEU is easier to fashion into a crude bomb but offers no advantages for more sophisticated, miniaturized designs. If Pyongyang is content with its current arsenal or modest growth, it would be better off restarting the existing plutonium production reactor. However, if Pyongyang wants to increase its arsenal substantially, it could expand the capacity of the current enrichment facility or build parallel clandestine facilities. Pyongyang cannot expand centrifuge capacity at will, however. It is limited by the need to import key materials and components—hence the international community must redouble its efforts to shut down Pyongyang's extensive illicit procurement network.

Even more troubling than an expansion of the North's nuclear arsenal is its potential export of fissile materials or the means of producing them, which now include centrifuge technologies. Moreover, by unveiling the LWR and enrichment facility, Pyongyang has complicated the diplomatic process by, in effect, redefining what is meant by denuclearization. Not only is it unlikely that Pyongyang will give up its nuclear arsenal anytime soon, but it will almost certainly insist on keeping its LWR program and centrifuges. Shutting down the plutonium program was within reach, but the same is not likely for the uranium program, because the justification for its peaceful nature is more credible than for the plutonium program, even though it is no less problematic.

Nevertheless, our Foreign Ministry host maintained that Pyongyang continues to support the denuclearization of the Korean peninsula as agreed to in the September

2005 Six-Party Joint Statement. As a starting point, he suggested that it would be helpful if Washington reaffirmed part of the October 2000 U.S.-North Korean Joint Communiqué. That document, which was the culmination of a long diplomatic process, stated that neither government would have hostile intent toward the other and confirmed the commitment of both to make every effort to build a new relationship free from past enmity.

It is time for the United States to conduct a thorough review of its policies on Northeast Asia, including but not limited to the nuclear issue. The fundamental and enduring goal must be the denuclearization of the Korean peninsula. However, since that will take time, the U.S. government must quickly press for what I call "the three no's"—no more bombs, no better bombs, and no exports—in return for one yes: Washington's willingness to seriously address North Korea's fundamental insecurity along the lines of the joint communiqué. Our Foreign Ministry host framed his no's in terms of no vertical or horizontal proliferation. When we asked specifically if Pyongyang would entertain the concept of three no's and one yes, he said, "If the U.S. government asks that question, I will answer it."

Pyongyang's revelation of the centrifuge facility makes it more challenging and more pressing than ever to ask that question.

SIEGFRIED S. HECKER is Co-Director of the Center for International Security and Cooperation at Stanford University. He was director of the Los Alamos National Laboratory from 1986 to 1997.

Next of Kim

North Korea, One Year Later

Victor Cha

Kim Jong-un (L) and his father, Kim Jong-il (R), watch a parade to commemorate the
65th anniversary of the founding of the Workers' Party of Korea, Pyongyang, North Korea,
October 14, 2010.

One year ago, the chubby and blubbering soon-to-be leader of the Democratic People's Republic of Korea was seen walking alongside the hearse that carried his dead father, Kim Jong Il. Kim Jong Un was young, inexperienced, unqualified, and bereft of any of the larger-than-life myths that had sustained his father's and grandfather's rules. And yet, just days later, he assumed power in the only communist dynasty in the world.

Today, the junior Kim can be seen riding high in Pyongyang. And last week, he became the first Korean to launch a domestically designed satellite into orbit on the back of a domestically designed rocket. But more broadly, some analysts see him as pushing his own version of reform. His new ways might not exactly be Gangnam style, but they are undeniably a break from the past. He promulgates high heels and miniskirts for women and commissions amusement parks and (pirated) Walt Disney productions for children. Never too busy to ride rollercoasters and frolic with school kids, the prince of Pyongyang also found time to take on a wife, Ri Sol-Ju, whom the New York Times compared to the British Duchess Kate Middleton.

Optimists look to these changes and to Kim's years of Swiss schooling—during which he took courses on democratic governance, wolfed down pizza, and came to idolize NBA stars—and declare that North Korea is ready for reform. This past spring, I participated in track-two meetings in New York at which North Korean officials sought out executives from Coca-Cola and Kentucky Fried Chicken to discuss opening branches in Pyongyong. Rumors that the regime is hatching a new economic policy only fuel speculation that Kim is "distanc[ing] himself from the regime of his father and grandfather," as one article in The Telegraph had it. Some onlookers even predict China-like reforms in Rason (a city near the Russian border) and Hwanggumpyong Island (an island near the Chinese border) that would create the next Hong Kong or Shenzhen, where low taxes, high returns, and reduced government intervention reign free.

Weathered North Korea watchers, however, will remember that similar predictions were made in 1994, when the 52-year-old Kim Jong Il took over after his 82-year-old father died. The journalist Selig Harrison believed that North Korea was signaling a coming transformation by sending officials abroad to learn about market economics. Likening the Kim regime to the Communist Party in China, Harrison remarked that "as Pyongyang gradually liberalizes its economy and opens up to the outside world," the ruling regime and the North Korean political system as a whole will transform. But believers in the irresistibility of Disney, Dior, and Coke have short memories.

BACK FROM THE BRINK

North Korea's political system, helmed by a young and unproven leader, faces severe challenges. The regime will not change because the West hopes that it will.

For optimists in the United States, North Korea's quiescence as the country's leadership changed this past year confirmed that Kim was on the right path. Last week's rocket launch from a snowy facility in the northwest corner of the country poured ice water on those expectations. And with presidential elections in the United States last month and in South Korea this month, Pyongyang is unlikely to be finished. A study I undertook at the Center for Strategic and International Studies found that Pyongyang has usually done something provocative within an average of 16–18 weeks of every South Korean election since 1992. For example, within four weeks of Lee Myung-bak taking the South Korean presidency in 2008, North Korea expelled all South Koreans from the joint industrial complex at Kaesong and tested two missiles. Pyongyang's election antics are not just reserved for other Koreans. In early 2009, U.S. President Barack Obama was welcomed into office with ballistic-missile and nuclear tests. Last week's successful rocket launch is thus only the first in a series of provocations that the Obama administration is likely to see.

Why? Because even an authoritarian dictator must justify his or her rule to the "selectorate," as the Georgetown professor Daniel Byman and the Dartmouth professor Jennifer Lind have written. Otherwise, they could "find a better deal from a rival leader." The current Kim's grandfather, Kim Il Sung, had revolutionary credentials as a guerilla fighter against the Japanese. And Kim Jong Il had a decade of training and preparation for the job. Without a day of military service, Kim Jong Un was grafted to the top of the power structure in his late twenties. Kim's regime is thus only as strong as his ability to prove to the elites that he is worthy. If he does not affirm his ability to actually do something—say a third and successful nuclear test—he will struggle to justify his rule.

The danger, however, is that decelerating from such a crisis this time will not be easy. In the past, the United States often provided the exit ramp. Based on my research of U.S.–North Korean negotiations since 1984, within an average five months of a provocation, Washington was usually back at the bargaining table. This diplomacy has often been for the express purpose of ratcheting down a crisis. So, after the October 2006 nuclear test, the George W. Bush administration returned to negotiations in January 2007 and reached a deal with the North Koreans the following month. But the Obama administration, having been burned thrice (first by the April-May 2009 missile and nuclear tests, then again in April 2012 by another missile test, and yet once more last week by a third missile test) is not interested in such diplomacy but rather in "strategic patience," or not negotiating with North Korea until it commits to denuclearization.

Perhaps that explains the Obama administration's relatively muted response to last week's missile test. The White House's bland condemnation of the test was a stark contrast to its stern announcement of a red line against the Syrian regime using chemical weapons, especially since last week's missile test indicated that North Korea's weapons program has come a long way in the last year. By successfully launching a payload into orbit, North Korea joined only China and Russia as non-allied countries that could potentially reach the United States with an intercontinental ballistic missile. It is probably just a few years before the country is able to load those missiles with a nuclear weapon.

Like the United States, South Koreans are fed up with negotiations. After North Korea torpedoed a South Korean navy ship and shelled one of its islands in 2010, the South Korean government and public are no longer willing to preach patience and stability, as they had been doing during the previous decade-long "Sunshine policy" toward North Korea. It is an open secret that South Korea has rewritten its rules of military engagement with its northern adversary. Seoul is now prepared to retaliate to the next military act, not just by returning fire but also by going after North Korean support systems and command structures. This escalation would not even require high-level political approval. In interviews with top officials, it was apparent that the military leadership could determine the steps to be taken based on the situation on the ground. Meanwhile, South Korea's newly-elected president, Park Geun-hye, has evinced a mild interest in more engagement with Pyongyang. But if Pyongyang tries to test the new leader, it will be very difficult for her to turn the other cheek.

CHINESE DIPLOMACY

China might be ready to step in where the United States and South Korea have demurred. Beijing's preferred solution to North Korean rambunctiousness has always been to make it more like China (or Vietnam)—that is, to push a slow process of economic reform that would get North Korea out of its attention-getting cycle of provocation and crisis. But despite all the economic assistance and food Beijing showers on its communist brother, Pyongyang bites the hand that feeds it. Recent high-level meetings between Chinese officials and Kim were preludes to more economic deals between the two countries. They might even presage a visit by Kim to Beijing to meet the newly ensconced Xi Jinping. But the day after the meeting with the Chinese, North Korea announced its rocket launch, which just goes to show that China can neither restrain Pyongyang nor reform North Korean leadership, no matter how much economic assistance it provides or how many bureaucrats it offers to train.

After all, every time Kim's father, Kim Jong Il, made a visit to China, his Chinese interlocutors urged him to tour factories and cities to see the benefits of capitalism with communist characteristics. Over a decade, Kim willingly walked through facilities that manufactured fiber optics, computers, telephones, lasers, and computer software. With each visit, Chinese and Western journalists and scholars proclaimed a new chapter in North Korea's economic transformation that would inevitably make it more peaceful. And each time, they were proved wrong. Kim invariably made the trips to appease his Chinese hosts (and to receive the requisite aid packages) but had no intention of changing. And all the while, he forged ahead with his ballistic-missile, chemical weapons, and nuclear programs.

China's long-term strategy remains to institute top-down economic reform in North Korea. But faced with short-term failures, China resorted to trying to bribe Pyongyang into returning to the six-party talks and holding off missile and nuclear tests. As last week's test showed, though, this is not sustainable either, so China has recently adopted a medium-term coping mechanism: engage with North Korea economically but solely for the benefit of Chinese economic interests, not as part of a reform agenda.

This medium-term solution is evident in the slew of mining contracts and further agreements to excavate coal, minerals, and other resources from North Korea to fuel China's two poor inland provinces, Jilin and Liaoning. In 2005, China and North Korea cooperated to build a "commercial corridor" associated with the Greater Tumen Initiative, which would connect Jilin Province to the seaport in Rajin, North Korea. China subsequently leased Rajin for ten years in 2010. In 2011, Chinese and

North Korean trade reached $6 billion, according to Scott Snyder, a senior fellow for Korea studies and the director of the Program on U.S.-Korea Policy at the Council on Foreign Relations. Meanwhile, in the same year, total Chinese investment in North Korea reached $98.3 million.That might sound like a lot, but this number is dwarfed by Chinese investments in South Korea ($1.2 billion), Vietnam ($437 million), and Mongolia ($890.7 million). In the end, Pyongyang's restrictions and inability to make rational economic decisions have confounded China's hope of seeing North Korean economic reform and peace. Only when the Kim regime decides to prize wealth and growth more than power will this vision be realized.

HERMIT NO MORE

Even as the nuclear and missile programs continue to grow unimpeded, the domestic situation inside the dark country seems unsettled. Presumably, there is some degree of infighting within the North Korean government, which resulted in the surprise sacking in July 2012 of Ri Yong-ho, the country's top military general. In fact, all of the military generals who walked with Kim aside his father's hearse last December are gone. Some interpret these unceremonious departures as evidence that the reform-minded Kim is trying to usurp power from the hardline military. Others suggestthat Kim, in a move to assert his authority, wanted to signal that he is fully able to silence rivals who challenge his power. More likely, Kim wants to strengthen his own patronage network by reclaiming some of the money that the military, presumably including Ri, was making through lucrative business activities awarded to them by Kim's father. This means that there are some very unhappy military generals in North Korea today.

Perhaps to befriend the military, Kim continues to pay lip service to his father's military-first (songun chongch'i) brand of rule. But he appears to have complemented this with a fundamentalist version of his grandfather's juche, or self-reliance, ideology of the Cold War. It could be that the bankruptcy of his father's rule compelled him to find a better idea to justify the family's continued rule. Fundamentalist juche ideology, or what I call "neojucheism," appeals because it reminds North Koreans of an era of relative economic development and affluence, when production levels outpaced those of the rival South, and Chinese and Soviet money poured into the country. Juche fundamentalism was, and will be, a time of deep ideological indoctrination, mass mobilization, and rejection of foreign influences. Indeed, Kim has made himself the physical reincarnation of his grandfather down to the Mao suit, protruding stomach, cropped hairdo, and hearty laugh.

But even as the regime's ideology is growing more hard-line, the society that Kim inherited is moving in a diametrically opposed direction. The biggest difference between the hermit kingdom of 1994, when Kim Jong Il took over, and the one of 2012 is the development of a market mentality among the people—something that grew out of terrible food shortages. Official and unofficial markets sprung up as people struggled to cope with the breakdown of the government's ration system. A study by the Peterson Institute for International Economics' Marcus Noland and his colleagues Stephen Haggard and Erik Weeks, found that recent defectors admitted that at least 50 percent of total food they consumed in North Korea came from sources apart from the government. That creates an independence of mind that is dangerous in a society such as North Korea's.

Other elements of modernity are starting to seep in, as well. Over one million North Koreans use cell phones, and more than 4,000 crawl the Web. Daily NK, one of the biggest new sites, attracts over 150,000 hits online per month for its timely insider information on North Korean issues. Thanks to expanded cell-phone access, North Korean "citizen journalists" operating between the Chinese-North Korean border can transmit bits of information more effectively both within the country and worldwide.

The peculiar part about these advancements in communication technology is that most of them are legal. The North Korean government promotes, to an extent, cell-phone use because it holds a 25 percent stake in Koryolink (the North Korean branch of the Egyptian telecommunications company Orascom Telecom). With the number of subscribers to Koryolink steadily rising, mostly in Pyongyang, phones are quickly finding a permanent place in daily life.

Where does all this lead? Toward a dead end for Kim, I think, and perhaps a nightmare loose-nukes scenario for the United States. The new leadership is exercising a more rigid ideology that seeks greater control over an increasingly independent-minded society and over disgruntled elements of the military. Meanwhile, its nuclear-bomb- and ICBM-making programs continue. All that is not sustainable. If Kim tried true reform and an opening North Korean society, however, he would immediately create a spiral of expectations that the regime would not be able to control. The young and untested leadership will try to navigate between these two perils. But it may prove too difficult. And if it does, Obama may find his pivot to Asia absorbed by a new crisis on the Korean peninsula.

VICTOR D. CHA is D.S. Song-KF Professor of International Affairs at Georgetown University and Senior Adviser for the Asia and Korea Chair at the Center for Strategic and International Studies. He is the author of The Impossible State: North Korea, Past and Future. This work was supported by the Academy of Korean Studies Grant (MEST) (AKS-2010-DZZ-2102).

The China Option

Progress in Pyongyang Must Go Through Beijing

Doug Bandow

Chinese and North Korean flags outside a restaurant in Ningbo, China, April 2016.

Among the challenges faced by the next president of the United States, perhaps none will be as serious as the question of how to deal with North Korea. The presence of U.S. forces on the Korean Peninsula is already a potential tripwire for war, and Pyongyang is seeking to develop the capability to strike the United States itself. And although U.S. officials routinely affirm that they will not accept the North as a nuclear power, it has become one nonetheless. Washington seems powerless to influence Pyongyang's behavior.

For many analysts and officials seeking a breakthrough with North Korea, China is the last hope. As Pyongyang's only ally and diplomatic and economic lifeline, China is thought to have a unique ability to influence the regime, and the United States has frequently sought its cooperation. Yet despite some deterioration in Chinese–North Korean relations in recent years, Beijing appears to have recently warmed to Pyongyang, relaxing economic controls imposed after the latter's nuclear test in early September. In order to convince China to change its Korea policy, the next U.S. administration should therefore try a new approach: addressing the rationale behind China's strategy.

SEE NO EVIL

Washington's North Korea policy is a wreck. The United States first faced the possibility of a nuclear North more than two decades ago, but hoped that the nightmare would never become reality. The country's derelict regime couldn't last forever, U.S. leaders reasoned. The end of the Cold War would transform North Korea, just as it had transformed the ex-communist countries of Eastern Europe. Officials assumed that the peninsula would be reunified, or that China wouldn't tolerate a northern nuke, or that Pyongyang could be bought off with aid and other benefits. Over the last quarter century U.S. policy thus oscillated between attempts to threaten, bribe, and isolate the North.

Hopes for change proved to be misplaced. Since the 1990s, North Korea has managed two dynastic successions. The regime, underwritten by China, has survived mass famine and a serious erosion of state institutions. Today, North Korea's economy, although still backward, is growing and some people are increasingly enjoying a small measure of prosperity despite international sanctions. The country's unique "social system," as North Koreans call it, shows no signs of disappearing, and the latest product of its nonpareil communist monarchy, Kim Jong Un, appears secure despite an unusually high number of defections and executions. His country, moreover, continues to develop nuclear weapons and ballistic missiles, having detonated its first warhead in 2006.

Indeed, Pyongyang now demands recognition as a nuclear state. Earlier this year, it informed China that it had no intention of abandoning nuclear weapons. And its arsenal is growing: the Rand Corporation estimates that the country could have as many as 100 nukes by 2020. As North Korea develops long-range missiles, South Korea will not be the only potential target; Pyongyang's goal is eventually to put the United States within range as well.

GOTTA KNOW WHEN TO HOLD 'EM…

The United States has so far found no effective strategy to prevent a nuclear North Korea. Negotiation is everyone's preferred approach, but it has broken down since the 2003 collapse of the "Agreed Framework," the Clinton-era denuclearization agreement. And even if it might have been possible to buy off Pyongyang decades ago, almost no one today believes that the regime is prepared to yield what it has gained at such substantial cost. Nukes, after all, protect North Korea against any U.S. attempt at regime change, generate international fear and respect, provide opportunity to extort its neighbors, and reward its military with the great power status conferred by the ultimate weapon.

Sanctions are the fallback option, but the North Korean regime's pain threshold is quite high, due to its totalitarian control over the population and relative isolation. In addition, Beijing has been unwilling to significantly ratchet up sanctions, fearing the consequences of a messy implosion just across the Yalu River, which separates China from North Korea. Indeed, if the results of a North Korean regime collapse turned out to be factional conflict, loose nuclear materials, and mass refugee flows, as China believes they would, Beijing might not be the only party wishing for the good old days of the Kim dynasty.

Because of the failure of sanctions, some analysts favor a preventive military strike on North Korea's nuclear facilities (Ashton Carter, as assistant secretary of defense in the Clinton administration, argued for this position). But that would be playing a game of chicken with millions of lives. Kim might be deterred from responding to a U.S. attack on his nuclear facilities for fear of provoking a war that could destroy his regime. On the other hand, Pyongyang has seen the United States routinely overthrow regimes it opposes, and it may have learned the lesson to seize the initiative, and strike after a U.S. assault if it believed full-fledged war to be inevitable. Although North Korea would lose the war, such a conflict could result in staggering casualties, especially among South Korean civilians.

KOREAN CENTRAL NEWS AGENCY / REUTERS

North Korean leader Kim Jong Un inspects a farm near Pyongyang in an undated photo, released September 2016.

If neither sanctions nor military intervention will work, that leaves the China option. China provides the vast bulk of trade with and investment in the North. Chinese food and energy supplies are particularly important for the country's survival. U.S. policymakers have long urged their Chinese counterparts to crush the North's windpipe, so to speak, and have been surprised when Beijing has refused to do so. For instance, Kelly Ayotte, Republican senator from New Hampshire, argued in 2013 that "we need to be clearer with China as to what our expectations are [regarding North Korea], because this is a danger to them." Senator John McCain of Arizona similarly complained in 2010 that "it's hard to know why China doesn't push harder."

Yet China's leaders are not stupid, and their position isn't difficult to understand. They have heard a long succession of U.S. officials insist, request, urge, and demand that Beijing do more about North Korea. The problem is, they don't believe it is in their nation's interest to do so. North Korea is Beijing's only military ally at a time when China is surrounded by treaty partners of the globe's most powerful state—a state that is attempting to make China the target of a Cold War–style containment system. Beijing is being asked to potentially allow its buffer to reunify with South Korea, which would leave a powerful U.S. ally—and U.S. military forces—on China's border. Along the way, the North could fall apart, spewing conflict, nukes, and refugees northward. Why would Chinese President Xi Jinping or anyone else in Beijing agree to Washington's request?

…AND WHEN TO FOLD 'EM

U.S. policymakers have only two real options: coerce China or convince China. Coercion seems unlikely to work when applied to the nationalistic government of an emerging great power. China is determined to overcome what it sees as decades and even centuries of humiliation at the hands of Western powers, and it would be difficult for United States to make its threats seem credible. Beijing's response to South Korea's decision to deploy the U.S.-made THAAD missile defense system was anything but conciliatory: China chastised Seoul and warmed to Pyongyang. Worse, launching economic war against China over North Korea—the Obama administration is reportedly considering sanctions on Chinese banks and other companies that deal with North Korea—would poison the entire relationship. Coercion is more likely to push Beijing and Pyongyang together.

The second course, that of convincing China, may remain a long shot, but it is still better than the alternatives. To succeed, Washington will need to listen to Beijing's concerns and respond accordingly. For example, Chinese officials argue that hostile U.S. policy has forced North Korea to pursue nuclear weapons, and insist that the North's nuclear program is not Beijing's responsibility anyway. Instead of confronting China, Washington should work with South Korea and Japan to develop a grand bargain package, focused on denuclearization, to offer to North Korea, for which Beijing's support would then be sought.

U.S. policymakers have only two real options: coerce China or convince China.

Such a package would require granting some concessions to Beijing. For instance, one of China's major concerns is that it would bear most of the cost of a potential North Korean implosion. The United States should therefore offer to share the cost of caring for refugees and accept the temporary intervention of Chinese military forces in North Korea, should the need arise (current doctrine presumes that South Korea would occupy the North before formally reunifying the peninsula). China and Chinese enterprises have also made substantial investments in the North, and the United States and especially South Korea should promise to recognize and protect these deals whenever possible.

Understandably, Beijing does not want to contribute to its own encirclement, and so it will be opposed to regime change in Pyongyang as long as South Korea remains a U.S. ally. At the very least, a grand bargain should thus state that if the North were to collapse, the United States would withdraw its forces from the peninsula in exchange for China accepting Korean reunification, rather than setting up its own puppet state in the North. Seoul might need to go further and pledge military neutrality. Although that would appear to be a major concession, the disappearance of North Korea would eliminate the justification for U.S. military presence on the peninsula. In the absence of a hostile North, the only plausible justification for continued U.S. troop presence would be containment of China. South Korea's recent dalliance with Beijing, moreover, suggests that Seoul would be unlikely to participate in an anti-China coalition. Washington and its allies may have to decide what is more important: a denuclearized Korean peninsula or the U.S.–South Korean alliance.

Finally, Washington should play international poker, indicating that the continued growth of the North Korea's nuclear arsenal would force it to reconsider its opposition to South Korean and Japanese nuclear arsenals. China may prefer not to disarm its ally, but in a world of second-best solutions, it might find the prospect of two powerful, nuclear-armed U.S. allies in its neighborhood even more frightening than the alternative. Beijing, which has resolutely opposed even modest Japanese re-armament, is likely to react particularly strongly to the prospect of Japan acquiring nuclear weapons.

NO EASY VICTORIES

A U.S.–Chinese deal on North Korea could still prove impossible. Beijing might not trust Washington to follow through on its commitments; both China and North Korea have seen what happened to former Libyan leader Muammar al-Qaddafi after he traded away his nukes and missiles under U.S. pressure. Even if Beijing did cut off Pyongyang, Kim might refuse to surrender, and the regime would stagger along, more isolated and hostile than ever.

Still, no fruitful option should be left untried, and China is very unlikely to go along with the United States if the latter does not attempt to address the former's concerns. Indeed, from Beijing's standpoint, it would be foolish to confront Pyongyang without some kind of agreement with the United States about what might come afterward.

The next U.S. administration cannot afford to ignore the Korean Peninsula in the hopes that the North Korea problem will go away. It won't. In another four years, North Korea is likely to be a serious nuclear power. It's time for Washington to play the China card.

DOUG BANDOW is Senior Fellow at the Cato Institute and former Special Assistant to President Ronald Reagan. He is the co-author of *The Korean Conundrum: America's Troubled Relations with North and South Korea* (Palgrave/Macmillan, 2004).

Unbalanced Alliances

Why China Hasn't Reined in North Korea

Sulmaan Khan

A South Korean security guard stands guard on an empty road which leads to the Kaesong Industrial Complex (KIC) at the South's CIQ (Customs, Immigration and Quarantine), just south of the demilitarised zone separating the two Koreas, in Paju, South Korea, February 11, 2016.

Diplomacy on North Korea has assumed all the comic predictability of a Samuel Beckett play. Leader Kim Jong Un tests a nuclear bomb; the world clucks in alarm. The United Nations lurches into action and hosts talks about having talks. Nothing substantive happens. And in Washington, policymakers and pundits remain mystified as to why China does not do more to rein in North Korea.

The reason is simple: Beijing still needs Pyongyang—all the more so given Washington's pivot to Asia. Perhaps more than any other capital, Washington should understand that the relationship between a great power and client state usually gives the upper hand to the latter. A great power can threaten, bribe, beg, and try to reason, but if it is convinced that the survival of a client state is crucial to its own national security, there is little it can do to change the client state's behavior. The weaker state is usually all too aware of this fact. The United States lived through this when it supported former Republic of China leader Chiang Kai-shek as a bulwark against the spread of communism. Similarly, Washington has little love for Saudi Arabia's toxic foreign policy or human rights records, but it sees the kingdom as a cornerstone of Middle Eastern stability.

China operates in much the same way with its client states. Pakistani militants attack Chinese workers in Baluchistan and traffic guns to Muslim separatists in Xinjiang, but since Pakistan provides China with a crucial access point to the Indian Ocean, Beijing can do little but lecture and cajole. Myanmar may be responsible for violent clashes and drug smuggling along the Chinese border, but, especially before the recent reform, commercial and geopolitical considerations pushed China to live with the junta. And in North Korea's case, China has had little choice but to ignore Pyongyang's excesses for decades.

North Korea's geostrategic significance is burnt deep into China's official mind. To be sure, there are other considerations. The two countries are economic partners with a $6.39 billion trade relationship as of 2014. China also fears a flood of North Korean refugees if the Kim regime were to collapse; the deluge, it is assumed, would overwhelm China's regional resources in the process and possibly spread discontent amongst China's ethnic Koreans. But these considerations pale in comparison to the geopolitical imperative.

Historically the Korean peninsula has been a staging ground for armies invading China. Japanese influence in Korea led to the Sino–Japanese War of 1894-45, which ended in defeat for China. The Korean War brought U.S. troops to the doorstep of the Chinese Communist Party, threatening the party's survival. These days, China is still determined to have a North Korean buffer against attack, and therefore supports the Kim regime so long as it provides one. The pivot to Asia deepens China's sense of insecurity, making the North Korean buffer all the more important.

A STRATEGIC REBALANCE

Washington's rebalance to Asia has only heightened Beijing's fears that the United States seeks to contain China. Beijing feels—quite understandably—as though it is being surrounded by hostile forces all along its coast. Talk of the China threat by politicians and pundits in Washington and Tokyo does little to assuage such concerns. In a world like this, Chinese policymakers have to take the risk of war and consequent attempts to invade China seriously. The North Korean buffer zone, vast and difficult to invade, affords China some protection at a point where it has always been vulnerable. The buffer is imperfect, but in a world where one might be confronted by the United States and Japan, every advantage counts.

This is not to say that China is happy with Pyongyang's behavior. South Korea has recently opened up discussions with the United States about implementing a Terminal High Altitude Area Defense system around the region after North Korea's latest round of missile tests; if Kim forces South Korea to deploy such a system, he will have harmed long-term Chinese interests by drawing the ire and military force of the United States and other allies to China's backyard. But for China, there remains no better option than supporting Kim's regime. The collapse of the North Korean statewould create a power void; no one knows what would fill it, but Beijing would fear increased American influence. If Kim proved truly unbearable, an adventurous Chinese leader might contemplate invading North Korea to depose the Kim regime and fill the resulting power vacuum, but such a move would scare Japan, South Korea, and the United States into adopting dangerous countermeasures. A nuclear-armed and volatile Kim regime is a bad option. But for China, it is the least worst option. So Kim does what he wants and China does nothing.

REUTERS

North Korean leader Kim Jong Un attends a banquet for contributors of the recent rocket launch, in this undated photo released by North Korea's Korean Central News Agency (KCNA) in Pyongyang on February 15, 2016

If the United States is serious about changing the status quo, it has three realistic options—two of which include China's assistance, and one which does not. With Beijing's help, the United States could revisit an idea that harkens back to the United States' Cold War-era strategy in Asia. Back then, Mao Zedong played Kim and the Soviet Union held China's role. One option the United States considered was a joint Soviet–American strike against China's nuclear facilities. The Soviets showed no interest (which they would later have cause to regret), but the concept could be revived. A new version of this plan would consist of a joint Chinese–U.S. strike on North Korea's nuclear facilities. It would only work, however, if Beijing were reassured about its own security. China would ask the United States to be more understanding on issues such as island building in the South China Sea, the reintegration of Taiwan, and China's claim to the Senkaku Islands. Washington would be reluctant to make any concessions on these fronts. Officials in the United States may see these issues as detached from North Korean policy, but to Chinese policymakers, they are inextricably linked and crucial to the nation's overall safety.

A variant on this option could include granting China approval for an invasion of North Korea, once tactical strikes take out the nation's nuclear facilities. Beijing could then attempt to reconstruct North Korea through regime change and the creation of a provisional Chinese government, followed by a successful transfer of power. This option would require a tremendous nation-building operation, and would set a discomfiting global precedent. But if Washington and Beijing are to cooperate on North Korea, this may be the least worst option for both. Such a plan would reassure China about that crucial security buffer; the reassurance, in turn, should allow Washington to avoid drastic concessions on other issues, making the option slightly more attractive to the United States. Such a move is sure to stoke the ire of Japan and, perhaps to a lesser extent, South Korea, but both could be convinced that a Chinese presence in North Korea is preferable to the Kim regime.

To be sure, for Washington, a denuclearized North Korea is likely not worth such concessions. For now, a rising China remains a far greater challenge than a flailing North Korea, and empowering the former to sign the latter's death warrant may not make much strategic sense. That leaves the option of rapprochement. As Chinese–Soviet relations deteriorated to the point of border clashes in 1968–69, Moscow asked Washington how it would feel about Soviet strikes on Chinese nuclear facilities. Instead of cooperating, U.S. President Richard Nixon and former Secretary of State Henry Kissinger sought rapprochement with Beijing. Chinese leader Mao Zedong, considered dangerous and untrustworthy, was still armed with nuclear weapons. But the Nixon–Kissinger team decided that it could live with a nuclear China; it was just one more card in the great balance of power game. Such an arrangement is not out of the question for contemporary North Korea.

[Image:3:inline]There are, of course, important differences between Mao's China and Kim's North Korea. But if Washington is serious about its pivot to Asia, and if the goal of that pivot is to balance against China, rapprochement with Pyongyang is an option worth contemplating. Allowing Pyongyang to remain nuclear while improving its relationship with the United States might provide Washington with added strength. North Korea is less strategically important to the United States than China was to the Soviet Union, but it is by no means insignificant. If Pyongyang were no longer isolated from Washington, Beijing too might have to reconsider its assertions of power in the region; knowing the United States was on decent terms with North Korea might cause China to hesitate before sending ships to the Senkakus, for example. And the United States could ease China's fears by making concessions from a position of strength. Accommodating China's interests in Central Asia, the Arctic, and even the South China Sea would be easier for Washington to stomach if it came by choice, rather than apprehension. U.S. allies would likely be shocked by rapprochement with North Korea, but foreign policy cannot be shackled to allies.

GETTING A REACTION

How Pyongyang would respond to overtures from Washington is unclear. Kim might be amenable if it meant that he could continue to do what he pleases, so long as he does not harm the United States and its allies. The benefits of a normal relationship—trade, investment, and perhaps even trips to Hollywood for Kim—might be tempting. And over the course of decades, improved ties might even better conditions for North Korean civilians. At any rate, it is difficult to see how a rapprochement is materially worse than the status quo. The United States already has to live with a nuclear North Korea; it might as well try to get along with the regime.

North Korea may not be worth these radical strategic shifts—in which case, the status quo remains the least worst option. But if Washington does decide to hold steady, expecting China to change its own tone on North Korea is laughable. China has interests and constraints when it comes to North Korean affairs. Washington can balance against China or have China's cooperation for a denuclearized North Korea. But it cannot have both. Deciding between unpalatable options does not come easily, but that is the business of statecraft. The failure to make that decision is why the United States is stuck, like a Beckett character, waiting for China and saying, "Nothing to be done."

SULMAAN KHAN is Assistant Professor of International History and Chinese Foreign Relations at the Fletcher School, Tufts University, where he also directs the Water and Oceans Program at the Center for International Environment and Resource Policy.

Trump and North Korea

Reviving the Art of the Deal

John Delury

KCNA

Deal with it: Kim Jong Un delivering a speech in Pyongyang, August 2016

In the next four years, North Korea is poised to cross a dangerous threshold by finally developing the capability to hit the continental United States with a nuclear missile. That ability would present a direct threat to the United States and could punch a hole in the U.S. nuclear umbrella in Asia: Japan and South Korea, doubtful that Washington would risk U.S. cities to defend Tokyo or Seoul, might feel they had no choice but to get their own nuclear bombs. U.S. President Donald Trump, while still president-elect, drew a redline at Pyongyang's feet, tweeting, "It won't happen!" But the real question is how to stop it.

Hawks argue that Washington should act now by imposing harsh new economic sanctions or undertaking preemptive military strikes. But neither option would end well. Slapping Pyongyang with still more sanctions would only encourage it to sprint toward the completion of a nuclear-tipped intercontinental ballistic missile. And military action could lead to the destruction of Seoul (which sits within range of North Korean artillery) and expose U.S. forces in Guam, Japan, and South Korea to devastating retaliation, potentially triggering a catastrophic war in one of the world's most populous and prosperous regions.

If the United States really hopes to achieve peace on the Korean Peninsula, it should stop looking for ways to stifle North Korea's economy and undermine Kim Jong Un's regime and start finding ways to make Pyongyang feel more secure. This might sound counterintuitive, given North Korea's nuclear ambitions and human rights record. But consider this: North Korea will start focusing on its prosperity instead of its self-preservation only once it no longer has to worry about its own destruction. And North Korea will consider surrendering its nuclear deterrent only once it feels secure and prosperous and is economically integrated into Northeast Asia. What's more, the world can best help most North Koreans by relieving their deprivation and bringing down the walls that separate them from the outside world. Washington's immediate goal should therefore be to negotiate a freeze of North Korea's nuclear program in return for a U.S. security guarantee, since that is the only measure that could enable Kim to start concentrating on economic development and the belated transformation of North Korea.

KCNA / VIA REUTERS

A test of a North Korean strategic submarine ballistic missile, April 2016.

Trump seems open to this approach to the North Korean conundrum. Even in his most hawkish moment, when he threatened to bomb North Korean targets during his failed presidential bid in 2000, he insisted, "I'm no war-monger," and argued that only negotiation would bring a lasting solution. And last year on the campaign trail, he said that he "would have no problem speaking" to Kim. A businessman at heart, Trump will not be likely to turn down a good deal.

Kim also appears ready to do business. After taking power in 2012, he unveiled a new national strategy that put equal emphasis on security and prosperity. So far, however, he has focused primarily on consolidating his domestic power and building up the country's nuclear arsenal. Trump can now help him pivot to the economy, as Kim appears to have wanted to do all along. However unlikely a pair the two might seem, Kim and Trump are well positioned to strike the kind of deal that could lower the grave risks both their countries (and the region) now face. Such a move would also allow Trump to reaffirm U.S. leadership in a region critical to U.S. interests, and to finally start resolving a problem that has bedeviled every U.S. president since Harry Truman.

Kim's interest in economic progress goes beyond mere sloganeering.

SINS OF THE FATHER

In order to understand why such a deal could work, consider how far North Korea has come over the past two decades. In 1994, the year Kim's father, Kim Jong Il, came to power, the country was heading into a perfect storm. The collapse of the Soviet Union three years earlier had abruptly ended Moscow's previously generous support. North Korea's other erstwhile Cold War benefactor—China—also cut back on its subsidies and even normalized relations with the North's principal enemy, South Korea. When massive floods hit, North Korea's already-stagnating economy went into a tailspin. Before long, the country was suffering a horrific famine that, according to the most conservative estimates, would take many hundreds of thousands of lives. Scrambling to survive, Kim called on his people to endure an "arduous march" through an era of "military-first politics." Kim gave power to his generals and rations to their troops, at the expense of party cadres and the rest of the population. He boosted defense spending even as his people starved. And he abandoned tentative reforms under pressure from hard-liners. His military-first strategy kept the regime alive and the country intact—but at a brutal cost.

By the time Kim died, in 2011, North Korea had recovered considerably—enough so that Kim Jong Un could use his inaugural address to signal an end to his father's military-first policies. Never again, he promised, would his people have to "tighten their belts." A year later, Kim launched a new doctrine, which called for "simultaneous progress" on nuclear deterrence and economic development. It was "a new historic turning point," Kim told the Party Central Committee in 2013, when North Korea could develop its economy and improve its living standards.

Kim's interest in economic progress goes beyond mere sloganeering. At the same time that he unveiled his strategy of "simultaneous progress," he appointed

Pak Pong Ju, a reformist technocrat, to be the country's top economic official. To improve efficiency, Kim decentralized control over management decisions to farms and factories. He set up a dozen "special economic zones" and has largely left the country's extensive informal markets alone to work their magic. Through high-profile visits to new shopping malls, high-rise apartments, and pop music concerts, he has publicly embraced Pyongyang's emerging consumer class. All these measures have helped the North Korean economy grow by a modest one to two percent per year since he took power—despite tight sanctions and limited foreign investment—and the capital city is booming, although much of the population elsewhere still languishes at near-subsistence levels.

Yet belying these efforts, Kim has focused his energy more on nuclear than on economic development. In 2016 alone, he staged two nuclear and 24 missile tests. Kim seems to be sticking to a general principle of international politics that puts security before prosperity. North Korea's leader will put the economy first—and open up the country in the way this would require—only if and when he starts feeling confident that he has secured his position at home and neutralized the threats from abroad. After five years in which he demoted generals, reshuffled top cadres, and even executed his own uncle, Kim seems to have accomplished the former goal. But so far, the latter remains out of reach.

North Korea's location at the crossroads of Northeast Asia gives it a natural advantage.

LET'S MAKE A DEAL

To get there, Pyongyang will need a breakthrough in its relationship with Washington. That was unlikely to happen as long as U.S. President Barack Obama remained in office: because of his belief that the regime could not outlive Kim Jong Il's death, and then the wishful notion that Beijing could solve the problem for him, Obama never showed much interest in striking a grand bargain with Pyongyang. Such indifference only encouraged Kim to maintain his father's reliance on nuclear weapons as a guarantor of his security.

With Kim now feeling far safer at home, the United States needs to help him find a nonnuclear way to feel secure along his borders. A comprehensive deal is the best way to accomplish this, but it will require direct dialogue with Pyongyang. Trump should start by holding back-channel talks. If those make enough progress, he should then send an envoy to Pyongyang, who could negotiate a nuclear freeze (and, perhaps, as a goodwill gesture on the part of Pyongyang, secure the release of the two U.S. citizens imprisoned in North Korea). Trump could then initiate high-level talks that would culminate in a meeting between Kim and himself.

In order to convince Kim to freeze the development of North Korea's nuclear weapons and the missiles that carry them, Washington will need to design a package of security guarantees and political incentives, along with the practical means to verify Kim's compliance. Trump should offer Kim substantive concessions, well beyond the food aid that Obama proposed to send in the 2012 Leap Day Deal (scuttled almost as soon as it was announced by a new North Korean satellite test). Trump could offer to scale back or suspend U.S.–South Korean military exercises and delay the deployment of new U.S. military assets to the Korean Peninsula. As long as the diplomacy moved forward, the United States could safely postpone these military moves. Trump could also suggest convening four-power talks among China, North Korea, South Korea, and the United States to negotiate and sign a treaty formally ending the Korean War, as Pyongyang has long demanded. Trump could further consider offering symbolic actions that would give Kim room to maneuver, such as setting up liaison offices in Washington and Pyongyang and moving toward the normalization of diplomatic relations.

The time for preemption passed long ago.

Direct negotiations are the only way to find out just what steps Kim is ready to take now and which will have to wait until mutual confidence grows. Whatever Kim's comfort level, however, Washington should, in the first phase, ask Pyongyang to halt further development of its nuclear and long-range ballistic missile programs and allow International Atomic Energy Agency inspectors back into the country to verify compliance. Negotiators would also have to tackle the dual-use dilemma: North Korea currently insists on its right to launch satellites, which the United States considers de facto ballistic missile tests. To separate the two issues, Trump should ask Kim to let Russia launch all his satellites for him (a solution Kim's father suggested to Russian President Vladimir Putin back in 2000). In return, the United States would officially acknowledge North Korea's sovereign right to a peaceful space program.

The bilateral discussions should go beyond nuclear security, however. Trump should press Kim to take concrete steps to improve North Korean human rights, such as relaxing restrictions on travel abroad, allowing foreign humanitarian organizations more freedom in North Korea, and closing political prison camps. Discussing how to manage the rise of China, meanwhile, might yield some useful surprises, since both Kim and Trump want to keep Beijing guessing. Making progress on these issues would prove the wisdom of Trump's campaign promise to talk to Kim so long as there was "a ten percent or a 20 percent chance that [he could] talk him out of those damn nukes."

KCNA / via REUTERS
Kim Jong Un at a meeting of the ruling party in Pyongyang, December 2016.

THE NEXT ASIAN TIGER

Initiating talks on a nuclear freeze would immediately relax tensions between Washington and Pyongyang and lower risks in the region. But even if both sides agreed on new security arrangements, that would not solve the long-term threat posed by North Korea's nuclear arsenal. It would, however, create an opening for further negotiation. The United States would then need to use it by moving swiftly to the crux of the deal: helping Kim plot a path to prosperity by integrating North Korea's economy into the region.

If the United States were to loosen sanctions in step with Kim's initial freeze and subsequent moves, North Korea's location at the crossroads of Northeast Asia would give it a natural advantage. Businesses in China's northeastern provinces and the Russian Far East would readily ship their goods through North Korea's ice-free port at Rason, a short trip from Busan, South Korea's international shipping hub. Building an oil and gas pipeline through North Korea would allow Russian energy companies to reach South Korean consumers more cheaply. International financial institutions could help Pyongyang stabilize its currency and improve its data collection, as well as providing development assistance. North Korea could also become a popular place for light industrial manufacturing, given its low wages and its industrious, disciplined, and educated work force (as demonstrated by the productivity of North Korean factory workers at the Kaesong joint industrial zone). Finally, Kim could attract foreign partners to help develop the country's rich natural resources, which include, by some estimates, trillions of dollars' worth of coal and iron ore, precious metals, and rare earths.

It's high time for Washington to recognize that Kim's regime is unlikely to collapse anytime soon.

Although Kim has already enacted some basic economic reforms, détente with the United States could usher in the next phase of North Korea's development. Such development would generate powerful new domestic business interests, which would slowly push the country toward more international cooperation. Convincing Kim to hand over his last bomb could take decades, and the world may never reach the perfect outcome of complete, verifiable, and irreversible denuclearization. But short of that, the United States could make huge progress in reversing the current trajectory of ever-rising capabilities and risks.

KIM HONG-JI / REUTERS

North Korean workers in the Joint Industrial Park in the Kaesong industrial zone, December 2013.

CRITICS AT HOME, ALLIES ABROAD

Should Trump attempt to break the North Korean logjam, he will get plenty of criticism from multiple directions. But he will also win support in the one place that really counts: South Korea.

Hard-liners in the United States would condemn Trump for throwing Kim a lifeline when (they would claim) North Korea is tottering on the brink of collapse. But such arguments do not stand the test of history. Wishful thinking about North Korea's imminent collapse has compromised U.S. strategy for far too long. Obama, envisioning a day when "the Korean people, at long last, will be whole and free," squandered the early years of Kim Jong Un's reign in the mistaken belief that the regime would not survive long following Kim Jong Il's death.

But survive it did, and it's high time for Washington to recognize that not only is Kim's regime unlikely to collapse anytime soon but economic sanctions have done more harm than good. The Obama administration tried many times to goad Beijing into imposing sanctions that would break Pyongyang's nuclear will, and U.S. officials hailed each new UN Security Council resolution sanctioning North Korea as a game changer. Yet eight years of effort have yielded only a dramatic increase in the North's nuclear arsenal and its ability to deliver those weapons. Because of its overriding interest in a stable, divided Korean Peninsula, China will never impose an economic embargo on its neighbor. Even if Beijing did enforce comprehensive sanctions, Kim would respond by doubling down on his nuclear weapons program. Targeted sanctions can slow proliferation somewhat, but wholesale sanctions designed to change North Korea's calculus have never worked and never will.

Another, more aggressive group of hard-liners will chide Trump for refusing to order preemptive strikes against North Korea's nuclear program. But the time for preemption passed long ago. The regime already possesses a modest nuclear arsenal and the means to hit targets in Guam, Japan, and South Korea. Its nuclear and missile programs are dispersed underground, underwater, and in other secret locations across the country.

Because the United States could not take out such weapons with a single blow, Pyongyang would almost certainly retain the ability to respond to any attack in kind—and respond it would. In a best-case scenario, Kim would retaliate by launching only conventional missiles and only against U.S. military installations in South Korea, and both Seoul and Washington would refrain from further escalation. Some Americans and South Koreans would be killed, but the fighting would at least stop there. Under an equally plausible worst-case scenario, however, the situation could quickly deteriorate into a catastrophe if North Korea unleashed artillery barrages on the civilian population in Seoul, triggering retaliatory attacks on Pyongyang. It's worth remembering that 20 years ago, General Gary Luck, then the commander of U.S. forces in Korea, estimated that a war with the North would take a million lives and do $1 trillion worth of damage to the South Korean economy. And that was before Pyongyang got the bomb.

None of the alternatives to a deal—doing nothing (waiting for North Korea to collapse), doing too little (relying on China to impose sanctions), or doing too much (starting a second Korean War)—holds any promise for success.

By contrast, not only is the ground ripe for a grand bargain, but should Trump pursue one, he will likely find a powerful ally in Seoul. Although South Koreans live under the constant threat of nuclear attack from the North, the public there firmly opposes preemptive military strikes against Pyongyang. If the United States unilaterally bombed North Korea, its alliance with the South might be the first casualty. Thanks to the downfall of South Korea's conservative president, Park Geun-hye, liberal politicians—who embrace comprehensive engagement as the only long-term solution to the conflict—are well positioned to win back the presidency this year. But even a conservative leader may well favor a moderate approach to the North, and so Trump can probably count on whoever becomes South Korea's next president to backstop a bold approach by Washington.

In January 2016, a few days after North Korea's fourth nuclear test, Trump said of Kim: "This guy doesn't play games, and we can't play games with him, because he really does have missiles, and he really does have nukes." Trump was right. Like it or not, North Korea's nukes are a reality. The United States needs a new strategy for dealing with Kim—and Trump is well placed to deliver it.

JOHN DELURY is Associate Professor of Chinese Studies at Yonsei University, in Seoul.

Getting Tough on North Korea

How to Hit Pyongyang Where It Hurts

Joshua Stanton, Sung-Yoon Lee, Bruce Klingner

Special delivery: unloading North Korean coal in Dandong, China, December 2010.

For the past quarter century, the United States and South Korea have tried to convince North Korea to abandon its nuclear aspirations. Beginning in the early 1990s, Washington attempted to bargain with Pyongyang, while Seoul pursued a strategy of economic engagement, effectively subsidizing Pyongyang with aid and investment even as it continued to develop nuclear weapons. Then, after North Korea tested an atomic bomb in 2006, the United States pressed the UN Security Council to impose sanctions on North Korea. Yet at the urging of South Korea and for fear of angering China, the United States failed to use its full diplomatic and financial power to enforce those sanctions. All along, the goal has been to induce North Korea to open up to the outside world and roll back its nuclear and missile programs.

This combination of sanctions and subsidies has failed. North Korea already possesses the ability to hit Japan and South Korea with nuclear weapons and will soon have the ability to hit the continental United States with one. Despite what some in Washington and Seoul want to believe, the country's leader, Kim Jong Un, is no reformer. He has staked his legitimacy on perfecting the nuclear arsenal his father and grandfather bought at the cost of billions of dollars and millions of lives. If he will disarm at all, he will do so only under duress so extreme that it threatens the survival of his regime.

To protect the United States and its allies from the North Korean threat and prevent further nuclear proliferation, the Trump administration must end the incoherent policy of simultaneously sanctioning and subsidizing Pyongyang. Instead, it should crack down on the foreign financial dealings of North Korean officials and companies and the foreign states that help them. The world is facing its greatest nuclear emergency since the Cuban missile crisis. It's past time for the United States to act decisively.

ROGUE STATE

For decades, North Korea has represented a second-tier crisis for the United States—never topping Iran, for example, as a nonproliferation priority, or Sudan as a humanitarian priority, or Iraq as a security priority. Every president since Bill Clinton has played for time, hoping that the North Korean regime would collapse while doing nothing to undermine it, and at times even propping it up with aid and by relaxing sanctions. The last three administrations cut a series of deals that traded hard cash for false promises. Time and again, North Korea agreed to dismantle its nuclear weapons program but did not.

In 1994, Clinton signed the first U.S. deal with Pyongyang: a pact, known as the Agreed Framework, that offered generous fuel aid and help building two expensive nuclear power reactors in return for promises from North Korea's then leader, Kim Jong Il, to halt both his uranium- and his plutonium-based nuclear programs. In 2002, U.S. President George W. Bush, having learned that Pyongyang was cheating by secretly enriching uranium, responded by stopping the flow of aid. After that, Kim pulled out of the agreement, withdrew from the Nuclear Nonproliferation Treaty, and restarted his plutonium reactor. Despite this history, Bush signed his own agreement with North Korea in 2007, under which he allowed North Korean entities to use the dollar system, provided more aid, relaxed sanctions, and removed the country from the list of state sponsors of terrorism. Within a year, Pyongyang balked at signing a verification protocol, and the deal collapsed as Bush left office.

Kim Jong Il toasts U.S. Secretary of State Madeleine Albright at a dinner in Pyongyang, October 2000.

U.S. President Barack Obama entered office promising to reach out a hand if Kim would unclench his fist. Within months, Kim answered by testing first a long-range missile and then a nuclear device. Yet Obama persisted in his outreach to Pyongyang. Under the 2012 Leap Day agreement, the United States promised North Korea aid in exchange for a freeze of its nuclear and missile tests. Just six weeks after agreeing to the deal, Pyongyang tested a long-range missile.

The lesson to be learned from all these experiences is clear: yet another piece of paper will not resolve the United States' differences with North Korea. After all, Pyongyang has already signed and then unilaterally withdrawn from two International Atomic Energy Agency safeguards agreements and the Nuclear Nonproliferation Treaty and violated an inter-Korean denuclearization agreement, the 1994 Agreed Framework, a 2005 joint statement, and both the 2007 and the 2012 agreements.

MONEY FOR NOTHING

While Washington negotiated deal after deal with Pyongyang, Seoul pursued a program of economic aid and subsidized investment in North Korea, hoping to draw it into the global economy, sow the seeds of capitalism, and gradually liberalize its regime. Between 1991 and 2015, Seoul poured at least $7 billion into Pyongyang's coffers. The United States contributed an additional $1.3 billion in aid, and private investment from China, South Korea, and Europe likely contributed billions more. The heyday of engagement, known in South Korea as "the sunshine policy," lasted from 1998 to 2008, under the presidencies of Kim Dae-jung and Roh Moo-hyun. The cash that the sunshine policy provided Kim came just in time to rescue him from a spiraling economic crisis that had already led to a major mutiny within the North Korean army.

The failure of engagement was just as inevitable as the failure of the Agreed Framework. Its premise—that capitalism would spur liberalism in a despotic state—was flawed. After all, over the past two decades, both China and Russia have cracked down on domestic dissent and threatened the United States and its allies abroad, even as they have cautiously welcomed in capitalism. In 2003, even as it cashed Seoul's checks, Pyongyang warned party officials in the state newspaper that "it is the imperialist's old trick to carry out ideological and cultural infiltration prior to their launching of an aggression openly." For the regime, engagement was a "silent, crafty and villainous method of aggression, intervention and domination." Given this attitude, it's no surprise that Kim Jong Il never opened up North Korea. The political change that engagement advocates promised was exactly what he feared the most.

U.S. relations with Pyongyang will have to get worse before they can get better.

North Korea did allow a few capitalist enclaves to be built. But while Pyongyang collected the financial windfall, it carefully isolated the enclaves from the rest of North Korean society. Starting in 2002, South Korean tourists booked overpriced and closely supervised hikes along the scenic but secluded Kumgang Mountain trail in North Korea's southeastern corner. (The tours abruptly ended in 2008, when a North Korean soldier shot and killed a South Korean woman as she took an unauthorized morning walk.) And beginning in 2004, South Korean companies employed thousands of North Korean workers at the Kaesong Industrial Complex, an inter-Korean factory park a few miles north of the demilitarized zone. By 2015, the companies in Kaesong employed over 54,000 North Koreans. (The regime probably stole most of the laborers' low wages.)

In 2016, after North Korea's fourth nuclear test and a missile launch, Seoul finally conceded that Pyongyang was probably using revenues from Kaesong to fund its nuclear program and withdrew from the project. The leading candidate in South Korea's presidential election this year, Moon Jae-in, has called for the Kaesong complex to reopen and expand, but a UN Security Council resolution passed in 2016 bans the kind of "public and private financial support" for trade with North Korea that kept the industrial complex afloat, absent approval from a UN committee, approval that the United States could—and should—block.

Engagement has not changed Pyongyang, but it has often corrupted the engagers. Take the case of the Associated Press. In 2012, when it opened a bureau in Pyongyang, it promised to chart "a path to vastly larger understanding," while following "the same standards and practices as AP bureaus worldwide," to "reflect accurately" the lives of the North Korean people. Yet it is the AP, not North Korea, that has been compromised, by submitting to censorship and broadcasting the regime's propaganda around the world, at the same time overlooking newsworthy events—such as an apartment collapse and a hotel fire—that took place just minutes from its bureau. Meanwhile, the foreign tour agencies that promote themselves as agents of glasnost have done little more than supply the North Korean government with hard currency—and, occasionally, hostages—while shuttling tourists through a circuit of propaganda spectacles. The Pyongyang University of Science and Technology was founded by Christian missionaries in 2010 to, in the founders' words, help North Korea "contribute as a member within the international community." But defectors have alleged that the regime is using the university to train hackers. And to avoid expulsion or imprisonment, aid workers in North Korea must collaborate with the government's discriminatory rationing system, which favors those citizens it deems the most loyal to the state.

The promised results of engagement have never materialized. Since the death of his father, Kim Jong Un has accelerated the pace of North Korea's nuclear and missile tests, stamped out foreign media, and tightened the seals on the country's already closed borders. He has expanded prison camps and carried out bloody purges, and he even seems to have sent a team of assassins to murder his half brother in a Malaysian airport earlier this year. Pyongyang's party elites are richer than they were ten years ago, but they also live in greater fear of falling out of favor with the regime and are defecting in greater numbers. Although there is no wide-scale famine of the type that ravaged North Korea's countryside in the 1990s, most North Koreans barely scrape together enough to eat.

North Korean society has changed in the past two-plus decades. Markets now provide people with most of their food, consumer goods, and information. Yet as the economists Marcus Noland and Stephan Haggard have documented, those changes have occured despite, not because of, official efforts. They have been driven by the country's poorest and most marginalized people, those who turned to smuggling to earn a living, often at the risk of death or life in a prison camp. The United States and its allies should focus on these signs of real change, not on brokering yet another deal with the regime that would only perpetuate the status quo.

Testing a missile engine in Cholsan County, North Korea, April 2016.

GOOD COP, GOOD COP

In 2006, after more than a decade of negotiations and aid shipments, North Korea conducted its first nuclear test. In response, the UN Security Council approved a series of sanctions resolutions, and the United States began a halfhearted campaign to use its own sanctions to pressure North Korea into disarming. Bush and Obama talked tough after various nuclear tests, but both failed to back up their words with action. Worse still, continued economic aid and investment canceled out much of the effect of the sanctions.

The lax enforcement of sanctions allowed Pyongyang to launder the money that paid for its nuclear arsenal and perpetuated its crimes against humanity through banks in the United States. Pyongyang earned much of that money from illicit activities and mingled dirty funds with legitimate profits to conceal the dirty money's origin. As reports from the UN and documents from the U.S. Justice Department confirm, North Korea continues to pay, receive, and store most of its funds in U.S. dollars. The U.S. Treasury Department could end this practice, because nearly all transactions denominated in dollars must pass through U.S. banks.

From late 2005 to early 2007, it did just that. Treasury Department officials warned bankers around the world that North Korean funds were derived in part from drug dealing, counterfeiting, and arms sales and that by transacting in those funds, banks risked losing their access to the dollar system. To show that they were serious, officials targeted Banco Delta Asia, a small bank in Macao that was laundering illicit funds for North Korea, and blocked its access to the dollar system. After that, other banks around the world froze or closed North Korean accounts, fearing similar sanctions or bad publicity. Even the state-owned Bank of China refused to follow the Chinese government's request to transfer funds from the tainted Banco Delta Asia to other accounts controlled by Pyongyang. As Juan Zarate, a former U.S. Treasury official, has explained, the U.S. effort "isolat[ed] Pyongyang from the international financial system to an unprecedented degree." The episode also showed that when the interests of Chinese banks diverge from those of the Chinese government, the banks will protect their access to the dollar system. As Zarate recounted, "Perhaps the most important lesson was that the Chinese could in fact be moved to follow the U.S. Treasury's lead and act against their own stated foreign policy and political interests."

Yet in early 2007, as part of Bush's effort to denuclearize North Korea, the Treasury Department returned to its policy of letting most of Pyongyang's dollars flow freely through the U.S. banking system. By July 2014, the Treasury Department had frozen the assets of just 43 (mostly low-ranking) people and entities in North Korea, compared with about 50 in Belarus (including its president and his cabinet), 161 in Zimbabwe, 164 in Myanmar (including its junta and its top banks), nearly 400 in Cuba, and more than 800 in Iran. Foreign banks that processed transactions for Cuba, Iran, or Myanmar risked getting hit with secondary sanctions and multimillion-dollar fines. The result was that many banks avoided doing business with those countries altogether. But doing business with North Korea posed no such risks and so continued freely, until last February, when Congress passed the North Korea Sanctions and Policy Enhancement Act. The law banned North Korean banks from processing payments through the dollar system. But because the restriction did not take effect until last November, it is too early to gauge its effects. It took three years for strong, well-enforced sanctions on Iran to begin to bite.

UN sanctions look strong on paper, but member states have often failed to enforce them. China, in particular, has made a show of voting for each round of sanctions, only to flagrantly violate each of them. China's state-owned companies have sold missile trucks to Pyongyang; its banks have laundered the regime's money; its government has allowed UNsanctioned companies and the North Korean hackers who attacked Sony Pictures in 2014 to operate on its soil; and its ports have allowed the transshipment of arms, materials for North Korea's nuclear and missile programs, and luxury goods headed to North Korea—all without fear of punishment.

China has made a show of voting for each round of sanctions, only to flagrantly violate each of them.

Other countries deserve a share of the blame, as well. Until 2016, South Korea let approximately $100 million a year flow into Pyongyang through Kaesong without questioning how Pyongyang used the money, despite UN resolutions requiring Seoul to ensure that the North Korean regime would not use South Korean funds for its nuclear program. The fleet of ships that North Korea uses to smuggle weapons has flown Cambodian and Mongolian flags; its nuclear and missile scientists have visited Indian and Russian laboratories; its slave laborers have toiled at Qatari construction sites, Malaysian mines, and Polish shipyards; its military has trained Ugandan pilots and built weapons for Iran and Namibia; its doctors have sold quack medicines in Tanzania; and its generals have bought Swiss watches. In testimony before a U.S. congressional committee in 2015, the scholar Larry Niksch estimated that North Korea receives over $2 billion a year from "various forms of collaboration" with Iran alone. The cash that Pyongyang has gained by disrupting sanctions enforcement may be modest by global standards, but it has been enough to keep the regime in power and advance its nuclear program.

TURNING THE SCREWS

North Korea's fourth nuclear test, in January 2016, forced the United States and South Korea to apply more coherent financial and diplomatic pressure. Seoul could hardly ask other governments to enforce the sanctions when it was violating them itself in Kaesong. Closing the industrial complex there allowed it to use its substantial diplomatic influence to persuade allies to crack down on North Korea.

In Washington, the passage of the North Korea Sanctions and Policy Enhancement Act forced the Obama administration to designate North Korea a money-laundering concern under the Patriot Act and label several North Koreans, including Kim, human rights abusers. Today, the U.S. Treasury Department has frozen the dollar assets of about 200 North Korean entities. This number represents progress, but it does not approach the level of pressure applied to Iran. Nor does it represent a determined effort to find and freeze North Korea's money-laundering network. Another UN Security Council resolution, passed in November 2016, aimed to coax wavering states to enforce UN sanctions against North Korea, but absent a threat of secondary sanctions, Fiji and Tanzania will continue to reflag North Korean ships, Iran and Syria will continue to buy North Korean weapons, Namibia will continue to host a North Korean arms factory, and Chinese banks will continue to launder North Korean cash.

In September 2016, in the wake of North Korea's fifth nuclear test, the United States for the first time indicted a Chinese firm for breaking UN and U.S. sanctions and seized its Chinese bank accounts. According to the indictment, the Dandong Hongxiang Industrial Development Company knowingly helped a sanctioned North Korean bank launder millions of dollars through U.S. banks. But the Obama administration stopped short of going after the Chinese banks that had facilitated the scheme, even though both UN sanctions resolutions and U.S. Treasury Department regulations obligated the banks to investigate and report the company's suspicious activities. That was a mistake: sanctions will not work if Chinese banks continue to break them, and Chinese banks will not enforce the sanctions until the United States begins penalizing violators. Indeed, it was secondary sanctions that isolated North Korea from 2005 to 2007, helped force Myanmar to accept political reforms in 2012, and got Iran to return to the negotiating table in 2014.

Damir Sagolj / REUTERS
What appear to be intercontinental ballistic missiles during a military parade marking Kim Il Sung's 105th birth anniversary in Pyongyang, April 2017.

BEEN THERE, TRIED THAT

Doves in the United States and South Korea still call for a return to economic engagement and even a halt to joint U.S.–South Korean military exercises, in the hope that North Korea will reciprocate by freezing its nuclear program. Yet Obama repeatedly attempted to negotiate, all for naught. In 2009, then former President Clinton flew to Pyongyang to meet with Kim Jong Il. He won the release of two American journalists and invited the North to denuclearization talks, but Pyongyang declined the invitation. Later that year, Stephen Bosworth, the U.S. special representative for North Korea policy, visited Pyongyang to invite the government back to the negotiating table and came back empty-handed. In 2013, Obama tried to send Robert King, the U.S. special envoy for North Korean human rights issues, to Pyongyang, but North Korea canceled the visit at the last moment. Shortly before the January 2016 nuclear test, US and North Korean diplomats discussed the possibility of starting negotiations for a peace treaty, but Pyongyang insisted that its nuclear program would not be on the agenda.

Diplomacy has failed because Pyongyang remains determined to build its nuclear arsenal. Resuming talks would achieve nothing, as Pyongyang will not freeze its nuclear and missile programs when it is so close to attaining an effective arsenal. Any

U.S. concessions without irreversible progress toward disarmament would do more harm than good. Suspending U.S.–South Korean military exercises would degrade the readiness of U.S. and South Korean forces at a time when North Korean missiles are still aimed at South Korean cities. And yet Pyongyang will use any resumption of exercises as an excuse to restart its nuclear reactors and missile tests. It will exploit any enforcement of UN sanctions, any interception of a North Korean arms shipment, any acceptance of a North Korean defector, or any criticism of North Korea's crimes against humanity in the same way.

North Korea now says that it will denuclearize only after the United States and South Korea negotiate a peace treaty with it to formally end the Korean War. But Pyongyang does not want peace, or even a peace treaty. It wants a peace-treaty negotiation—the more protracted and inconclusive, the better. By drawing the United States into a peace process, the North hopes to blunt criticism of its crimes against humanity, legitimize its regime, get South Korea to lower its defenses, induce the United States and the UN to lift sanctions, and eventually get U.S. forces to withdraw from South Korea. Yet Pyongyang would ultimately rebuff U.S. requests for verification and would meet any new concessions with yet more demands and more provocations.

NO MORE MR. NICE GUY

The only remaining hope for denuclearizing North Korea peacefully lies in convincing it that it must disarm and reform or perish. Doing that will require the United States to embark on an unrelenting campaign of political subversion and financial isolation. The United States should begin by fining and sanctioning the Chinese banks that illegally maintain relationships with North Korean banks and fail to report suspicious North Korean transactions to the U.S. Treasury Department. The Treasury Department should also require banks to report North Korean ownership of offshore assets. The United States and South Korea should facilitate high-level defections by North Korean diplomats of the kind that exposed large parts of Pyongyang's money-laundering network last year. As Fredrick Vincenzo, a commander in the U.S. Navy, argued in a paper last October, the United States and South Korea should try to convince elites in Pyongyang that they have a future in a free, democratic, united Korea, and that in the event of war, the United States will hold them accountable for any attacks on civilian targets in South Korea. The United States and South Korea should also threaten to prosecute those involved in Pyongyang's ongoing crimes against the North Korean people and promise clemency for those who mitigate them.

Because Pyongyang has so consistently reneged on its agreements, the United States must continue to pursue the regime's assets until it has permanently and verifiably disarmed. Until then, Washington should work with UN aid agencies to allow Pyongyang to buy and import only the food, medicine, and other goods required to meet the humanitarian needs of the North Korean people. Washington should release blocked North Korean funds only in exchange for verified progress toward the freeze, disablement, and dismantlement of Pyongyang's nuclear and missile programs; the withdrawal of the artillery that threatens Seoul; and humanitarian reforms. As long as North Korea remains a closed society, outside inspectors will find it impossible to verify its disarmament. Only financial coercion stands any reasonable chance of getting North Korea to take the path that sanctions forced on Myanmar: incrementally opening up its society.

Effective sanctions require years of investigation and coalition building; they cannot be turned on and off in an instant. So this strategy will take time, determination, and a willingness to accept that U.S. relations with Pyongyang will have to get worse before they can get better. The same is true of U.S. relations with Beijing. In response to tough sanctions on North Korea, China will likely impose import tariffs on goods from South Korea, Japan, and the United States; increase its domestic anti-American rhetoric; take aggressive military steps in the Pacific; and attempt to circumvent the sanctions by sending food and other goods to Pyongyang. Yet Beijing wants neither a major trade war nor a military conflict. And Chinese banks and trading companies have shown that they value their access to the U.S. economy more than their business with North Korea.

China will be most likely to put diplomatic and financial pressure on North Korea if it believes that failing to do so will lead the United States to destabilize the regime on its northeastern border. Accordingly, Washington must make clear to both Kim Jong Un and Chinese President Xi Jinping that it would prefer the regime's chaotic collapse to a stable, nuclear-armed North Korea. The missing ingredient in U.S. diplomacy with Pyongyang has been not trust but leverage—and the willingness to use it. Washington must threaten the one thing that Pyongyang values more than its nuclear weapons: its survival.

JOSHUA STANTON is an attorney in Washington, D.C., and was the principal drafter of the legislation that later became the North Korea Sanctions and Policy Enhancement Act of 2016.

SUNG-YOON LEE is Kim Koo-Korea Foundation Professor in Korean Studies at Tufts University's Fletcher School of Law and Diplomacy.

BRUCE KLINGNER is Senior Research Fellow for Northeast Asia at the Heritage Foundation.

Atoms for Pyongyang

Let North Korea Have Peaceful Nuclear Power

Richard Rhodes and Michael Shellenberger

DAMIR SAGOLJ / REUTERS

Military trucks drive through downtown Pyongyang in preparation for Kim Il Sung's birthday, April 2017.

Earlier this month, U.S. President Donald Trump said that "under the right circumstances," he would meet with North Korean President Kim Jong Un, who continues to increase his nation's nuclear arsenal. With the recent election in South Korea of President Moon Jae-in, who campaigned for renewed negotiations between the two Koreas, the circumstances might indeed be just right.

Kim Jong Un has repeatedly stated that he wants the same thing North Korea's previous leaders—his father, Kim Jong Il, and grandfather Kim Il Sung—wanted: first, assurance that North Korea won't be invaded again, and second, electricity for economic development to replace the hydropower capacity the United States destroyed with massive strategic bombing in the first years of the Korean War, which was fought from 1950 to 1953. These were the two demands North Korea made, and the Clinton administration agreed to, in 1994, when North Korea pledged to stop producing plutonium in exchange for nuclear power plants.

North Korea's president is fully aware that attacking the United States would be tantamount to suicide. In 2000, as President Kim Jong Il told a South Korean newspaper publisher, "[Our] missiles cannot reach the United States, and if I launched them the U.S. would fire a thousand missiles back and we would not survive. I know that very well. But I have to let them know I have missiles. I am making them because only then will the United States talk to me." Shortly thereafter, during a visit to North Korea by Secretary of State Madeleine Albright, he agreed to a moratorium on missile construction.

The 1994 energy-for-weapons agreement worked until the 9/11 terrorist attacks, after which U.S. President George W. Bush claimed that North Korea was part of a so-called axis of evil with Iraq and Iran. Two years later, the United States invaded Iraq. North Korean leaders quite rationally concluded that Iraq's mistake was not its pursuit of a weapon but rather its failure to build one. They conducted their first nuclear weapons test three years later, in 2006.

Washington's continued pursuit of a failed strategy is evidence that it, not Pyongyang, is the irrational actor.

The Obama administration largely continued the Bush administration's hardline approach to North Korea, to even worse results. Not only is North Korea closer than ever to producing an intercontinental ballistic missile that can reach the United States—its people remain mired in poverty thanks in part to a lack of abundant or reliable electricity. Satellite images show a brightly lit South Korea—one-third of whose power comes from nuclear power plants—casting a glare over an almost entirely dark North Korea.

Washington's continued pursuit of a failed strategy is evidence that it, not Pyongyang, is the irrational actor. Threatening North Korea with military action, as Trump has done, only deepens its leaders' conviction that they need a sizable nuclear deterrent to protect themselves. By contrast, promising not to attack—and helping North Korea gain access to nuclear energy in exchange for limiting its nuclear arsenal and missile development—gives it reason to stop threatening its neighbors and creates a powerful economic incentive for it to cease exporting missiles and other military contraband.

Constructive engagement is critical for achieving peace on the Korean peninsula and, eventually, freedom for the North Korean people. The failure of the United

States to impose democracy in Afghanistan and Iraq stands in marked contrast with the gradual, multi-decade transition from dictatorships to democracy by many other nations around the world, from Europe to Latin America to much of Asia.

Indeed, there is no mystery to how peaceful and gradual regime change occurs. Rising prosperity increases popular demands for freedom and inspires the children and grandchildren of hereditary dynasties to loosen their grip on power. South Korea is no exception. Even though it regularly held elections, that U.S. ally was effectively a military dictatorship until 1987, when a national referendum approved a new constitution that allowed direct elections, including that of the president. Between 1980 and 1990, per-capita income nearly quadrupled, from $1,778 to $6,642.

Conservative hawks who seek a military solution to the Korean problem are not the only ones at fault. Liberal doves who oppose nuclear power are equally to blame. Since the Carter administration, Democrats have sought to restrict access to nuclear energy by poor nations and to punish nations such as India and Pakistan that acquired a weapon after the nuclear nonproliferation treaty (NPT) was ratified, blocking their efforts to scale up nuclear energy production. Democrats have long sought to prevent nations—even those that have already become nuclear-weapons states—from reprocessing spent nuclear fuel because they fear the separated plutonium might be used for weapons, even though the NPT explicitly gives its signatories the right to do so and reactor-grade plutonium is unreliable for weapons use.

As an outsider, Trump has the opportunity to break from both extremes and finally realize the "Atoms for Peace" vision that U.S. President Dwight Eisenhower outlined at the United Nations in 1953, five months after the end of the Korean War. Eisenhower, a former general deeply committed to alleviating the conditions that lead to military conflict, called for nuclear power development to supply "abundant electrical energy in the power-starved areas of the world." Working through the United Nations' International Atomic Energy Agency (IAEA), the United States provided nations with research reactors and the training to use them, while maintaining oversight of weapons-grade materials.

Given Trump's bellicose rhetoric toward North Korea, his moving to open negotiations with the Hermit Kingdom may seem unlikely. Yet he has frequently criticized the U.S. invasion of Iraq as well as the Obama administration's handling of North Korea, and he is a professed supporter of nuclear energy. That industry, despite having significant export potential, is currently struggling for survival in the United States against heavily subsidized renewables and cheap natural gas.

In seeking an atoms-for-peace deal with North Korea, Trump can build on humankind's successes in reducing the threat of nuclear conflict. Thanks in large measure to an agreement negotiated by another Republican president, Ronald Reagan, the United States and Russia have reduced their total number of operational nuclear warheads from 30,000 in the late 1960s to 1,500 today. The CIA estimates that more than 30 nations have the technical capacity to develop nuclear weapons. Only nine have chosen to do so. In short, for more than 70 years, nations have successfully avoided the use of atoms for war. What's missing now is the expansion of atoms for peace—on the Korean peninsula and beyond.

RICHARD RHODES is the author of the Pulitzer Prize-winning history *The Making of the Atomic Bomb*. MICHAEL SHELLENBERGER is president of Environmental Progress, a research and policy organization.

Kim Jong Un's Quest for an ICBM

The State of North Korea's Missile Program

Jeffrey Lewis

North Korean Supreme Leader Kim Jong Un watches a missile launch at an undisclosed location, released March 2016.

North Korea is on track to conduct a record number of missile tests this year, with the ultimate goal of developing an intercontinental ballistic missile (ICBM) capable of delivering a nuclear warhead to the continental United States. During his 2017 New Year's Day speech, North Korean Supreme Leader Kim Jong Un said that his country had "entered the final stage of preparation for the test launch of an ICBM." North Korean state media outlets have repeatedly asserted that despite international protests, the country has the right to conduct such a test at the time of its choosing. And during an April 15 parade in Pyongyang, the regime showed off two different kinds of vehicles, six apiece, each carrying large missile canisters apparently designed to carry ICBMs.

No one doubts that Kim Jong Un wants an ICBM; many, however, wonder whether his missileers are close to delivering one that works. North Korea today has at least four paths to a working ICBM, and although each has its drawbacks, taken together, they suggest a country that will likely succeed before too long.

WHY BUILD A MISSILE?

There are obvious reasons for North Korea to seek the capability to strike the United States with a nuclear weapon. Washington is Pyongyang's primary adversary and the one power in the world that threatens Kim Jong Un with the fate that befell Libyan dictator Muammar al-Qaddafi and Iraqi President Saddam Hussein: forcible regime change. The North Koreans believe that Qaddafi, who was toppled by a NATO intervention in 2011, made a fatal mistake by abandoning his nuclear weapons program in 2003 and that Hussein, who was deposed in 2003, doomed himself by allowing the United States to build up its forces in neighboring countries before the Iraq war. Pyongyang wants nuclear weapons both as a deterrent against invasion and as a part of its strategy for repelling one. If war was to break out, North Korea would likely use large numbers of nuclear weapons against U.S. forces in Japan and South Korea, hoping to shock the United States and blunt an invasion.

A threat to use nuclear weapons against U.S. forces throughout South Korea and Japan would be credible only if North Korea is also capable of striking the United States—U.S. officials have suggested that Kim Jong Un would be committing suicide by using nuclear weapons in this way, but they do so safe in the knowledge that Washington and other U.S. cities are out of North Korea's reach. That is why the development of an ICBM is an essential component of Pyongyang's nuclear strategy.

THE SCUDS ARE ALRIGHT

The basis of North Korea's missile force was a pair of Soviet-manufactured Scud-B missiles provided by Egypt in the late 1970s. Pyongyang is believed to have reverse engineered the Egyptian Scuds in order to create missiles of its own. Today, short-range Scud missiles form the bulk of North Korea's arsenal and have been sold to countries around the world, including Egypt, Iran, Pakistan, Syria, Vietnam, Yemen, and the United Arab Emirates. North Korea has also created a series of longer-range missiles using Scud-based technology, including the Nodong medium-range ballistic missile as well as space-launch vehicles—carrier rockets used to reach outer space—that Western analysts call the Taepodong and Taepodong-2.

The Scud-B missiles that North Korea imported could carry a 2,200-pound payload just under 200 miles. Today, the country's extended-range Scuds can carry a half-ton payload more than 600 miles, while the Nodong, a larger version of the basic Scud missile, can deliver a similar-sized payload just under 750 miles. North Korea's most recent missile test, on May 29, was of a Scud-C missile with improved guidance that is more accurate than the regime's other short-range Scud missiles.

KCNA / REUTERS

Kim Jong Un inspects a Hwasong-12 rocket in an undated photo, released May 2017.

North Korea has used this basic technology to develop a launcher, which it calls the Kwangmyongsong and the United States calls the Taepodong-2. In theory, Pyongyang could use the Taepodong-2 as an ICBM, and a three-stage version might travel over 9,000 miles—capable of hitting the East Coast of the United States. But the process of assembling and fueling North Korea's space launchers is lengthy and requires the use of a massive gantry. Such a missile would be vulnerable during its long preparation to launch—an obvious drawback that limits its strategic value. These problems have led North Korea to develop alternative missile systems. One of these is an ICBM called the KN-08.

MUSUDAN-CE THE NIGHT AWAY

After the collapse of the Soviet Union in 1991, North Korea sought more advanced technologies for its missile program—technologies that would scale better than those in the Scud missiles supplied by Egypt. During the 1990s, reports emerged that engineers from Russia's Makeyev Missile Design Bureau, which had designed the Soviet Union's submarine-launched ballistic missiles (SLBMs), were helping Pyongyang to copy a Soviet-era SLBM called the SSN-6. The United States calls the North Korean version of this missile, which appeared in the middle of the following decade, the Musudan.

The Musudan uses more powerful propellants than the Scud, which allows North Korea to build longer-range missiles that are compact enough to be carried by vehicles. But it is also a far more complicated missile. Soviet designers needed to keep the SS-N-6 short enough to fit inside a submarine launch tube, so they submerged the engine inside the fuel tank. This complex design has proved hard for North Korea to replicate. All but one of Pyongyang's six or eight attempts to launch a Musudan have failed. (It is not always easy to tell what has been launched if it explodes.)

Just as North Korea has attempted to create an ICBM using Scud-based technologies, it has also tried to make one based on the Musudan. Despite the challenges associated with this design, North Korea seems to have used a pair of the submerged engines as the basis for its KN-08, an ICBM that would be able to deliver a nuclear weapon–sized payload to Washington.

No state that has developed an ICBM has been unable to develop a reentry vehicle capable of delivering a warhead.

North Korea conducted a ground test of the KN-08 engine in 2016, demonstrating that the engine works in a controlled environment. But it has yet to conduct a flight test, which is necessary to demonstrate that all the components of the missile would function properly in a realistic launch scenario.

Given the Musudan's awful track record, there are many reasons to think that the first KN-08 flights will fail. Some experts, such as Markus Schiller of ST Analytics, doubt that it can ever be made to work given the engineering challenges posed by the engine. Nevertheless, when Kim Jong Un discussed North Korea's readiness to conduct an ICBM test this year, the KN-08 was probably the missile he had in mind.

The KN-08 represents a more plausible path to an ICBM than the Taepodong-2. But both missiles emerged from a process of taking existing rocket engines designed by someone else and attempting to use them to cobble together an ICBM. On March 18, North Korea showed something new—a ground test of a new engine that the country's officials said was completely indigenous (although assistance from countries such as Iran cannot be ruled out). The government's statement called the event "a historic day which can be called the March 18 revolution." The new engine appears to use the same propellants as the Musudan, but without the complicated submerged-engine design that has bedeviled North Korea's engineers.

The statement also warned that "the whole world will soon witness what eventful significance the great victory won today carries." This was apparently a reference to the Hwasong-12 intermediate-range ballistic missile, which North Korea tested on May 14. Based on images of the missile, my colleagues and I at the Center for

Nonproliferation Studies believe the Hwasong-12 uses the new "March 18" engine and is capable of carrying a nuclear weapon about 3,000 miles—just short of the technical definition of an ICBM (3,400 miles) and capable of striking Guam and the Aleutian Islands. Although the Hwasong-12 is not an ICBM, it represents a domestic capacity to design engines that should ultimately manifest itself in far more capable missiles.

KCNA / REUTERS

Kim Jong Un watches a ground test of the "March 18" engine in an undated photo, released March 2017.

ON SOLID GROUND

Finally, there is North Korea's rapidly developing solid-fueled missile program. The Taepodong-2, KN-08, and Hwasong-12 all use liquid-fueled engines, which must be fueled prior to launch. Liquid-fueled rockets are typically less mobile and require a larger number of support vehicles, whereas solid-propellant rockets, although they are less powerful, arrive from the factory fully fueled and offer more mobility. Before 2015, North Korea had tested only a few, relatively small, solid-fueled ballistic missiles. But in the past two years, it has successfully tested a two-stage medium-range missile that can be launched from a submarine and, beginning this year, a variant that is launched from land. North Korea's new generation of solid-fueled missiles represents a far more survivable missile force than its existing Scuds and Nodongs.

It is hard to say how quickly North Korea might develop a solid-propellant ICBM. The major challenge of building such missiles lies in casting motors in the large diameters necessary for them to travel long distances. The diameter of North Korea's missile is 1.5 meters—an important threshold that, although it represents progress, is well short of the larger diameters needed for an ICBM.

North Korea almost certainly has a compact fission warhead capable of fitting on a future ICBM. Pyongyang claimed that its most recent nuclear test, in September 2016, was for the purpose of standardizing a warhead small enough to arm its ballistic missile force. This was the same language North Korea used earlier in the year when Kim Jong Un posed in front of a mockup of a compact nuclear warhead next to a KN-08—the message clearly being that North Korea had tested the warhead that would arm its ICBM. With five nuclear tests under its belt, North Korea's claim is line with the progress that other nuclear powers had made at similar points in the development of their programs. For instance, China, by the time of its fifth nuclear test, had both built a nuclear weapon small enough to be delivered by a missile and developed the basic principles for the massive thermonuclear weapon it would test next.

The major question now is not whether the warhead is small enough to mount on an ICBM—it is—but whether it is rugged enough to survive the shock, vibration, and extreme temperatures that a nuclear warhead would experience on an intercontinental trajectory, in which it would be shot into space and then reenter the earth's atmosphere. A successful intercontinental launch would involve not only the durability of the warhead itself but that of the reentry vehicle—the part of the ICBM that protects the warhead from the incredible heat generated by reentering the atmosphere.

Some analysts, including within the U.S. intelligence community, have expressed doubt about whether North Korea's current reentry vehicle would survive an ICBM's journey. But no state that has developed an ICBM has been unable to develop a reentry vehicle capable of delivering a warhead. The warhead fitted to the Hwasong-12 experienced heat loads similar to those of an ICBM (although for a shorter period of time) and survived. Separately, North Korea has published images of an apparently successful ground test of a reentry vehicle last year. Similar doubts were expressed about China's nuclear warheads in the 1960s, prompting China's leaders to arm a missile with a live nuclear weapon and launch it across the country to dispel any lingering doubts. Fortunately, North Korea has not chosen to take such a step.

WAITING ON KIM

Any and all of these programs could lead to a functioning ICBM. North Korea could test a KN-08 or a converted Taepodong-2 at any time, although a first KN-08 flight test is likely to fail. Or North Korea could wait to test a far more capable ICBM, based on either the engine displayed on March 18 or the solid-fueled missile program.

North Korea's state media has stated that the country could test an ICBM at "any time and anywhere determined by the supreme headquarters of the DPRK"—a reference to Kim Jong Un. Kim's decision, however, will be as much political as technical. Does Kim value a quick demonstration of a crude capability? Is he willing to wait for a more credible ICBM? Or will he wait, hoping to explore diplomatic options to reduce tension on the peninsula? Only time will tell.

JEFFREY LEWIS is a scholar at the Middlebury Institute of International Studies and the founding publisher of the *Arms Control Wonk* blog.

© Foreign Affairs

Japan's North Korea Options

Will Tokyo Equip Itself for a Preemptive Strike?

J. Berkshire Miller

A Japanese destroyer in Sagami Bay, southwest of Tokyo, Japan, October 2015.

Earlier this month, North Korea launched four ballistic missiles toward Japan. Three of them landed within Japan's exclusive economic zone, less than 200 miles from the country's coast, in an area frequented by Japanese fishing boats. The missile test, North Korean state media claimed, was aimed at "the bases of the U.S. imperialist aggressor forces in Japan." By demonstrating that it could carry out a so-called saturation attack—one in which a massive barrage of missiles would overwhelm Japan's defenses—Pyongyang sought to weaken the credibility of the military deterrent that Japan, the United States, and South Korea have erected against it.

North Korea has conducted dozens of missile tests and three nuclear tests since Kim Jong Un took office in late 2011. Over the same period, Pyongyang's missile capabilities have grown and its arsenal's vulnerability to attack has diminished.

Last August, North Korea successfully tested a submarine-launched ballistic missile. In February, it tested an intermediate-range ballistic missile propelled by solid fuel—a technological leap that would allow Pyongyang to dramatically reduce the signs of an impending launch, helping to insulate its missiles from preemptive strikes. The Kim regime is now attempting to create a nuclear warhead small enough to attach to the tip of a missile, a step toward its ultimate goal of creating an intercontinental ballistic missile that could deliver a nuclear bomb to the continental United States. Through an elaborate shell game involving mobile missile launchers and the diversification of its launch sites, North Korea has sought to sow doubts in the United States, Japan, and South Korea about the potential efficacy of preemptive action.

All of these developments have worried Japanese policymakers, deepening a long-standing debate in Tokyo over the country's security posture. At issue is whether enhancing Japan's missile defense capabilities will be enough to meet the threat and whether Tokyo should equip itself for a preemptive strike against North Korea—a move that could raise China's ire and create domestic controversy due to Japan's own constitutional constraints.

ISSEI KATO / REUTERS

Japanese Prime Minister Shinzo Abe in the Diet after reports of a North Korean missile test, Tokyo, March 2017.

WHERE JAPAN STANDS

Japan's current defense against North Korean missiles is based on a two-tiered system. In the Sea of Japan, Japanese destroyers equipped with the Aegis missile defense system serve as the country's frontline interceptors. Land-based Patriot Advanced Capability-3 (PAC-3) batteries provide a second layer of protection. This system is effective in some respects, but it is becoming increasingly insufficient in light of the North's expanding capabilities—especially its potential capacity for a saturation attack in which multiple missiles would be launched at different targets.

As Japan's strategic position has deteriorated, Japanese policymakers' interest in new military capabilities has grown, placing a long-standing technocratic debate over how to respond to the North Korean threat at the center of the country's politics. On the same day as Pyongyang's missile test, Japanese Prime Minister Shinzo Abe told the Diet that the threat posed by North Korea had reached a "new stage." A day later, Itsunori Onodera—the chair of the ruling Liberal Democratic Party's committee dealing with the North Korean missile threat and a former defense minister—underscored the need for Japan to start considering offensive options. "If bombers attacked us or warships bombarded us, we would fire back," he told Reuters. "Striking a country lobbing missiles at us is no different." (Many opposition politicians, such as Akihisa Nagashima, a key Democratic Party member of the Diet and a former vice-minister of defense, agree that Japan's defense posture is in need of reform, though the nature of the changes is contentious.)

Japan's constitution does not necessarily prohibit the country from carrying out a preemptive strike.

In the coming months, the Liberal Democratic Party will present a report to the government outlining Japan's options for dealing with the North Korean threat. Tokyo has already committed $1 billion to upgrading its PAC-3 interceptors, and it is also considering deploying land-based Aegis systems to complement its sea-based capabilities. In February, Japan conducted a successful joint test with the United States of the Standard Missile-3 Block IIA system—a missile interceptor tied to the Aegis system that, if deployed in Japan, would improve the country's missile defenses both on land and at sea.

Many in Tokyo are now considering adding a third layer to Japan's missile defenses by asking Washington to deploy the Terminal High Altitude Area Defense (THAAD) system to Japan. THAAD's sophisticated radar and its ability to destroy incoming projectiles at a high altitude would reduce the leakage produced by intercepted missiles, limiting the damage that their debris would cause in populated areas—an advantage that would be even more valuable in the event of a nuclear attack. (The United States is currently deploying THAAD to South Korea, in a move that China has opposed.)

Such measures would be useful, but they might not be enough to deter a North Korean attack or to withstand a particularly sophisticated one. That is why Japanese policymakers are also debating acquiring weapons that would allow their country to destroy North Korean missiles before they are launched, perhaps in conjunction with the United States—a capability that Japan now lacks. Japan could buy Tomahawk missiles from the United States, for example, or it could use the F-35A fighter, which Japan is slated to procure in the coming years, to strike North Korean targets. Precision guided missiles, such as Lockheed Martin's Joint Air-to-Surface Standoff Missile, are another option. The best choices among these preemptive options are those pieces that would work well with Japan's destroyers in the Sea of Japan, such as the F35A and Tomahawk cruise missiles.

KIM HONG-JI / REUTERS

People watch a news report on a North Korean missile test at a train station in Seoul, South Korea, February 2017.

TALK ISN'T CHEAP

The debate over whether to acquire these kinds of weapons will probably intensify in the coming months if North Korea steps up its provocations. That will likely complicate the debate over revising Japan's pacifist constitution, which has kept Tokyo from maintaining a traditional military since the end of World War II. It has also prohibited Japan from procuring offensive weapons systems, such as intercontinental ballistic missiles and long-range strategic bombers, which would exceed the minimum level of force needed for the country's self-defense. The document has been a lightning rod for criticism from conservatives who claim that it is overly prohibitive. Revising it appears to be one of Abe's major goals; whether he will be able to do so before he leaves office is unclear. Time running out is not as much of an issue as it was before:

Abe could theoretically remain in office until 2021, thanks to a change in the LDP's rules, which now permit a third term for the party's leader.

Even in its current form, however, Japan's constitution does not necessarily prohibit the country from carrying out a preemptive strike against a threat from North Korea. The constitution may permit preemptive actions when they are the only way to safeguard Japan's security against an imminent danger and when they are carried out with a proportional amount of force. What's more, although the prevailing interpretation of the constitution places the overseas deployment of Japanese forces with the aim of using force beyond the limits of self-defense, it does not explicitly rule out striking overseas targets using equipment based in Japan. This leaves the door open for lawmakers and lawyers to justify using preemptive weapons. In any case, the procurement and deployment of weapons such as cruise missiles would not in itself need to fulfill the constitution's requirements for the use of force.

But there are challenges to gaining preemptive strike capabilities that go beyond the constitution. First, it's not clear whether such capabilities—even when combined with a U.S.-led surgical strike—would be able to neutralize Pyongyang's missile programs, which are being developed to withstand preemptive attacks. Second, the costs associated with such a strike, which would probably include retaliatory actions by North Korea against Japan and South Korea, may outweigh the benefits. And finally, Japan's development of preemptive capabilities would raise eyebrows among pacifists in Japan and among officials elsewhere in the region—especially in China—and help feed into false narratives about Japan's alleged remilitarization. Beijing would also likely protest the deployment of THAAD or other missile defense systems to Japan. Even though these arguments from China would ring hollow in light of Beijing's own ability to strike Japan, it will be hard for Tokyo to bolster its national security without exacerbating broader tensions in northeast Asia. Japanese officials and their allies in South Korea and the United States should continue to publicly discuss their options anyway, if only to signal to Pyongyang that its escalations will not be met with silence.

J. BERKSHIRE MILLER is a Tokyo-based International Affairs Fellow at the Council on Foreign Relations and a Senior Fellow on East Asia at the EastWest Institute.

Caught in the Middle

The North Korean Threat Is Ultimately Seoul's Problem

Katharine H.S. Moon

U.S. President Donald Trump arrives for a joint news conference with South Korean President Moon Jae-in in the Rose Garden of the White House in Washington, D.C., June 30, 2017.

After sending a missile over Japan on Tuesday morning, North Korea has returned to threatening the United States, claiming its latest provocation was only a prelude to what awaits Guam. To be sure, Pyongyang takes pleasure at taunting the most powerful country in the world with its growing nuclear capabilities, but the United States would be simply wrong to assume that it is the ultimate target of North Korea's belligerence.

For the United States, a nuclear armed North Korea undercuts its security and traditional policy objectives, such as nonproliferation, and destabilizes the East Asia region. But for South Korea, it is an existential threat. Given the high tensions of late, Seoul fears being dragged into a war or, at the very least, falling victim to limited military exchanges between Washington and Pyongyang.

South Korea faces a triad of pressures—from its enemy in the north, its superpower ally across the Pacific, and its largest trading partner, China. President Moon Jae-in, however, who has been in office for only three months, has been dealing with the stresses remarkably well. In the early weeks of his presidency, Moon took a softer rhetorical approach toward the volatile Donald Trump, fully agreeing with the U.S. president's suggestion to tighten allied coordination and impose tougher sanctions on Pyongyang. The new South Korean leader surprised those who had assumed that as a pro-engagement, liberal opposition leader, he would go easy on North Korea. After Pyongyang conducted an ICBM test in early July, Moon emphasized that "more than just a statement" was needed and then proposed that Seoul and Washington conduct a decapitation missile-firing drill, which would prepare for the elimination of the top North Korean leadership in case of war.

But Moon had also insisted, upon assuming office, that South Korea suspend and review the full deployment of the advanced U.S. anti-missile defense system known as THAAD (Terminal High Altitude Area Defense), which had already begun prior to his presidency. To his North Korean counterpart, Moon extended several olive branches, ranging from generous humanitarian assistance, military dialogue to reduce border tensions, and the reunion of families divided by the demilitarized zone. (Pyongyang has rejected all offers thus far.) Moon's gestures are notable for avoiding the self-righteous and superior attitude of his predecessor, the impeached and deposed Park Geun-hye. Pyongyang excoriated her, and interpreted her pursuit of preparations for unification to mean its collapse or its forced absorption by South Korea. Still, inter-Korean relations fell to a new low during Park's tenure.

In August, Moon began hardening his rhetoric toward Washington, declaring that he would never let South Korea get embroiled in another peninsular war. He boldly stated that any U.S. military action against North Korea would require South Korean consent. Although most national leaders reserve the right to assert national sovereignty, South Korean presidents have rarely been so explicit about telling Washington what it can or cannot do. Moon may be hoping to be more assertive in dealing with both North Korea and the United States to avoid getting trapped by either's initiatives.

This contrasts with the previous administration, which tended to wait for Washington to take the lead on North Korea. But former President Barack Obama's "strategic patience" approach frustrated South Koreans and made them anxious to formulate an effective policy against North Korea. Moon, on the other hand, has now made it clear that he will take a tough approach toward Pyongyang while keeping the door ajar for dialogue. On August 17, he announced that he would enforce a "red line" for North Korea's nuclear capabilities, which no world leader has been willing to do. In a speech, he explained that the threshold would be "completing the development of an intercontinental ballistic missile and being able to weaponize it with a nuclear warhead." At the same time, Moon has sought to counter Trump's wild impulsiveness in order to prevent war and to keep the possibility of inter-Korean dialogue open.

What might make Moon more effective in his approach to balance openness with toughness is to upgrade the South Korean military. In late July, after a series of missile tests from Pyongyang, Seoul requested talks with Washington about increasing the payload of South Korean missiles. Boosting the power of its missiles would heighten Seoul's ability to destroy underground bunkers or nuclear sites in North Korea. Seoul also seeks to build nuclear submarines to counter the North's improvements in submarine-launched ballistic missiles, which are part of Pyongyang's efforts to diversify its nuclear arsenal, increase strategic flexibility, and reduce the vulnerability of its land-based systems.

More recently, Moon commanded the ministry of defense to enhance war readiness in the case of a North Korean incursion or attack. His call for comprehensive defense reform serves two purposes. It will strengthen its position against North Korea and also put it in a better position to take over operational command from the United States should war break out. Both are intended to increase South Korean sovereignty and command over its own security.

Moon's biggest challenge at the moment is dealing with domestic calls for nuclearizing South Korea by reintroducing U.S. tactical nuclear weapons or building its own arsenal. Although the idea of building nuclear weapons is usually supported by the conservative opposition, it is gaining broader traction. In September 2016, a Gallup survey found that 58 percent of South Koreans supported the development of a home-grown nuclear arsenal and only 34 percent opposed it. Although Moon's administration is adamantly against nuclearization, he was also anti-THAAD but has since relented and allowed for its full deployment.

Given Pyongyang's rollout of missile tests and nuclear devices, and Trump's "America First" rhetoric and inconsistency on foreign policy, it is likely that South Koreans' support for nuclearization will grow. This of course would violate the 1992 Joint Declaration on Denuclearization on the Korean Peninsula signed by Seoul and Pyongyang, but the latter had already broken its promise decades ago. Nevertheless, a homegrown South Korean nuclear arsenal would likely trigger a nuclear arms race in East Asia and lead to the breakdown of the nuclear umbrella that the United States has maintained for over half a century. It would also eliminate South Korea's moral high ground and political justification for demanding the North's denuclearization. For now, Moon has continued to toughen his stance. After North Korea's saber rattling on Tuesday, Seoul responded by sending eight rockets toward the North Korean border and releasing images of its own missile tests.

The nuclear standoff with North Korea is also putting pressure on South Korea's troubled economy. Young people, especially, despair over joblessness and whether they can have a viable future. South Korea's unemployment rate for those 15-24 years of age experienced the highest increase among all OECD countries between December 2016 and April 2017.

China, in taking advantage of the situation, is using economic tools to punish Seoul for deploying THAAD. It has successfully called on citizens to boycott South Korean products that are produced by large conglomerates such as Hyundai, Kia, and the Lotte Group, whose land holdings in South Korea were used by the Korean government to house the THAAD system. Lotte Shopping Group reported an 88 percent drop in second quarter earnings in China compared to the same period last year. Nearly 30 percent of Lotte's sales outside South Korea come from China. It was reported in September that the Chinese retaliatory boycott has seriously hurt Hyundai Motors, too. A 41 percent drop in sales in the first seven months of this year hurt cash flow and caused the temporary closing of four manufacturing plants. Chinese tourism to South Korea has been prohibited and lucrative cultural products—from Kpop to classical music concerts—have been unilaterally blocked. South Korea has lost an estimated $4.7 billion in tourism earnings from Chinese visitors based on 2016 spending figures.

International pressure for China to enforce tough sanctions against North Korea has not made a substantial dent in slowing or stopping the advancement of Pyongyang's nuclear capability. And yet, China's unofficial sanctions against South Korea are causing real economic pain to chaebol (family-owned conglomerates), cultural entrepreneurs, and average workers alike at a time when good diplomatic relations with Beijing are critical for Seoul's geopolitical and domestic economic goals.

On the other side of the Pacific, the Trump administration is intent on pushing tougher trade demands on both China and South Korea while pressing each to deal collaboratively with the nuclear challenge from North Korea. This puts South Korea on a tough path: it must balance its security and economic priorities while also improving relations with two indispensable powers. Seen in this light, it is no wonder that the North, sensing a lack of solidarity among those who could rein it in, has decided in recent weeks to test the strength of the alliance.

KATHARINE H.S. MOON is Professor of Political Science at Wellesley College and Nonresident Senior Fellow at the Brookings Institution. She is author of *Protesting America: Democracy and US-Korea Relations.*

China's North Korean Liability

How Washington Can Get Beijing to Rein In Pyongyang

Zhu Feng

U.S. President Donald Trump and Chinese President Xi Jinping attend the bilateral meeting at the G20 leaders summit in Hamburg, Germany, July 8, 2017.

On July 8, at the G-20 summit in Hamburg, U.S. President Donald Trump held a cordial press conference with Chinese President Xi Jinping where they discussed how they would address the growing threat of North Korea. Just days before, on July 4, as many Americans were observing Independence Day, North Korea announced that it had successfully tested an intercontinental ballistic missile capable of reaching Alaska. This was likely on Trump's mind at the summit when he told this Chinese counterpart that he believed the two of them would "come to a successful conclusion" in reining in Pyongyang. The key challenge, of course, is how they will get there.

For over two and a half decades, international efforts to curb North Korea's nuclear ambitions have been in vain. Pyongyang has repeatedly and blatantly violated its multiple commitments to denuclearize and shows no willingness to fulfill its promises to do so. Make no mistake: a North Korea with nuclear weapons is not a problem just for the United States and China but a collective one. Former U.S. President Barack Obama's policy of "strategic patience" failed. Now, as U.S. Secretary of State Rex Tillerson has made it abundantly clear, particularly during his visit to Beijing in March, the Trump administration hopes to change the U.S. approach to North Korea. But as much as Washington has failed to rein in North Korea, so has China. Beijing must face the reality that the Kim family's nuclear and missile programs are opposed to Chinese interests and a threat to regional stability. As momentum once again builds in Beijing to reassess its relationship with North Korea, it is time for China to make a significant shift in its policy, once and for all.

AN UNSUSTAINABLE STATUS QUO

China-North Korean relations have been slowly souring since the end of the Cold War. North Korea ceased being China's ally long ago when Beijing decided, against Pyongyang's objections, to normalize its ties with Seoul in 1992. A recent example of their dysfunctional relationship is the killing of Kim Jong-nam, former leader Kim Jong-il's eldest son, by North Korean agents in Malaysia. Its heavily publicized nature signaled Pyongyang's utter disrespect for Beijing, under whose protection the elder Kim had lived in Macau.

China has long offered various forms of support to the North based on their shared history, but the relationship has turned into a heavy burden for China, holding Beijing back from playing a greater role in the global and regional order.

Beijing is, of course, highly aware of the costs if it continues to keep Pyongyang within its fold. The completely divergent paths they have taken to fulfil their basic goals of peace and development since early the 1990s have kept the two countries apart. For today's Chinese, North Korea today is reminiscent of the deplorable era under Chairman Mao Zedong. But for North Koreans, China is an "accomplice" to American imperialism. Despite this, Beijing has not been ready yet to "give up" North Korea, since doing so would require an explicit policy decision, such as pulling its lifeline to North Korea or literally deeming it a "public threat."

Trump once complained of China's failure to put enough pressure on Pyongyang. Although his warm meeting in April with Xi at Mar-a-Lago gave the impression that the two leaders were inclined to work together in "harnessing" North Korea, China's lack of determination in fully abandoning North Korea may disappoint the Trump administration.

North Korea's increasingly belligerent behavior has irritated China to an ever-greater extent. Pyongyang conducted 15 missile tests in 2015 and 33 in 2016, and so far in 2017, it has tested ten. In 2016, Pyongyang conducted two nuclear tests despite ever-increasing international pressure. Although North Korea's aim is to destroy the United States, China's capital is also well within range of some of Pyongyang's Scud missiles. It would only take one unpredictable official in the military chain or some such for North Korea to turn on a nominal ideological ally in the most drastic way. The threat of a nuclear attack is not the only thing China must worry about; the risk of a North Korean nuclear accident spewing radiation across the Chinese border could spell catastrophe in megacities such as Shenyang in the Liaoning province, which has over eight million people and is located just 124 miles from the North Korean border.

Chinese public opinion toward North Korea is also worsening, with many Chinese now critical of Beijing's long-standing indecision to deal adequately with Pyongyang. A growing number of Chinese citizens believe that the North is a bad actor that poses a severe threat to China's security interests, according to polls conducted by the Global Times. Another portion of the Chinese populace believes that Beijing should not assume the responsibility for denuclearizing the Korean Peninsula—Washington should. China's only role, they believe, is to support reconciliation while bolstering negotiations, even if many Chinese are aware that such a limited role for China is remarkably inconsistent with the real threat posed by the North.

Concern over North Korea has also been on the rise in South Korea, leading Seoul to allow the U.S. deployment of the Terminal High-Altitude Air Defense ballistic missile defense system, against China's strong protestations. This is because THAAD interceptors are capable not only of shooting down North Korean missiles but also of obstructing missiles launched from China. This growing geostrategic complexity triggered by Pyongyang requires that Washington and Beijing not distract themselves with this negative spillover and focus on finding a workable solution.

This is what a great many Chinese citizens want. When Beijing recently shuttered the Chinese branches of the South Korean-owned Lotte supermarket chain, providing land for the THAAD deployment, the move was viewed domestically as unconstructive. Although Beijing also managed to stir up Chinese nationalistic fervor by insisting that THAAD is a threat to China's national security, it was arguably little more than a cleverly engineered political ruse. Actual popular resentment toward North Korea is surging, and Beijing's passive North Korea policy is increasingly under fire domestically. For example, the Chinese academia and media are largely and distinctively divided over how Beijing should approach Pyongyang, and considering that many Chinese media outlets are wholly state owned, this signals that the likelihood of a reassessment of China's commitment to North Korea is slowly but firmly gaining favor in Beijing.

INCREMENTAL HELP

It is fortunate that just as Chinese public opinion is turning against the North, the Trump administration has begun pushing China to get tougher on Pyongyang. And since ties between Beijing and Seoul have reached their lowest point in history, this is yet another reason why China needs to reconsider its impotent and misguided policy of trying to balance the two Koreas against one another.

Trump has made himself clear: the failed Six Party Talks of yesteryear are over, and North Korea's continued actions in contempt of the international community mean that U.S. strategic patience is over. As a result, all options are now on the table. Chinese leadership should view this as an opportunity not only to improve ties with the United States but also to change its official stance on North Korea.

Yet the debate in Beijing is partially stymied by feelings that U.S. animosity toward China remains unchanged, so China should do little to help the United States solve the North Korea issue. Of course, this faction opposes China's unilateral action to pressure North Korea. Such opposition no doubt adds to the Chinese government's hesitation to utilize a number of economic tools at its disposal, such as ending oil deliveries to the North. But if the two powers could maintain a forward-looking approach to regional security, they could work together to ensure that North Korea truly feels the pain of international sanctions. Beijing's suspension of coal imports from the North, for example, was a big blow to Kim Jong-Un's regime, as Pyongyang has used most of its income from coal imports to develop its nuclear weapons.

In this regard, Trump needs to understand the complexity of China's thinking on North Korean policy. Getting China to take more responsibility on North Korea requires both a gentle and a hard push. The Trump administration has made it clear that it will not tolerate a nuclear North Korea—but Beijing has heard this before. Despite the rhetorical flourish, to the experienced Chinese diplomat, the Trump administration's policy sounds quite a lot like those of Presidents George W. Bush and Obama: a desire to achieve denuclearization but an unwillingness for this to come at the cost of war on the peninsula. Chinese President Xi Jinping is similarly bound by the strategic logic of China's long-standing approach to its petulant neighbor— avoiding the dangers and uncertainty of war and instability by looking past the present consequences of North Korea's actions. Xi's view of North Korea is still dominated by the fear of a reunified Korea under Seoul, which may want U.S. forces to remain in the country. This is a legitimate concern, but it is possible, given Trump's isolationist stance, that he might consider not stationing U.S. troops above the 38th parallel or deploying offensive capabilities to a unified Korea.

The real difference that Beijing and Washington must overcome, however, is China's fear of chaos in North Korea spilling over its own borders. Such instability could spell an unmanageable situation involving all sorts of crises: civil war, famine, and mass displacement, not to mention the danger of fissile material and biological weapons falling into even more unstable hands. Of course, some Chinese hardliners take this view even further, suggesting that it would be foolish for China to take the North Korean burden off the back of its greatest competitor. They argue that, considering that the United States is in many ways a thorn in the flesh to Chinese interests in areas such as Taiwan and the South China Sea, it would be against China's national interests to release the United States from this problem.

Today, many within China believe that Beijing must reevaluate its relationship with both Koreas, which essentially means abandoning Pyongyang. It is both the strategic and the moral choice. Choosing South Korea, a democracy with a strong economy, will place China on the right side of history. China's lack of clear direction on this issue is beginning to negatively affect its reputation, with Beijing seen by the international community as reluctant to cooperate or behave responsibly. These are not traits that behoove a rising power.

BEIJING'S ONE POLICY OPTION

Going forward, China has three options: it can work more closely with the United States on getting tougher on North Korea, continue to drag its feet and avoid rocking the boat, or reinforce its alignment with Russia and use North Korea as a piece in a geopolitical chess game against the United States and South Korea. Of these options, only the first choice aligns with China's long-term interests to integrate with the international community. The question is how to ease Beijing's hesitations regarding this choice. In other words, how can the hawks in Beijing be brushed aside to make way for a more decisive and progressive policy while continuing to save face for all decision makers?

There are no easy answers, but the U.S.-China bilateral relationship is certainly a priority for Xi, particularly because of the strong anti-China elements within the Trump administration. The best way to improve the relationship is by cooperating on North Korean denuclearization, which would bring China the added benefit of increased regional security.

Economic pressure is another avenue forward in solving the North Korea problem. There are many avenues for implementing sanctions: reducing North Korea's coal and oil imports, shutting down North Korean front companies operating in China, expelling North Korean laborers toiling away in Chinese factories, barring Chinese banks from doing any further business with Pyongyang's moneymen, and cracking down on a host of other avenues for cash to reach Kim Jong-un. China has halted operations for many if not all of these activities at one point or another over the last 15 years, sometimes simultaneously. But now is the time for China to be utterly comprehensive, to seal all the cracks and thus send a clear signal to North Korea—and the Trump administration—that Beijing will not stand idly by. Such pressure, of course, will not work on its own. Beijing and Washington must cooperate or at least coordinate their efforts for engagement with Pyongyang to demonstrate that Kim can still choose a diplomatic solution to resolve these tensions. As Pyongyang grows ever more belligerent, it becomes increasingly urgent for Beijing and Washington to restore cooperation over North Korea.

ZHU FENG is Director of the Institute of International Studies and Executive Director of the China Center for Collaborative Studies of the South China Sea at Nanjing University.

August 9, 2017

The Wolf of Pyongyang

How Kim Jong Un Resembles a CEO

David Kang

Kim Jong Un waves at participants in the Sixth Congress of the Democratic Women's Union of Korea, November 2016.

Western commentators often treat North Korean Supreme Leader Kim Jong Un as a joke. In private conversations I have heard U.S. administration officials and military leaders occasionally refer to him as a "fat boy," a "young playboy," and a "laughingstock." Ambassador to the UN Nikki Haley has even publicly questioned whether he is crazy. Yet calling the North Korean leader names is a mistake, not because it is rude but because it underestimates his abilities. Kim is no buffoon. To treat him like one is to misunderstand the threat posed by North Korea and its leader—an especially grave mistake today, as tensions between Pyongyang and Washington flare up on a regular basis.

A better way to view Kim is as a new CEO taking over a company—call it North Korea, Inc. Doing so allows observers to bypass discussions of his mental health (and the focus on him as a dictator) and instead to examine his qualities as a leader. In the business world, the role of the CEO is central to any company's success. An incoming CEO, especially one entering a struggling company, must take control and lead. He must provide his company with a vision and guide its implementation. A new CEO needs to motivate his employees, explain to them where the company is going and why, and regularize processes of performance and evaluation so that expectations are clear. He needs to do this while also culling the ranks and eliminating dead weight and petty factionalism in the ranks of middle management. An effective leader identifies the malcontents, fires, sidelines, or motivates them, and rewards and promotes those who share his agenda and can move his vision forward. In short, a good CEO is able to get everybody marching in the same direction.

These are precisely the steps that Kim is taking. Kim has survived six years as leader of North Korea while instituting a clear personal vision for the country's direction. He is apparently unthreatened by any internal challenges to his rule, and indeed looks to be comfortably in charge in Pyongyang. The North Korean government shows no signs of collapsing and seems more stable now than under his father, Kim Jong Il. The debate about whether Kim is rational is harmful to U.S. foreign-policy making because it diverts outsiders from addressing the real issues with North Korea—its active nuclear weapons program and horrific human rights abuses—and obfuscates Kim's proven ability to lead his country down a path that external pressure has been powerless to weaken. Viewing Kim as CEO, rather than as an ordinary political leader, also emphasizes the non-political aspects of his rule—what leaders in any organization must do to create expectations and stability.

By making economic development a key element of state ideology, Kim has signaled a break from the past.

NORTH KOREA, INC.

Perhaps the most important thing that a new CEO must do is to articulate a bold and clear vision that serves as a metric and motivator for the rest of the firm. Kim's vision for North Korea is clearly articulated in the byungjin line. Adopted by the Workers' Party of Korea (WPK) Central Committee in April 2013, byungjin calls for the simultaneous development of North Korea's economy and its nuclear weapons, replacing the so-called military-first doctrine of Kim Jong Il. By making economic development a key element of state ideology, Kim has signaled a break from the past. Under Kim Jong Il and his predecessor, Kim Il Sung, North Korean propaganda emphasized the people's strength in the face of adversity and willingness to suffer for the sake of their country. This positive spin on hardship justified an enormous range of practices, from a campaign pressing North Koreans to eat two meals per day in 1991, when the country was struck by famine, to various worker mobilization campaigns. Kim Il Sung had called for North Koreans to sacrifice for the sake of the country as far back as the Chollima campaigns of the 1950s, in which ordinary North Koreans were drafted into work units for mass construction and infrastructure projects; people were urged to "donate" their labor and work 18-hour days, and were even required to time their bathroom breaks.

Kim Jong Un, by contrast, has said that North Koreans "should no longer be hungry." Typical of this approach is a speech from 2015:

> *The most important task facing us today is to improve the people's standard of living at an earlier date. Our people have so far waged an intense struggle to build socialism ... they have never enjoyed a plentiful life to their heart's content. Whenever I am reminded of my failure to provide a rich life to these laudable people, who, in spite of their difficult living conditions, have firmly trusted and followed only our Party and remained faithful to their pure sense of moral obligation to the great Comrades Kim Il Sung and Kim Jong Il, I cannot get sleep.... We should provide our people, who have entrusted their all to the Party and stood by it in braving all manner of trials and hardships together with the Party, with the most abundant and happiest life in the world.*

This focus on material comfort instead of selfless sacrifice marks a clear change in tone from the past. And, although this is rhetoric, it is consequential nonetheless—Kim cannot gesture at economic improvement without raising expectations among those from the top of the party to the bottom of the country's social hierarchy. Byungjin does not mean that Kim has embarked on wholesale economic reforms—far from it. But it does mean that Kim has explicitly linked his legitimacy to his ability to make good on the promise of both economic development and the pursuit of nuclear weapons. Under his direction, North Korea is moving forward on both. Given the West's near-exclusive focus on North Korea's nuclear and missile programs it is easy to overlook its economic initiatives. Kim has increased the autonomy granted to state-owned factories over what they produce and how they find suppliers and customers, and North Korean farm workers can now sell any their surplus once they meet government quotas. Western analysis of a parade held on April 15, however, was almost solely concerned with assessing the military hardware on display.

Widely overlooked was the fact that in the two-and-a-half-hour-long parade, the military segment lasted for only twenty minutes. The other two hours emphasized economic successes, such as the opening of new shopping districts and new government-approved markets (Jangmadang), as well as environmental challenges and simple celebrations of the Kim family. When Kim was seen standing on a balcony to review the parade, standing either side of him were Hwang Pyong So, vice marshall of the Korean People's Army, and Pak Pong Ju, premier of North Korea and most important official in charge of the economy.

KCNA / REUTERS

Kim Jong Un visits a foodstuff factory in Pyongyang, January 2016.

Indeed, a week before the April parade, the Kim government told some 200 foreign journalists to wake up at 5 AM and leave their cellphones and laptops in their hotel rooms. Their minders put them on buses and, after a two-hour security check, dropped them off just past the Chinese embassy in downtown Pyongyang. Given the security, the secrecy, and the tensions with the United States, reporters had originally guessed that they might be preparing to see a nuclear test or a new intercontinental ballistic missile. Instead, they were shown to Ryomyong Street, a new luxury housing and shopping district, proudly referred to by state media as "green" and "energy efficient." The meaning of the display could not be more clear: Kim was emphasizing how important business, the economy, and quality of life (at least in Pyongyang) is to his vision. As Prime Minister Pak Pong Ju said in a speech at the event, "The completion of this street is more powerful than 100 nuclear warheads."

A NEW NORMAL

If Kim, as a young CEO, has articulated a new vision for North Korea, Inc., so too has he dramatically changed the corporate culture in order to implement it. When Kim took power in December 2011, so little was known about him that even his age was indeterminate. But today, he has proved that he has the skills of a much more experienced leader. Kim has begun to create predictability and regularity in the North Korean government. He has created processes and clarified priorities, most importantly by identifying the byungjin line. And he has dealt with middle management, firing some top officials, rewarding some, and moving others around. In doing so, he has improved his country's ability to pursue and achieve his goals.

If Kim has articulated a new vision for North Korea, Inc., so too has he dramatically changed the corporate culture in order to implement it.

One of the ways that Kim has begun to change his government's culture is by regularizing its bureaucratic processes. Kim has instituted reforms to expand the scope of the private economy and attempt to rein in military expenditures, for example. But a CEO's leadership is perhaps more important in large, symbolic actions. Under Kim Jong Il, there were no regular party meetings or New Year's Day speeches, and other organizational practices fell into disuse. Before May 2016, when Kim Jong Un held the Seventh Party Congress, the WPK had gone 36 years since its last official meeting, the Sixth Party Congress in 1980—this despite party rules stipulating that a congress be held every four years. He has also suggested the Eighth Congress would be held in 2020, returning the WPK to its mandated schedule. All of this appears aimed at creating more consistency, and systematized, regularized bureaucracy.

In addition to the congresses, Kim has renewed the tradition of giving an annual New Year's Day speech. Kim's first speech, on January 1, 2013, was the first since his grandfather's final address in 1994. Significantly, Kim gave the speech from the KWP Central Committee building, emphasizing that he intends to cement the party's preeminence over other institutions. And at the Seventh Party Congress, Kim announced the first five-year plan since the early 1980s. The economist and North Korea watcher Rüdiger Frank calls this suite of changes a "new normal," one that is reviving many elements of Kim Il Sung's rule.

Kim has also been hard at work reshaping his senior staff. Due to the opacity of North Korean politics, it can be difficult for outside observers both to follow Kim's personnel moves and to interpret their meaning—in December 2013, the purge and execution of Kim's uncle Jang Song Thaek, then believed to be the second most powerful man in North Korea, prompted wide speculation that Kim was in the midst of massive power struggle and that his position was weak. But since then Kim has consolidated his power, and the purge now looks to have been a dramatic show of force. In other cases, supposedly purged officials have shown up later in powerful positions. Vice Marshal Choe Ryong Hae, thought to have been purged in October 2015, reappeared in official photographs in January 2016. Ri Yong Gil, the former army chief of staff, was even reported to have been executed in February 2016 before appearing at the Seventh Party Congress a few months later to receive his four-star generalship.

KCNA / REUTERS

Kim Jong Un waves during a WPK party conference in Pyongyang, April 2012.

Indeed, there may be no better evidence of how badly outside observers have misunderstood Kim's moves than the number of supposed purges that have later turned out to be nothing of the sort. Given the opacity of North Korea's bureaucracy, it is no surprise that Westerners have been guilty of overinterpretation. But if one views Kim as a CEO taking over a company, it is no surprise that there is so much staff turnover. Kim is likely finding people he can work with, trying them out in different positions, and slowly consolidating his own senior executive team. Like a good corporate executive, he is identifying leaders, culling middle management, and instituting regular institutional processes throughout the government.

There are, of course, multiple reasons for Kim's moves—most important, that Kim is ensuring his own survival and eliminating enemies. But to view his moves solely as those of a dictator consolidating his power is to overlook how important it is for any leader to find an executive team he trusts and can work with. By understanding personnel changes first as an outcome of internal power struggles, outsiders are often led to embarrassing overreactions about alleged purges.

IT'S NO JOKE

North Korea's leader seems secure in his own power and unintimidated by outside threats. Donald Trump's inauguration as president of the United States set off an unprecedented flurry of commentary about whether Washington and Pyongyang were close to war, and has continued essentially unabated through the first six months of Trump's administration. But North Korea, which has spent seven decades under threat from the United States, seemed quite comfortable with Trump's saber-rattling. Indeed, Washington is playing into Kim's hands, justifying his byungjin line with its aggressive rhetoric and equal emphasis on nuclear weapons as well as economic development.

There is also good evidence that, despite international sanctions on North Korea and Pyongyang's resistance to Chinese-style market reform, the country's economy has stabilized and is even growing. Although any measures should be used with caution, the Bank of Korea claims that North Korea's economy grew 3.9 percent in 2016, the fastest rate since 1999. The famine has ended and no imminent crisis looms. Reforms, halting as they are, continue to move forward. According to the research group Beyond Parallel, North Korean households now earn nearly 75 percent of their income from markets. Foreign trade is increasing, too: India is now North Korea's third-largest trade partner, and Russian-North Korean trade grew 73 percent in the first two months of 2017. Some of this is a result of events and decisions taken before Kim became leader in North Korea, but the point remains that Kim is continuing down a path of economic reform as a central element of his leadership vision.

Viewing North Korea as a joke ignores the reality of Kim's tenure. Judging him as a CEO provides a much more accurate way to assess his leadership style, and by that measure he seems to be firmly in control, setting a vision and surrounding himself with the people he needs to succeed. There is recurrent speculation in the West both about whether Kim Jong Un himself is a weak dictator clinging to power and whether his regime is on the brink of collapse. Viewed as a CEO, however, Kim does not appear threatened, and neither does his government. Indeed, both appear increasingly stable. Kim's rule is comprehensive and addresses issues beyond the U.S. threat to North Korean security, and he seems to be making progress on the economic aspects of his vision. This progress, moreover, has occurred despite tremendous external pressure put on the country. The outside world is looking at a long relationship with Kim Jong Un and North Korea—it should at least try to understand him.

DAVID C. KANG is Professor of International Relations and Business at the University of Southern California, where he also directs the Korean Studies Institute and the Center for International Studies. His latest book, "American Grand Strategy and East Asian Security in the 21st Century," will be published by Cambridge University Press later this year.

The Korean Missile Crisis

Why Deterrence Is Still the Best Option

Scott D. Sagan

Kim Jong Un waves during a celebration of the founding of the ruling Workers' Party of Korea in Pyongyang, October 2015.

It is time for the U.S. government to admit that it has failed to prevent North Korea from acquiring nuclear weapons and intercontinental ballistic missiles that can reach the United States. North Korea no longer poses a nonproliferation problem; it poses a nuclear deterrence problem. The gravest danger now is that North Korea, South Korea, and the United States will stumble into a catastrophic war that none of them wants.

The world has traveled down this perilous path before. In 1950, the Truman administration contemplated a preventive strike to keep the Soviet Union from acquiring nuclear weapons but decided that the resulting conflict would resemble World War II in scope and that containment and deterrence were better options. In the 1960s, the Kennedy administration feared that Chinese leader Mao Zedong was mentally unstable and proposed a joint strike against the nascent Chinese nuclear program to the Soviets. (Moscow rejected the idea.) Ultimately, the United States learned to live with a nuclear Russia and a nuclear China. It can now learn to live with a nuclear North Korea.

Doing so will not be risk free, however. Accidents, misperceptions, and volatile leaders could all too easily cause disaster. The Cold War offers important lessons in how to reduce these risks by practicing containment and deterrence wisely. But officials in the Pentagon and the White House face a new and unprecedented challenge: they must deter North Korean leader Kim Jong Un while also preventing U.S. President Donald Trump from bumbling into war. U.S. military leaders should make plain to their political superiors and the American public that any U.S. first strike on North Korea would result in a devastating loss of American and South Korean lives. And civilian leaders must convince Kim that the United States will not attempt to overthrow his regime unless he begins a war. If the U.S. civilian and military leaderships perform these tasks well, the same approach that prevented nuclear catastrophe during the Cold War can deter Pyongyang until the day that communist North Korea, like the Soviet Union before it, collapses under its own weight.

DANGER OF DEATH

The international relations scholar Robert Litwak has described the current standoff with North Korea as "the Cuban missile crisis in slow motion," and several pundits, politicians, and academics have repeated that analogy. But the current Korean missile crisis is even more dangerous than the Cuban one. For one thing, the Cuban missile crisis did not involve a new country becoming a nuclear power. In 1962, the Soviet Union was covertly stationing missiles and nuclear warheads in Cuba when U.S. intelligence discovered the operation. During the resulting crisis, Cuban Prime Minister Fidel Castro feared an imminent U.S. air strike and invasion and wrote to Soviet Premier Nikita Khrushchev advocating a nuclear strike on the United States "to eliminate such danger forever through an act of clear legitimate defense, however harsh and terrible the solution would be." When Khrushchev received the message, he told a meeting of his senior leadership, "This is insane; Fidel wants to drag us into the grave with him!" Luckily, the Soviet Union maintained control of its nuclear weapons, and Castro did not possess any of his own; his itchy fingers were not on the nuclear trigger.

Kim, in contrast, already presides over an arsenal that U.S. intelligence agencies believe contains as many as 60 nuclear warheads. Some uncertainty still exists about whether North Korea can successfully mount those weapons on a missile capable of hitting the continental United States, but history cautions against wishful thinking. The window of opportunity for a successful U.S. attack to stop the North Korean nuclear program has closed.

At the time of the Cuban missile crisis, both the American and the Soviet nuclear war plans were heavily geared toward preemption. Each country's system featured a built-in option to launch nuclear weapons if officials believed that an enemy attack was imminent and unavoidable. This produced a danger that the strategist Thomas Schelling called "the reciprocal fear of surprise attack." That fear was why Khrushchev was so alarmed when a U.S. U-2 spy plane accidentally flew into Soviet airspace during the crisis. As he wrote to U.S. President John F. Kennedy on the final day of the crisis: "Is it not a fact that an intruding American plane could be easily taken for a nuclear bomber, which might push us to a fateful step?" Today, the world faces an even more complex and dangerous problem: a three-way fear of surprise attack. North Korea, South Korea, and the United States are all poised to launch preemptive strikes. In such an unstable situation, the risk that an accident, a false warning, or a misperceived military exercise could lead to a war is alarmingly high.

Another factor that makes today's situation more dangerous than the Cuban missile crisis are the leaders involved. In 1962, the standoff included one volatile leader, Castro, who held radical misperceptions of the consequences of a nuclear war and surrounded himself with yes men. Today, there are two such unpredictable and ill-informed leaders: Kim and Trump. Both men are rational and ruthless. Yet both are also prone to lash out impulsively at perceived enemies, a tendency that can lead to reckless rhetoric and behavior.

The same approach that prevented nuclear catastrophe during the Cold War can deter Pyongyang.

This danger is compounded because their senior advisers are in a poor position to speak truth to power. Kim clearly tolerates no dissent; he has reportedly executed family members and rivals for offering insufficiently enthusiastic praise. For his part, Trump often ignores, ridicules, or fires those who disagree with him. In May, The New York Times reported that Trump had described his national security adviser, Lieutenant General H. R. McMaster, as "a pain" for subtly correcting him when he made inaccurate points in meetings. And in June, the spectacle of U.S. department secretaries falling over themselves to declare their deep devotion to Trump and flatter him on live television during the administration's first full cabinet meeting brought to mind the dysfunctional decision-making in dictatorships. Any leader who disdains expertise and demands submission and total loyalty from his advisers, whether in a democracy or in a dictatorship, will not receive candid assessments of alternative courses of action during a crisis.

President John F. Kennedy signs a proclamation for the interdiction of the delivery of offensive weapons to Cuba during the Cuban missile crisis, October 1962.

TONE-DEFCON

Trump's poor decision-making process highlights another disturbing contrast with the Cuban missile crisis. In 1962, strong civilian leaders countered the U.S. military's dangerously hawkish instincts. When the Joint Chiefs of Staff recommended an immediate air strike and an invasion of Cuba, Kennedy insisted on the more prudent option of a naval blockade. Together with his subsequent refusal to retaliate with an air strike after an American U-2 spy plane was shot down over Cuba, Kennedy's approach reflected the best kind of cautious crisis management.

Now, however, it is the senior political leadership in the United States that has made reckless threats, and it has fallen to Secretary of Defense James Mattis (a former general) and senior military officers to serve as the voices of prudence. In early August, Trump warned: "North Korea best not make any more threats to the United States. They will be met with fire and fury like the world has never seen." By appearing to commit to using nuclear force in response to North Korean threats, he broke sharply with U.S. deterrence policy, which had previously warned of military responses only to acts of aggression. Vice President Mike Pence, Secretary of State Rex Tillerson, and un Ambassador Nikki Haley have not echoed Trump's "fire and fury" rhetoric, but they have repeated the worrying mantra that "all options are on the table."

That phrase may sound less threatening than Trump's comments, but it still leaves itself open to misinterpretation. To some listeners, it just suggests that Washington is considering limited military options. But from a North Korean perspective, the statement implies that the United States is contemplating launching a nuclear first strike. This would not be an altogether unreasonable conclusion for Pyongyang to draw. In 2008, U.S. President George W. Bush stated that all options were on the table when it came to U.S. tensions with Iran, and when a reporter explicitly asked Bush whether that included "nuclear options," Bush simply repeated himself: "All options are on the table." The Obama administration made a commitment, in its 2009 Nuclear Posture Review, not to use nuclear weapons against any non-nuclearweapons state that was in compliance with its nonproliferation commitments. But then Secretary of Defense Robert Gates quickly added that "because North Korea and Iran are not in compliance with the Nuclear Nonproliferation Treaty, for them, all bets are off. All options are on the table."

Such rhetoric is dangerous. The U.S. government must convince Kim that an attack on the United States or its allies would spell the end of his regime. But it is equally important that U.S. leaders acknowledge loudly and often that it would be a disaster for the United States to start a war. If those in White House do not do so, the civilian and military leadership in the Pentagon should more forcefully and publicly make this point.

To back this rhetoric up, the United States should take some military options off the table, starting with a preventive nuclear war. A preemptive strike, the use of force when a country considers an adversary's first strike imminent and unavoidable, can sometimes be justified strategically and legally as "anticipatory self-defense." But preventive war—starting a war to prevent another country from taking future action or acquiring a dangerous capability—is rarely justified and arguably contrary to the UN Charter.

U.S. milita ry officers are trained to follow orders from political authorities, unless they are clearly unconstitutional. The Constitution, however, says nothing about what to do if a president's orders are legal but also crazy. This leads to bizarre situations, such as the response that Admiral Scott Swift, the commander of the U.S. Pacific Fleet, gave when he was asked at a seminar at the Australian National University in July if he would launch a nuclear strike against China "next week" if Trump ordered him to do so. The admiral should have said that the hypothetical scenario was ridiculous and left it at that. Instead, he answered, "Yes."

The current Korean missile crisis is even more dangerous than the Cuban one.

Trump's volatility has produced a hidden crisis in U.S. civil-military relations. In 1974, during the final days of Richard Nixon's presidency, when Nixon had become morose and possibly unstable, Secretary of Defense James Schlesinger told the chairman of the Joint Chiefs of Staff, General George Brown, that if Nixon gave military orders, Brown should contact Schlesinger before carrying them out. Schlesinger's action was extraconstitutional but nonetheless wise, given the extraordinary circumstances. The U.S. government faces similar dangers every day under Trump. Mattis and senior military leaders should be prepared to ignore belligerent tweets, push back against imprudent policies, and resist any orders that they believe reflect impetuous or irrational decision-making by the president. Their oath, after all, is not to an individual president; it is to "support and defend the Constitution of the United States." The Constitution's 25th Amendment lays out procedures on how to relieve an impaired president of his responsibilities. If senior military leaders believe at any time that Trump is impaired, they have a duty to contact Mattis, who should then call for an emergency cabinet meeting to determine whether Trump is "unable to discharge the powers and duties of his office" and thus whether to invoke the 25th Amendment.

WHAT YOU DON'T KNOW CAN HURT YOU

One similarity with the Cuban missile crisis is that those Americans who think the United States should attack North Korea exaggerate the prospects that U.S. military action would succeed and underestimate the costs of a war. In 1962, the CIA and the military assumed that there were no nuclear weapons in Cuba and, on that basis, recommended air strikes and an invasion. But the intelligence assessment was wrong. Well over 60 nuclear warheads, gravity bombs, and tactical nuclear weapons had already arrived in Cuba, and one missile regiment was already operational by the time the Joint Chiefs were advising military action. Any attack on Cuba would almost certainly have led to nuclear strikes on the United States and against invading U.S. forces.

Today, U.S. intelligence finds itself once again in the dark. It does not know the status of North Korea's warheads or the locations of its missiles. For example, when the North Koreans successfully tested an intercontinental ballistic missile in late July, it came as a complete surprise to the United States and demonstrated that North Korea can now build such missiles, store them, take them out of storage, and launch them, all before the United States could react. Yet U.S. military leaders have failed to pour cold water on the idea of a U.S. first strike. Instead, they have added fuel to the fire.

Consider the complaint expressed by General Joseph Dunford, the chairman of the Joint Chiefs of Staff, at the Aspen Security Forum in July that "many people have talked about the military options with words such as 'unimaginable.'" Dunford insisted that, to the contrary, "it is not unimaginable to have military options to respond to North Korean nuclear capability. What's unimaginable to me is allowing a capability that would allow a nuclear weapon to land in Denver, Colorado.... And so my job will be to develop military options to make sure that doesn't happen." Dunford should have reinforced deterrence. Instead, he created a redline that Kim may have already crossed.

The military's job is to come up with options. That involves thinking the unthinkable. But it is also military leaders' responsibility to offer brutal honesty to political leaders and the public. When it comes to the current conflict with North Korea, that means admitting that there are no military options that do not risk starting the most destructive war since 1945.

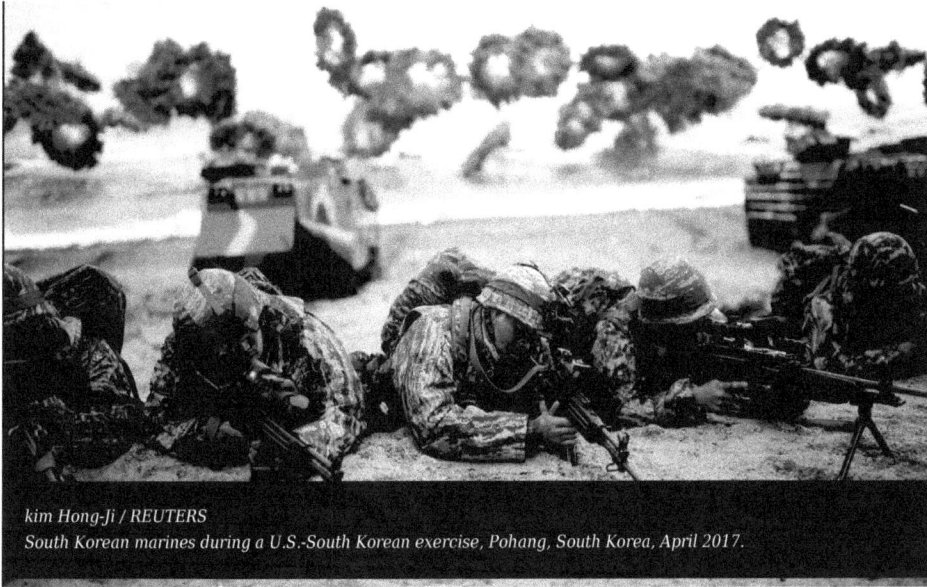

kim Hong-Ji / REUTERS
South Korean marines during a U.S.-South Korean exercise, Pohang, South Korea, April 2017.

WHY THERE'S NO MILITARY SOLUTION

Some Trump supporters, including former un Ambassador John Bolton and Trump's evangelical adviser Robert Jeffress, have argued that a U.S. strike to assassinate Kim is the best solution. Any attempt to "decapitate" the regime, however, would be a gamble of epic proportions. The history of unsuccessful U.S. decapitation attempts, including those launched against the Libyan leader Muammar al-Qaddafi in 1986 and the Iraqi leader Saddam Hussein in 1991 and again in 2003, warns against such thinking. Moreover, Kim may well have ordered his generals to launch all available weapons of mass destruction at the enemy if he is killed in a first strike—as did Saddam before the 1990–91 Gulf War. There is no reason to think that the North Korean military would fail to carry out such an order.

U.S. leaders should also resist the temptation to hope that limited, or "surgical," conventional attacks on North Korean missile test sites or storage facilities would end the nuclear threat. Proponents of this course believe that the threat of further escalation by the United States would deter North Korea from responding militarily to a limited first strike. But as the political scientist Barry Posen has argued, this argument is logically inconsistent: Kim cannot be both so irrational that he cannot be deterred in general and so rational that he could be deterred after having been attacked by the

United States. Moreover, even a limited attack by the United States would appear to North Korea as the beginning of an invasion. And because no first strike could destroy every North Korean missile and nuclear weapon, the United States and its allies would always face the prospect of nuclear retaliation.

Mattis and senior military leaders should be prepared to resist any orders that they believe reflect impetuous or irrational decision-making by the president.

Nor can missile defense systems solve the problem. The United States should continue to develop and deploy missile defenses because they complicate North Korean military planning, and any missiles that Pyongyang aims at U.S. or allied military targets are missiles not aimed at American, Japanese, or South Korean cities. But military leaders should be candid about the limits of U.S. ballistic missile defenses. Most such systems have failed numerous tests, and even the most effective ones, such as the Terminal High Altitude Area Defense, or THAAD, system, could be overwhelmed if North Korea fired multiple missiles—even dummy missiles—in a salvo at one target. That is why North Korea has been practicing launching several missiles simultaneously. Any prudent U.S. planner should therefore assume that in the event of an attack, some North Korean nuclear-armed missiles would reach their targets. Even in the best-case scenario, in which only a few North Korean nuclear weapons penetrated U.S. defenses, the consequences would prove catastrophic.

Estimating the potential fatalities in a limited nuclear strike is difficult, but the nuclear weapons scholar Alex Wellerstein has designed a useful modeling tool called NUKEMAP, which uses data from the Hiroshima and Nagasaki bombings to provide rough estimates of how many people would die in a nuclear strike. After North Korea conducted its sixth nuclear test, in early September, Japanese, South Korean, and U.S. intelligence agencies reportedly provided a range of estimates of the weapon's explosive yield, with an average estimate of around 100 kilotons. According to NUKEMAP, a single 100-kiloton nuclear weapon detonated above the port city of Busan, in South Korea (which was shown as a target in a recent North Korean press release), would kill 440,000 people in seconds. A weapon of that size detonated over Seoul would kill 362,000; over San Francisco, the number would be 323,000. These estimates, moreover, include only immediate blast fatalities, not the deaths from fires after a nuclear detonation or the longer-term deaths that would result from radioactive fallout. Those secondary effects could easily cause the number of dead to double.

Even if a war were limited to the Korean Peninsula, the costs would still be unacceptable. According to a detailed study published in 2012 by the Nautilus Institute, a think tank based in California, North Korea has thousands of conventional artillery pieces along the demilitarized zone that by themselves could inflict some 64,000 fatalities in Seoul on the first day of a war. A major attack on South Korea could also kill many of the roughly 154,000 American civilians and 28,000 U.S. service members living there. If the North Korean regime used its large arsenal of chemical and biological weapons, the fatalities would be even higher. Finally, there are a number of nuclear power plants near Busan that could be damaged, spreading radioactive materials, in an attack. All told, one million people could die on the first day of a second Korean war.

KCNA

A military drill in North Korea, March 2016.

ACCIDENTAL WAR

Even if the United States forswore preventive conventional or nuclear strikes, the danger of an accidental war caused by the mutual fear of a surprise attack would remain. South Korea increasingly (and quite openly) relies on a strategy of preemption and decapitation. In 2013, General Jeong Seungjo, the chairman of the South Korean Joint Chiefs of Staff, announced that "if there is a clear intent that North Korea is about to use a nuclear weapon, we will eliminate it first even at the risk of a war," adding that "a preemptive attack against the North trying to use nuclear weapons does not require consultation with the United States and it is the right of self-defense." A white paper published by the South Korean

Ministry of National Defense in 2016 featured an illustration of several missiles being fired at and a group of South Korean commandos attacking the "war command" building in Pyongyang. (Unsurprisingly, the North Koreans have similar ideas about preemption: in April 2016, in response to U.S. and South Korean military exercises,

North Korean state media reported that "the revolutionary armed forces of [North Korea] decided to take preemptive attack as the mode of its military counteraction…. The right to nuclear preemptive attack is by no means the U.S. monopoly.")

Reducing the risk of war will require an end to U.S. threats of first-strike regime change.

In such a tense environment, one government's preemptive-war plan can look a lot like a first-strike plan to its enemies. Would Seoul see the movement of Pyongyang's nuclear missiles out of the caves in which they are stored as a drill, a defensive precaution, or the start of an attack? Would Pyongyang mistake a joint U.S.–South Korean exercise simulating a decapitation attack for the real thing? Could an ill-timed inflammatory tweet by Trump provoke a military response from Kim? What if a radar technician accidentally put a training tape of a missile launch into a radar warning system—which actually happened, creating a brief moment of panic, during the Cuban missile crisis? Add in the possibility of an American or a South Korean military aircraft accidentally entering North Korean airspace, or a North Korean nuclear weapon accidentally detonating during transport, and the situation resembles less a Cuban missile crisis in slow motion than an August 1914 crisis at the speed of Twitter.

The fear of a U.S. attack explains why Kim believes he needs a nuclear arsenal. Pyongyang's nuclear weapons development undoubtedly appeals to Kim's domestic audience's desire for self-sufficiency. But that is not its primary purpose. Kim's spokespeople have stressed that he will not suffer the fate of Saddam or Qaddafi, both of whom gave up their nuclear programs only to be attacked later by the United States. The North Korean nuclear arsenal is not a bargaining chip. It is a potent deterrent designed to prevent a U.S. attack or disrupt one that does occur by destroying U.S. air bases and ports through preemption, if possible, but in retaliation if necessary. And if all else fails, it is a means for exacting revenge by destroying Kim's enemies' cities. That may sound implausible, but keep in mind that Castro recommended just such an attack in 1962.

KEEP CALM AND DETER ON

Living with a nuclear North Korea does not, in Dr. Strangelove's terms, mean learning "to stop worrying and love the bomb." On the contrary, it means constantly worrying and addressing every risk. U.S. policy should aim to convince Kim that starting a war would lead to an unmitigated disaster for North Korea, especially as his own ministers and military advisers may be too frightened of his wrath to make that argument themselves. The United States should state clearly and calmly that any attack by North Korea would lead to the swift and violent end of the Kim regime.

Kim may be under the illusion that if North Korea were to destroy U.S. air bases and kill hundreds of thousands of Americans, Japanese, and South Koreans, the American public would seek peace. In fact, it would likely demand vengeance and an end to Kim's regime, regardless of the costs. Such a war would be bloody, but there is no doubt which side would prevail. There are few, if any, military targets in North Korea that the United States could not destroy with advanced conventional weapons in a long war. And the Kim regime cannot ignore the possibility of U.S. nuclear retaliation.

The more difficult challenge will be convincing Kim that the United States will not attack him first. Reducing the risk of war will therefore require an end to U.S. threats of first-strike regime change. In August, Tillerson told reporters that the United States did not seek to overthrow Kim unless he were to begin a war. Other American leaders should consistently echo Tillerson's comments. Unfortunately, the Trump administration's rhetoric has been anything but consistent.

Should the United States succeed in bringing North Korea back to the negotiating table, it should be prepared to offer changes to U.S. and South Korean military exercises in exchange for limits on—and notifications of—North Korean missile tests and the restoration of the hotline between North and South Korea. The United States should also continue to extend its nuclear umbrella to South Korea to reduce the incentive for Seoul to acquire its own nuclear arsenal. Some have argued for a return of U.S. tactical nuclear weapons to air bases in South Korea, but such weapons would be vulnerable to a North Korean first strike. A better option would be to keep nuclearcapable bombers at Guam on ground alert. Or the United States could borrow a tactic it used in the wake of the Cuban missile crisis. To assuage Moscow, Washington promised to remove its Jupiter ballistic missiles from Turkey after the crisis. But to reassure Ankara, it also assigned some submarine-based missiles to cover the same retaliatory targets in the Soviet Union that the Jupiter missiles had and arranged for a U.S. submarine to regularly visit a Turkish port. Today, occasional U.S. submarine calls at South Korean harbors could enhance deterrence without provoking North Korea.

In 1947, the American diplomat George Kennan outlined a strategy for the "patient but firm and vigilant containment" of the Soviet Union. Writing in this magazine, he predicted that such a policy would eventually lead to "either the breakup or the gradual mellowing of Soviet power." He was right. In the same way, the United States has deterred North Korea from invading South Korea or attacking Japan for over 60 years. Despite all the bluster and tension today, there is no reason why Kennan's strategy of containment and deterrence cannot continue to work on North Korea, as it did on the Soviet Union. The United States must wait with patience and vigilance until the Kim regime collapses under the weight of its own economic and political weakness.

SCOTT D. SAGAN is Caroline S. G. Munro Professor of Political Science and a Senior Fellow at the Center for International Security and Cooperation at Stanford University.

Preventing Nuclear War With North Korea

What to Do After the Test

Van Jackson

Smoke rises from burnt banners during an anti-North Korea rally in central Seoul, South Korea, September 10, 2016.

Few anticipated that 2016 would see such unprecedented missile and nuclear testing in North Korea, most recently its fifth and largest ever test, reportedly coming in at 10 kilotons. But none of this should have come as a surprise. Under Kim Jong Un, North Korea's approach to developing its strategic forces is markedly different—more aggressive—than it was under his father or grandfather. The striking change puts the Korean Peninsula on a path to nuclear war unless the U.S.South Korean alliance can adapt to the constraints of deterrence and defense against a second-tier nuclear-armed adversary.

Whereas Kim Jong Il's North Korea conducted 18 missile tests during his 18-year reign, the last four years under Kim Jong Un have already seen 35 missile launches and three nuclear tests. In word and deed, Kim Jong Un has laid bare his intentions to mate nuclear warheads to long-range missiles, pursue a hydrogen-based nuclear bomb, and develop a submarine-launched ballistic missile capability, which has long been considered the gold standard of an assured retaliatory capacity. Gone are the days in which it is possible to speculate that North Korea's nuclear weapons were mere symbols or bargaining chips, or that the threat of nuclear attack was "deeply hypothetical," as a White House spokesperson during the George W. Bush administration once described it.

North Korea's nuclear program is now more accelerated, less constrained, and more openly linked to its missile program than at any point in its history. Pyongyang is rushing to deploy a nuclear force that can ensure the regime's survival by guaranteeing that any attempt to replace it or invade to North Korea leads to nuclear war. But Washington and Seoul are dealing with North Korea as if it were still the 1980s.

For a long time, North Korea's foreign policy playbook has included recurring small, isolated, and deniable attacks against South Korean and U.S. targets. Historically, these attacks were backed by a willingness to wage conventional war if the alliance retaliated. These days, the stakes are even higher; those same kinds of attacks are backed by a willingness to risk nuclear war. In turn, the alliance's policy playbook has historically involved nuclear threat-making, a willingness to impose regime change and unify the Korean Peninsula in the event of conflict, and continuous preparations to deploy large-scale military forces to make good on the threat.

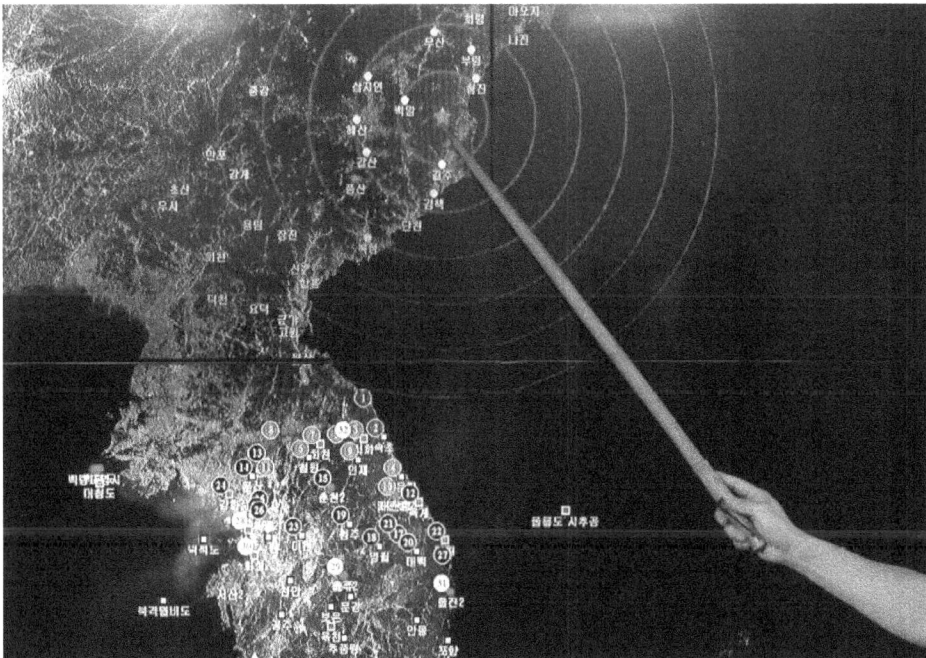

KIM HONG-JI / REUTERS

Ryoo Yong-gyu, Earthquake and Volcano Monitoring Division Director, points at where seismic waves observed in South Korea came from, during a media briefing at Korea Meteorological Administration in Seoul, South Korea, September 9, 2016.

Following this playbook, the alliance still routinely signals actions it is prepared to take against North Korea, from deploying nuclear-capable B-52 bombers, to dispatching aircraft carriers, to mobilizing hundreds of thousands of ground forces to invade and occupy Pyongyang. Yet going down either of those paths—U.S. nuclear first use or regime change—removes incentives for North Korean nuclear restraint in the event of conflict. By holding to its old ways, the alliance is unintentionally making any conflict more likely to go nuclear.

The Korean Peninsula's best chance of avoiding a mushroom-cloud fate is by adapting to—not downplaying—the unique risks and requirements of deterrence against a second-tier nuclear-armed adversary. The alliance, and the United States in particular, must thread the eye of a tiny needle by fashioning a credible deterrent without igniting a nuclear war. Two steps toward adaptation are in order: reducing the role of nukes in alliance military signaling and planning and curbing the objectives and scope of conflicts that break out.

LESSER EVILS

To refrain from nuclear signaling, the United States and South Korea will have to make several adjustments, including ending B-52 deployments to the peninsula, swapping nuclear-umbrella consultations with South Korea for gray-zone consultations, and creating greater distance from the prospect of U.S. nuclear first use.

The United States has a tradition of deploying B-52s—strategic bombers capable of carrying nuclear payloads—from Guam to the Korean Peninsula whenever it wishes to rattle its sabers at the North. The implication that Washington might be willing to use nuclear weapons gives North Korea incentive to place its nuclear weapons on alert, as Kim Jong Un ordered this past April. This was never really a problem in decades past, before North Korea had nearly deliverable nuclear weapons, but times have changed. And North Korean nukes or no, the alliance's dramatic conventional superiority over North Korea moots any military need to resort to nuclear use. Moreover, as I explain in my book, Rival Reputations, there is no evidence that the B-52 flights have even changed North Korean perceptions of the alliance in a desirable way; the history of how the B-52 has been used in Korea—following incidents in which the alliance takes no real action in response to a North Korean attack—makes the flights more likely to signal fecklessness than resolve.

Nuclear signaling toward North Korea also takes subtler forms than the B-52 flight, such as publicly advertised nuclear-umbrella consultations between the United States and South Korea. Since the 1970s, the United States has pledged to extend its nuclear deterrence capability to select allies, including South Korea. Such efforts were ramped up in the wake of two North Korean strikes in 2010, when alliance officials established new consultation mechanisms to assure South Korea of the United States' commitment and to coordinate their respective defense policies on North Korean nuclear weapons. As recently as February this year, the United States hosted what is now termed the Deterrence Strategy Committee with South Korea, which media statements characterized as burnishing U.S. nuclear forces to assure South Korea of their availability.

But since the United States neither needs nukes to destroy North Korea nor wishes to instigate North Korea's nuclear trigger, consultations aimed at assuring South Korea of America's commitment would be better spent on a more acute problem: working through when and how the United States would help South Korea respond to North Korean provocations, guerilla attacks, and limited-scope military campaigns. These are threats that live in what many policymakers now describe as a gray zone of conflict. They are concrete problems that South Korea actually faces, and whose occurrence gives rise to national angst about the credibility of the United States' commitments. Following North Korea's torpedo attack on a South Korean naval vessel in the Yellow Sea and an artillery attack against the South Korea–held Yeonpyeong Island in 2010, for example, South Korean officials openly questioned the viability of extended deterrence and introduced the idea of an independent South Korean nuclear weapons program. Since North Korean behavior—not simply the presence of nukes—is the primary concern, consultations with South Korea would be better if they focused on realistic problems rather than reifying unrealistic nuclear promises.

DAMIR SAGOLJ / REUTERS

A painting is seen around the site where a shell landed during the 2010 North Korean attack on the island of Yeonpyeong which lies on the South Korean side of the Northern Limit Line (NLL), in the Yellow Sea April 9, 2014.

Further, the B-52 deployments and nuclear umbrella consultations are mere instruments made possible by a larger U.S. policy of withholding so-called negative security assurances from North Korea. The United States' 2010 Nuclear Posture Review effectively promised all adherents of the Nuclear Nonproliferation Treaty (NPT) that it would not engage in nuclear use against them under any circumstances. As a declaratory policy, this amounted to a carefully crafted threat by omission. The United States does not extend its assurance of no first use to noncompliant states, meaning that nuclear strikes against North Korea remain possible as a matter of policy. Yet it is difficult to imagine a scenario in which a U.S. president sees either prudence or necessity in launching nuclear strikes—let alone preventive nuclear strikes—against North Korea, which makes the threat of doing so dubious.

There is of course no guarantee that restrictions on U.S. nuclear signaling would induce North Korean restraint in the event of conflict, but they would nudge North Korea (and the United States) away from reckless action by making nuclear weapons less salient to thinking about, planning for, and waging potential conflicts on the peninsula.

CHILL

These measures may help reduce the nuclear temperature in the Korean Peninsula, but they do not address the need for a credible deterrent against the military adventurism of a nuclear-armed North Korea. The emerging situation presents a paradox. On the one hand, the alliance must demonstrate resolve by imposing unacceptable costs on North Korea for acts of aggression. At the same time, the alliance must do everything in its power to ensure that the regime in Pyongyang does not believe that the alliance seeks to destroy or replace it; those conditions would be a nuclear casus belli.

These seemingly contradictory requirements—of demonstrating resolve and conveying only limited aggressive intentions—can be reconciled by shoring up deterrence against low-level violence short of war and giving a new mandate to U.S. forces in Korea (USFK).

North Korea has a long history of unreciprocated small-scale violence—more than 1,300 incidents resulting in more than 1,600 casualties since 1961—which has convinced Pyongyang elites over time that there is no great risk in small, isolated, and deniable attacks. North Korea must be disabused of this notion by swift, concentrated retaliation in the event of future attacks; there is simply no other way to establish deterrence against transgressions short of war.

The role of USFK, meanwhile, must shift from its traditional role as tripwire—that is, a political symbol designed to ensure the dispatch of large-scale U.S. reinforcements in the event of war—to one capable of fighting and winning limited military campaigns on its own. Every year, USFK leads Key Resolve and Foal Eagle, major military exercises involving thousands of troops from throughout the region. USFK's 28,500 troops are simply not designed to win a war on their own. But North Korea knows that large-scale flows of forces into South Korea are a prelude to regime change and attacks on Pyongyang, even if that is not what the alliance intends. Worse, North Korean diplomats warned the United States in 1994—a decade before the country had nuclear arms—that "we will not give you time to collect troops around Korea to attack us … if it is clear you are going to attack, then we will attack." This threat should be taken at face value; if the regime believes it faces imminent demise, North Korean nuclear first use becomes much more likely. The implication for USFK is that it must prepare to achieve military objectives short of regime change and reunification without the support of massive reinforcements because to do otherwise is to risk unintentionally incentivizing a North Korean nuclear attack.

The greatest challenge for the next generation of U.S. and South Korean policymakers is not denuclearization or peaceful unification of the Korean Peninsula. These are noble visions, but they don't match facts on the ground. Instead, the alliance must adapt to the evolving requirements of deterrence against a nuclear-armed adversary. This means demonstrating a greater willingness to meet violence with violence, marginalizing the role of U.S. nuclear weapons as much as possible, and self-limiting both the ends and the means of military conflict to avoid nuclear strikes based on misperceptions or unintended signals.

Former Secretary of Defense William Perry once wrote, "We must deal with North Korea as it is, not as we wish it to be." With North Korea now an emergent threat, heeding his advice is more important than ever.

VAN JACKSON is an Associate Professor at the Asia-Pacific Center for Security Studies (APCSS) and an Adjunct Senior Fellow at the Center for a New American Security (CNAS). He is the author of *Rival Reputations: Coercion and Credibility in US-North Korea Relations* (Cambridge University Press). The views expressed are his own.

© Foreign Affairs

Changing North Korea

An Information Campaign Can Beat the Regime

Andrei Lankov

DANNY MOLOSHOK / REUTERS

U.S. journalists Euna Lee and Laura Ling embrace their families after being freed from months of detention in North Korea, Los Angeles, United States, August 5, 2009.

North Korea, a small country with no economic potential to speak of, has for two decades been a major irritant to the international community. Its nuclear weapons program puts the international nonproliferation regime at risk and threatens to provide assorted rogue states and terrorist groups with the nuclear technology they have long sought. In April, Pyongyang conducted a missile test, and a nuclear test followed in May. In July, however, Kim Jong Il signaled a readiness to talk by inviting former U.S. President Bill Clinton to visit Pyongyang and retrieve two American journalists detained in North Korea since March. Still, this dramatic event was no indication that North Korea is planning to give up its nuclear program.

In considering the North Korean nuclear question, U.S. policymakers and experts typically fall into two camps. The optimists believe that negotiating with Pyongyang will set North Korea on the path of Chinese-style political and economic reforms, help it become a "normal state," and convince it to abandon its nuclear ambitions. The pessimists insist that only relentless pressure will cause Pyongyang to denuclearize. The optimists (such as Christopher Hill, who once led U.S. negotiations with North Korea and is now ambassador to Iraq) favor talks and compromise. The pessimists (such as John Bolton, former U.S. ambassador to the United Nations) prefer coercive sanctions. Pyongyang's recent provocations seem to confirm the pessimists' view for now, but at other times the optimists have seemed vindicated, and the pendulum has swung back and forth frequently over the years. In any event, neither camp's approach is likely to work.

The optimists' position rests on two false hopes: that Pyongyang, like Beijing in the late 1970s, might oversee a process of economic reform and that, with patience and goodwill, the international community can convince it to abandon its nuclear program. But Kim and his entourage believe that Chinese-style reforms are not a viable option—and they are probably correct. Market reforms in North Korea would require relaxing domestic surveillance and would spread information about South Korea's prosperity. Because North Koreans would be exposed to the much higher standard of living enjoyed by their neighbors, a kindred people who speak the same language, they would start to question Pyongyang's legitimacy. So major reforms would more likely push North Korea the way of East Germany in the 1980s—namely, toward collapse—than the way of China's economic boom. It is neither paranoid nor irrational, then, for Pyongyang to resist change and maintain its Stalinist institutions and policies.

Because the economic system it strives to preserve is inherently inefficient, Pyongyang is dependent on aid from the outside world. But in order to retain his lock on power, Kim prefers that aid to come with as few conditions as possible—hence, his nuclear and missile programs, which make North Korea an international threat that great powers seek to mollify with billions in aid.

Pyongyang cannot do away with these programs. That would mean losing both a powerful military deterrent and a time-tested tool of extortion. It would also relegate North Korea to being a third-rate country, on a par with Mozambique or Uganda. This is the reason that Pyongyang has rejected South Korea's "Vision 3000" plan, which proposed raising North Korea's per capita GDP (currently estimated at between $500 and $1,700) to $3,000 through a generous aid and investment program—on the condition that Pyongyang denuclearize. That condition—along with the various connections to the South that such investment would inevitably create—seemed to Pyongyang more threatening than enabling. For 15 years, North Korea's leaders have deftly stuck to a single strategy: start negotiations, squeeze aid out of the international community by making incremental concessions (while trying to cheat), and then walk away from the talks and stage a provocation or two—only to return in exchange for more payoffs.

The pessimists correctly recognize this pattern, but they, too, hold an unrealistic belief: that external coercion can be effective. The idea of a military invasion is a nonstarter except perhaps in the very unlikely event that North Korea is shown to have transferred fissile material to terrorists. Sanctions, meanwhile, can be effective only if they are supported and enforced by all major states—especially China and Russia, with which North Korea conducts slightly more than half of its external trade. This is not going to happen, however, if only because Beijing and Moscow are far more worried about North Korea's potential instability than its acquisition of nuclear weapons. The Chinese and the Russians do not believe that Pyongyang would attack them. To them, North Korea's nuclear program is merely an indirect threat. To be sure, the approach of Chinese and Russian diplomats might elicit anger from their more concerned U.S. and Japanese counterparts. But this seems to them far less troublesome than the prospect of a North Korean collapse, which would send refugees, arms, and perhaps even fissile material into neighboring states.

Notwithstanding China and Russia, some have argued for shrinking Kim's coffers by imposing financial sanctions on foreign banks that do business with his regime. But even severe financial pressure would be unlikely to create serious political stress. A shortage of luxury goods would not lead North Korean elites to challenge Kim, for they understand that to generate any instability is to risk toppling the whole system and therefore losing their own status and comforts. Such elites would be willing to accept a less luxurious lifestyle for a while. The main victims of financial sanctions would be ordinary North Koreans, whose suffering has not hurt the regime historically. Even after three to five percent of the population starved to death in the late 1990s, there were no signs of political unrest. Terrified and isolated, the North Koreans did not rebel; they died quietly.

When it comes to dealing with North Korea, in other words, the United States and its allies have no efficient methods of coercion at their disposal. The regime is remarkably immune to outside pressure. Its leaders cannot afford change, so they will make sure their state continues to be an international threat, using nuclear blackmail as a survival tactic while their unlucky subjects endure more poverty and terror. The North Korean nuclear issue cannot be resolved in isolation; it is a part of the broader North Korean issue. And that can only be resolved with a radical transformation of the regime. Since outside pressure is ineffective, change will have to come from the North Koreans themselves. The United States and its allies can best help them by exposing them to the very attractive alternatives to their current way of life.

KIM'S WEAKENING INFORMATION MONOPOLY

This is a well-tested approach: it is, essentially, the one that allowed liberal democracies to win the Cold War. Americans sometimes credit containment with cracking the Soviet Union, but it was the West's economic prosperity and political freedom that irrevocably undermined popular support for communism. This approach might be even more efficient in the case of North Korea.

The income gap between North Korea and South Korea is much larger than the disparity that existed between the Soviet Union and the developed West in the 1960s or 1970s. Whereas North Korea's per capita income is estimated (generously) to be between $500 and $1,700, South Korea's is about $20,000. This disparity makes Pyongyang especially vulnerable because the regime bases its legitimacy not on religious grounds, as do some rogue states, but on its ability to ensure the material well-being of its subjects.

Long aware of this vulnerability, North Korean leaders have taken information control to extremes unprecedented even among communist dictatorships. Since the late 1950s, it has been a crime for a North Korean to possess a tunable radio, and all radios sold legally are set only to official broadcasts.

In libraries, all nontechnical foreign publications, such as novels and books on politics and history, are placed in special sections accessible only to users with proper security clearance. Private trips overseas are exceptional, even for government officials. North Korea is the world's only country without Internet access for the general public (although there is a small, growing intranet system maintained by the government). These measures seek to ensure that the public believes the official portrayal of North Korea as an island of happiness and prosperity in an ocean of suffering. (South Korea suffers "under the yoke of U.S. domination and subjugation, its sovereignty wantonly violated," reports the official North Korean news agency.) On top of this information blockade are various levels of daily surveillance. Travel beyond one's hometown requires police approval, and overnight visitors need to register with the authorities ahead of time. Changing jobs is possible only by government mandate.

But conditions have slightly improved in recent years, and North Korea is no longer the perfect Stalinist state it was under Kim Jong Il's father, Kim Il Sung, who died in 1994. Since Kim Jong Il took over in the mid-1990s and famine killed approximately two million people, the country has been more vulnerable to domestic dissent and open to outside influences. The devastation and chaos of the famine undermined the state surveillance system. Today, badly paid officials overlook prohibited activities—such as travel, smuggling, or migrant work—in exchange for bribes. There is also a booming black market for all kinds of consumer goods, as state industry became paralyzed in the 1990s following the sudden loss of Soviet economic aid. Today, 70-80 percent of the average North Korean family's income is generated through private economic activities. (The rest is still allocated by the state through elaborate rationing systems.)

Further weakening the regime's monopoly on information in recent years has been the continued influence of South Korea. A tiny but growing proportion of North Koreans have learned of South Korean prosperity thanks to smuggled South Korean consumer goods, including tunable radios and DVDs of movies and television shows. And those North Koreans who have spent time in China as illegal refugees—an estimated 500,000 since the mid-1990s—have both witnessed the impressive results of the Chinese reforms and heard of South Korean prosperity from the ethnic Koreans who populate the Chinese borderlands and from the South Koreans who travel there. Thus, rumors about foreign affluence are spreading, undermining Pyongyang's control over its population. The system is disintegrating from below, albeit slowly.

THE POWER OF EXCHANGE

Truth is subversive in regimes built on lies and isolation. So to crack Pyongyang's control over information and bring about pressure for change from within, truth and information should be introduced into North Korean society. The U.S. government and its allies can do this through two seemingly contradictory strategies: engagement and subversion.

As the Cold War demonstrated, cultural exchanges can be effective in transferring forbidden knowledge and fostering critical thinking. The citizens of the communist bloc learned of the West's quality of life through various sources, including foreign broadcasts and smuggled dissident literature but also, crucially, from government-approved interactions. For example, when Soviet censors allowed theaters in the late 1970s to screen White Line Fever, an American movie about trade union activism, Soviet audiences—including myself, then a teenager—could not fail to notice that "oppressed" workers in the United States lived better than midranking party apparatchiks in the Soviet Union. Occasional encounters with Western tourists and students became topics of endless conversation. So did the stories of the select few Soviet citizens allowed to visit the West or even "fraternal countries" in the Soviet bloc where knowledge of Western life could be more easily obtained. Thus informed, the Soviet people came to conclusions that varied greatly from the official propaganda. Exchanges of this type would have the same effect on North Koreans today. Indeed, they might be even more powerful because North Koreans' major point of reference is South Korea, once a poorer part of the same country. The U.S. government should therefore spearhead initiatives that bring foreigners to North Korea and take North Koreans abroad.

Academic and student exchanges can bring young members of the North Korean intelligentsia into contact with the outside world. Away from police surveillance (and close to Internet-equipped computers), they would learn much about the true workings of the world. If dozens or hundreds of North Koreans studied subjects such as water treatment, finance, or rice agriculture in, for example, New Zealand, Poland, or Vietnam, they would inevitably be exposed to truthful information about the world. (The United States should be careful, of course, not to expose North Koreans to technology that might be militarily valuable to their regime. Exchanges that teach about agriculture, light industry, foreign languages, economics, and medicine would be the most mutually advantageous.)

It is possible that only the scions of the North Korean elite would be allowed to participate in such programs, since the leadership seeks to benefit itself and its friends. But this would still be worth encouraging, as those involved might develop a more independent mindset and share some of their newly acquired knowledge with the less privileged back home. Because the North Korean government is reluctant to send students to the United States, Washington should encourage—and even provide financial support for—such programs in other countries. As I know from personal experience, however, diplomats in such countries are afraid of angering their U.S. ally by appearing to be soft on North Korea. Hence, a clear sign of approval from Washington is necessary.

Of course, the North Korean regime might be disinclined to support any initiative with subversive potential. But since the immediate-term beneficiaries of such initiatives would be self-interested members, relatives, and clients of the ruling class, they would likely support opportunities for exchange and professional training even if they posed longer-term risks to the system.

The importance of encouraging North Korean rulers to support exchanges is one reason why talks with the regime are important, whether through the six-party structure or not. Although talks will not solve the nuclear issue, they can reduce the likelihood of confrontations and support an environment conducive to exchange and interaction.

Hard-liners in the United States would likely criticize exchanges as a form of "appeasement," but they would be missing the point. Although compromises may be unpalatable at times, exchanges with North Korea would ultimately weaken the regime's physical and ideological grip on the population. Engagement is necessary, but its goals should be realistic. The objective would not be to disarm North Korea's leaders or persuade them to become enlightened autocrats—no such miraculous transformation will happen in the near term. Rather, the goal would be to spread knowledge about the modern world to North Korea's common people and lower-level elites, those without a vested interest in perpetuating the brutality of the current system.

Engagement would require making some controversial tradeoffs. Consider the Kaesong Industrial Complex, a fenced-off industrial compound outside of North Korea's second-largest city, Kaesong, several miles from the border with South Korea, where some 40,000 North Koreans work for South Korean companies, supervised by South Korean managers. This project has been criticized by some in the United States; Jay Lefkowitz, the George W. Bush administration's special envoy on human rights in North Korea, wrote that "there is ample cause for concern about worker exploitation" at Kaesong. But although the jobs there may pay meagerly according to South Korean standards, they are by far the best-paying regular employment in North Korea. And although they provide Kim's regime with some money, they also bring a large number of North Koreans into direct contact with their cousins from the South. As these North Korean workers get to observe the South Koreans' dress and possessions and hear their conversations, they become more likely to realize the dishonesty of Pyongyang's propaganda.

DEFECTORS AND DIGITAL TOOLS

There are other ways besides open engagement to weaken the North Korean regime through the spread of information. Some were employed with great success during the Cold War, and others have become available only recently, thanks to advances in technology. As during the Cold War, radio broadcasts remain a reliable method of disseminating information. An increasing number of tunable radios are being smuggled into North Korea, and these are being used by the small fraction of North Koreans who, assured of their basic physical sustenance, are able to take an interest in politics. For this small but important minority, the United States should support radio broadcasts that provide news, history, and opinion.

North Koreans' perceptions of the world are shaped perhaps primarily by foreign videos and DVDs smuggled into the country—especially from South Korea—by profit-seeking Chinese merchants. Although often illegal, videos and DVDs are watched widely. It makes sense, then, to support the production of documentaries specifically tailored to the tastes of the North Korean audience. Such documentaries should inform North Koreans about daily social and economic life in South Korea, North Korean contemporary history (known to North Koreans only through distorted official claims), and political matters such as reunification. In addition, lighter videos and DVDs can educate North Koreans about the real world even if their chief purpose is simply to entertain.

Thanks to the digital revolution, digitized videos and books could easily be sent to and circulated among North Koreans. This represents a great advance since the era of samizdat, the Soviet underground's practice of retyping and carbon-copying banned books for secret distribution. It creates an opportunity to do something that was unthinkable during the Cold War: put entire libraries within the reach of North Korean intellectuals and introduce them to a world of knowledge the regime has denied them for decades. The necessary environment is developing: despite a U.S. ban on the sale of Pentium-class personal computers to North Korea, more affluent North Koreans are buying such computers used from China.

Instead of continuing the current harmful restrictions, the United States should encourage the spread of computers inside North Korea. The U.S. ban has failed to advance its ostensible goal—namely, to keep computers from North Korean military engineers and government-employed hackers. Yet the ban has unintentionally inhibited the circulation of digital information among the people. This is a shame, for even without access to the Internet, computers remain a powerful tool of emancipation, thanks to flash drives, DVDs, and the like. The United States should allow—and encourage—cheaper personal computers to be sold or donated to North Korea without much hassle. Such low-market computers—which would not be of great harm even if they fell into government hands—would help create an environment in which unauthorized information spread faster and more easily.

Broadly, the U.S. government should be cultivating a political opposition and alternative elite that could one day replace the fallen Kim regime. Due to many factors, including information control and police surveillance, those few North Koreans who are politically aware hardly constitute a community of dissenting intellectuals. An increasing number of North Koreans have doubts about the system, but they remain isolated and terrified. Washington should focus, therefore, on aiding the dissident community in South Korea, where some 16,000 North Korean defectors live. Most of them are farmers from impoverished borderland provinces, but there are some young intellectuals and even a few established academics among them. The younger generation could be given internships and scholarships, including for postgraduate studies at South Korean and other universities. This would make them the first generation of modern North Korean professionals. Meanwhile, older defector-intellectuals could be connected to creative circles, periodicals, radio stations, and publishing houses. Centers promoting such connections could operate overseas but would usually be best placed in South Korea—not least because few North Korean defectors speak a language other than Korean.

Washington might have to lead such efforts because South Korean society is remarkably indifferent to the plight of the refugees. Despite regular rhetoric calling for the reunification of the Korean Peninsula, South Koreans and their leaders are ambivalent about prompting reform in the North. South Koreans fear the political risks and financial burdens associated with North Korea's implosion and seem to prefer the status quo while hoping that the North Korean problem will somehow solve itself.

IN LIEU OF QUICK FIXES

Combining engagement, information dissemination, and support for emigres is the only way to promote change in North Korea. This approach, however, might be a hard sell to most Americans. It is likely to bring about only barely visible, incremental change—at least until the situation reaches a breaking point, which could be many years away. Granting a scholarship to a farmer's son, promoting the concert tour of a North Korean tenor, and donating funds to a small radio station run by defectors are not glamorous diplomatic initiatives. Nor will they yield the sort of demonstrable, quantifiable results sought by bureaucracies that are accountable to the public.

But the American public should recognize that there are no quick fixes to the North Korean problem. For two decades, Washington has searched for those, sometimes by way of concessions to Pyongyang, sometimes by way of threats. Both approaches have failed and—given the goals of the North Korean regime, as well as its hold on power today—would fail again and again. Only low-profile and persistent efforts aimed at promoting change from within will make a difference. North Korea is often described as the last outpost of Cold War politics. So why not seek to change that by using the policies that won the Cold War in the rest of the world?

ANDREI LANKOV is Associate Professor of History at Kookmin University, in Seoul. A Kookmin University new-faculty grant supported his research for this article.

A Korea Whole and Free

Why Unifying the Peninsula Won't Be So Bad After All

Sue Mi Terry

The unfinished New Yalu River bridge that was designed to connect China and North Korea, Dandong, China, September 11, 2016.

When Kim Il Sung, North Korea's founding ruler, died in 1994, many outside observers predicted that his state would die with him. That never happened, of course, and his son Kim Jong Il managed to keep the regime alive until his own death, in 2011. When his son Kim Jong Un took the reins that year, numerous Korea watchers again predicted a collapse. Once again, they were proved wrong. Despite its extreme poverty, North Korea is still very much alive and a major threat to its southern neighbor.

But cracks are appearing. Last December, Kim Jong Un took the unprecedented step of publicly executing his uncle Jang Song Thaek, the second most powerful official in the regime. Although Jang's removal may help strengthen Kim's rule in the short run, it could have the opposite effect in the long run, convincing North Korean elites that the 31-year-old heir to the throne is too hotheaded to be trusted. The regime's patrons in China, meanwhile, were undoubtedly unsettled by the execution of Jang, who was Pyongyang's chief envoy to Beijing and a proponent of Chinese-style reforms.

But Beijing is unlikely to start putting more pressure on Pyongyang, at least not anytime soon. China's leaders may not like the current regime, but they like the alternative far less. North Korea's collapse would likely flood China with refugees and precipitate a military intervention that would bring South Korean and U.S. forces to China's border. So Beijing sees supporting Kim as its least bad option.

Seoul, for its part, has also traditionally avoided doing anything to destabilize Pyongyang, and for similar reasons. For South Korea's leaders, living with the North's occasional pinprick attacks and the ever-present threat of another war is preferable to bearing the crippling social and financial burdens that would accompany reunification.

Even the United States and Japan, which have much less to fear from North Korea's demise, have quietly decided to live with the regime. Both the Clinton and the George W. Bush administrations struck generous aid deals with Pyongyang in exchange for limits on its nuclear program. Japan agreed to spend $1 billion as part of one of those deals, the 1994 Agreed Framework, to finance two light-water nuclear reactors in the North (a project that was formally suspended in 2002), and Tokyo has contributed generous amounts of food aid. Policymakers in Washington and Tokyo know that they have little leverage to bring down the North Korean regime. But they also fear the regional chaos that regime change would bring.

Such concerns are legitimate, and all outside parties need to take them into account when planning for the regime's inevitable demise. Even under the best of circumstances, the reunification of North and South Korea will prove more expensive and challenging than that of East and West Germany, given how far apart the two Koreas are in terms of their economies, education levels, and ideologies.

But it is a mistake to conclude that reunification should therefore be avoided. Contrary to popular belief, a merger would not spell disaster for South Korea, nor would it pose an unacceptable risk for the United States, China, and Japan. Rather, it would produce massive economic and social benefits for the peninsula and the region. There can be only one happy ending to the long-running saga of the North: the emergence of a single, democratic Korea. Outsiders should do all they can to promote and plan for this outcome.

THE GOOD, THE BAD, AND THE UGLY

Reunification is likely to come about in one of three basic ways. The scenario South Koreans hope for most is a soft landing, in which Pyongyang adopts the Chinese economic model, eschews militarism, and undertakes a gradual rapprochement with Seoul. The second scenario is far less attractive: North Korea, staggering under the weight of economic and social forces, implodes and gets absorbed by South Korea. The third scenario is even worse: the peninsula could be reunified through military conflict, in which, following a major attack from the North, South Korean and U.S. forces finally destroy the regime. Of these three outcomes, a soft landing is the least likely, given how little interest Kim has shown in reform. The third scenario is also improbable; for all his pugnacity, Kim is no more suicidal than his father or his grandfather was. That leaves the second scenario, a hard landing, as the most plausible. So that's what policymakers should plan for.

The collapse of Kim's regime would pose many immediate problems, the most pressing of which, from the standpoint of the United States, being how to secure North Korea's nuclear weapons. U.S. and South Korean forces would have to maintain the command structure of North Korea's army in order to prevent factional fighting and attacks by die-hard elements. They would also need to provide security, food, and basic public services, such as water, electricity, and telecommunications, in order to avert a humanitarian crisis that would send the long-suffering North Korean population flooding across the borders into China and South Korea and across the sea to Japan.

These are major challenges, but with enough planning, South Korea—backed by the United States, the UN, and other international actors—could deal with them. In fact, South Korea's Ministry of Unification, in cooperation with U.S. defense officials, has spent decades preparing to do just that. In the event of the North Korean regime's collapse, South Korea's large, well-equipped, and highly trained military should be able to rapidly assume control of North Korea and provide basic services until a civilian government takes over. The task would prove all the easier if South Korea could involve China in the planning process. So far Beijing has refused to publicly entertain the possibility that the Kim regime may not last forever. But even without Chinese participation, South Korea and its partners should be able to handle the fallout of collapse.

The real fear of South Koreans, however, is not that Seoul won't be able to deal with the immediate effects of an implosion; it is that the financial price would ruin them. Reuniting Korea would likely cost more than reunifying Germany did: the Halle Institute for Economic Research has estimated Germany's bill at $1.9 trillion over 20 years. According to South Korea's finance ministry, reunification would consume seven percent of South Korea's current GDP—a share equal to $80 billion—every year for a minimum of ten years. An advisory body appointed by South Korean President Lee Myung-bak in 2011 put the price tag of reunification even higher, at over $2 trillion. Whatever the final figure, there is little doubt that the endeavor will prove expensive and that the difficulties will be exacerbated by the social challenges of integrating an isolated, impoverished, and brainwashed population.

WHEN TWO BECOME ONE

Although South Koreans tend to focus on the obvious costs, those costs would be outweighed by the benefits of reunification. Most immediate among these would be the disappearance of Northeast Asia's primary source of instability. Assuming that the regime's nuclear weapons and ballistic missiles could be secured and its army peacefully demobilized, its dissolution would leave not only Seoul but also Washington and Tokyo much more secure. The United States would no longer have to worry about North Korea selling nuclear weapons abroad or drawing U.S. forces into a second Korean war. Japan would no longer have to fear North Korean missile strikes or the abduction of more of its citizens. And South Korea could stop worrying about North Korea's artillery pulverizing Seoul, its navy torpedoing South Korean ships, or its commandos targeting South Korean leaders.

Even China would have reason to rejoice. It could replace its unrequited transfers of fuel, food, and other goods to Pyongyang with capital investments that yielded income. And once it stopped propping up the most despotic regime in the world, Beijing would find it far easier to portray itself as a responsible international stakeholder.

The end of the Kim regime would also have huge humanitarian benefits, freeing 25 million people from the grip of the world's last remaining Stalinist state and integrating them into a modern democracy. The majority of North Korea's 80,000 to 120,000 state prisoners could leave the government's slave-labor camps, where most have been consigned for political, rather than criminal, offenses. Average North Koreans could move from a starvation diet, both literally and intellectually, to the plentiful availability of food, information, consumer products, and all the other benefits of modern capitalism. South Koreans, an intensely nationalist people, would also finally get to celebrate the reunification of the Korean family. Korea would once again become a single state, as it was from the year 668, when the Silla dynasty unified the three Korean kingdoms, until 1945, when the Soviet Union and the United States divided it at the 38th parallel.

But the greatest benefits for the South would be economic. Reunification would be far more profitable than is commonly assumed. For starters, Seoul could sharply reduce its defense spending, which currently stands at $30 billion a year, or 2.5 percent of GDP—a figure that excludes the $1 billion it gives every year to Washington to help cover the costs of the U.S. military's presence on the peninsula. South Korea could end universal conscription and shrink its 680,000-man military to 500,000 personnel or fewer, freeing large numbers of young Korean men to enter the work force years earlier than they currently do. Also joining them would be the 1.1 million people, most of them young, that North Korea now employs in its military.

The prospect of extra young workers should be especially tantalizing given the rapid aging of South Korea's population. Thanks to the country's growing wealth, life expectancy in South Korea has reached 81 years and continues to improve, whereas its birthrate, at only 1.2 children per woman, is among the lowest in the world. As a result, according to projections by the Organization for Economic Cooperation and Development, by 2050, South Korea will have the second-oldest population in the developed world, with nearly seven people over the age of 65 for every working-age adult. Absent reunification, the number of South Koreans aged 15 to 64 will start to decline in 2017; by 2030, so will the overall population.

In North Korea, by contrast, 91 percent of the population is currently younger than 65, and the fertility rate is higher than in the South, at 2.0 children per women. Following reunification, North Korea would add more than 17 million potential workers aged 15 to 64 to the nearly 36 million already in the South. South Korea could thereby avoid turning to Southeast Asia or other regions for low-wage workers, who would be hard to assimilate. South Korean firms could even move their factories from China to North Korea, where wages would be even lower initially.

Reunification would yield big gains in the mining sector. South Korea's high-tech economy is among the most advanced in the world, but the country possesses virtually no mineral wealth and must import 97 percent of its energy and mineral needs. North Korea, by contrast, has vast deposits of coal, uranium, magnesite, and rare-earth metals—together valued at $6 trillion—but it cannot currently access them. With technology from the South, however, this mother lode could be unlocked at last, providing a welcome boost to the global economy.

A reunified Korea would also boast a newly expanded domestic market, experience a spike in tourism revenues—since some of the most scenic parts of the peninsula lie in the North—and see its sovereign risk rating improve. As the risk of war finally disappeared, credit would become cheaper and foreign capital would flow more freely into the country.

Once the landmine-fortified demilitarized zone vanished, moreover, trade would get easier and cheaper. South Korea currently functions as an island economy, paying high transportation prices for raw materials. With the border gone, a long-envisioned gas pipeline from Vladivostok to Seoul could finally be built, sending badly needed Russian oil and gas south. Energy costs, which drag down the South Korean economy, would fall dramatically. Korean companies could also begin shipping goods to China and Russia over land.

Over time, a reunified Korea, with a hard-working population of 75 million, could emerge as a consumer and industrial powerhouse—the Germany of Asia. As two economies became one, abundant new investment opportunities would arise. According to a 2009 report by Goldman Sachs, within 30 to 40 years, the peninsula, if reunified, could overtake France, Germany, and even Japan in terms of GDP. South Korea's current trading partners—especially the biggest two, China and the United States—would benefit immensely from this newfound source of economic vitality.

NEIGHBORHOOD WATCH

Despite all these benefits, selling Korea's neighbors on the geopolitical consequences of reunification will be difficult. Leaders in China fear losing a bulwark against U.S. power, but Washington could assuage these concerns by privately assuring Beijing that following reunification, no U.S. troops would be stationed north of the current demilitarized zone—or on any part of the peninsula, if that's what it takes to win Chinese support. Nationalist South Koreans might insist on this anyway; relieved of the threat from the North, they could well demand that Washington withdraw its forces.

Although such a move might feel jarring in Washington, it would not be a foreign policy setback. If anything, the departure of U.S. forces would represent a happy culmination of the long U.S. commitment to the peninsula, which began in the dark days of the Korean War. The United States could still hedge against Chinese expansionism from its bases in Japan and Guam, and it would undoubtedly maintain good relations with a reunified Korea, just as it does with a reunified Germany.

As for Beijing, its ties with Seoul are already better in some ways than its vexing relations with Pyongyang—and they should stay that way after reunification. Historically, Korea was a tributary state of China, and although that submissive relationship will never be reestablished, China need not fear reunification. The new Korea would become an even better trade partner, and given its desire to avoid a hostile relationship with its giant neighbor to the north, it would likely triangulate its foreign policy between Beijing and Washington.

Japan, for its part, would no doubt look askance at the emergence of a stronger, single Korean state. Nearly 70 years after World War II, the Japanese–South Korean relationship remains fraught thanks to Japan's dark colonial legacy. But the emergence of a democratic, capitalist Korea would not truly threaten the region's other big democracy. In fact, reunification would give Tokyo a golden opportunity to dispel anti-Japanese sentiment among Koreans by donating food and medicine and sending aid workers and medical personnel. Japan already ranks as one of the top foreign aid donors in the world, and it could win considerable goodwill by helping rebuild the North.

READY FOR REUNIFICATION

Given all these advantages, the international community should promote reunification, not postpone it. There may be little that any outsider can do to make Pyongyang change course. But regional powers, notably South Korea and the United States, should stop propping up the Kim dynasty in return for fleeting assurances of better behavior, as they have in the past; Kim Jong Un is no more likely to keep these promises than his father or his grandfather was.

Nor should the West resist the urge to tighten sanctions or retaliate proportionately in response to North Korea's provocations for fear of destabilizing the country. Even if the North were to implode now, that would be preferable to allowing the state to limp along for decades and waiting for reforms that will never come. South Korea has the most to gain from reunification, so it should confront the prospect with confidence, not trepidation. South Korean President Park Geun-hye caused a stir earlier this year when she called reunification a possible "bonanza," and she gave a major pro-unification speech in Germany (a symbolic choice) at the end of March. Her government should continue with its public relations campaign to get South Koreans educated and excited about the benefits of reunification—a task that is particularly important as the younger generation in South Korea grows increasingly wary of it. And Park should make good on her pledge to stay resolute in the face of the North's threats and provocations, even as she attempts to establish a renewed dialogue with the Kim regime and pursue initiatives such as holding cross-border family reunions. Seoul should not shy away from retaliating—which it has never really done—the next time Pyongyang torpedoes a South Korean vessel or shells a South Korean island for fear that doing so could destabilize or aggravate North Korea. Even China would be well advised to stop pouring resources into Pyongyang, unless a new cadre of reform-minded rulers takes power.

To get China and Japan on board, the United States and South Korea should launch a diplomatic initiative aimed at preparing for the contingency of an unexpected collapse. Washington and Seoul should augment their joint military planning by crafting a comprehensive political, diplomatic, economic, and legal strategy for reunification. Both governments should designate diplomatic and political representatives to come up with a civilian counterpart to the joint military plans that would be activated in the event of a conflict with or instability in the North. Both states have much to offer: South Korea's Ministry of Unification and other agencies could contribute years of expertise on precisely this scenario, and the United States could contribute the lessons learned from its experiences, good and bad, with nation building in Germany, Japan, Kosovo, Iraq, and Afghanistan.

Once the United States and South Korea develop a common vision, they should encourage Japan to join the planning. Tokyo has legitimate interests in the future of the peninsula and would benefit from preparations designed to address its concerns, such as the prospect of a massive influx of refugees by sea. Japan's logistical support and economic assistance would prove crucial during reunification.

As a final step in this process, the trilateral dialogue among the United States, South Korea, and Japan should expand to include China and possibly Russia. All these key players should be asked to bear some of the costs of reunification in return for a say in how the new Korea behaves in the region. For example, China and Japan could be asked to contribute to the North's reconstruction—the former could help develop the North by providing discounted electricity and assistance in rebuilding infrastructure, and the latter could provide humanitarian and financial aid, investment, and expertise—in return for a guarantee that Seoul will not keep North Korea's nuclear arsenal. Striking such a deal would solve two big problems: South Korea's fears about the costs of integrating North Korea and the rest of the region's fears about an unleashed Korea as a military and economic competitor.

The Kim regime will probably not come to a neat end; the collapse of a state is always messy, and it will be particularly so for a regime so militarized and desperate. But that reality should not blind outside powers to the many upsides of what will come after, nor should it cause them to put off planning for the inevitable. In fact, the best way to cope with future instability in the North and reduce the costs of reunification is for the principal powers to start cooperating now. North Korea has the worst government on the planet. Despite all the challenges a transition will entail, everyone will benefit immeasurably from the rise of a new Korea, whole and free.

SUE MI TERRY is a former analyst at the CIA and a Senior Research Scholar at Columbia University's Weatherhead East Asian Institute.

www.ingramcontent.com/pod-product-compliance
Lightning Source LLC
Chambersburg PA
CBHW081150270326
41930CB00014B/3095

* 9 7 8 0 8 7 6 0 9 7 2 4 3 *